'Ian Clayton has created one of the best ⋯
ever written. That's a big claim, yet the ⋯
everything here is small-scale, local, personal, and very often funny. In telling the story of his life as a modestly successful writer, broadcaster, traveller and record collector, he manages to tell the whole story of music in Britain, from the music halls to the Artic Monkeys, from folk to NWOBHM, and beyond, to Eastern Europe and Africa. You'll find yourself smiling in recognition at so much. Wonderful stuff.' – Alan Lewis, Record Collector

'A great story, of a great and interesting life. And weirdly enough it's a life we might all have. Or have had. Or have thought about. From Featherstone to the world. I love this book. It resonates with me in so many ways, and I reckon it will resonate with most of the people who read this.' – Boff (Chumbawumba), ROCKnREEL

'A fantastic book.' – Aled Jones, BBC Radio 2

A music-powered helter-skelter of living and learning, as perceptive as a Bob Dylan lyric and as earthy as a Bessie Smith blues.' – Val Wilmer

'Ian's book is of a piece with the man – generous, funny and wise – written with a tenderness that only the strongest can aspire to. He describes it, astutely, as the soundtrack to a life and the music embraces everything from half-forgotten music-hall songs to the outer limits of jazz, blues and folk. But beneath these sounds he hears the secret music of the common people – from the mining towns of Yorkshire to the Mississippi Delta – the joy of community and the devastation of loss and betrayal. The final chapter – about Billie Holiday Clayton – is the bravest piece of writing I've ever read. It is, as Lady Day sang, but beautiful.' – Alan Plater

'A fascinating and thoughtful narrative that reveals how the author's passion for music has enriched and shaped his life. The records he listened to as a boy later inspired a pilgrimage through the Deep South, during which he visited the room where Bessie Smith died and juggled walnuts in front of Muddy Waters' house. In a funny yet poignant style, he describes meetings with musicians such as Van Morrison and his relationship with his grandparents. This is a moving memoir that stirs our deepest feelings of nostalgia. We get only glimpses of the author's history, but through these highly personal memories, constantly resonant with music, he has somehow bared all.' – Rebecca S Bundhum, New Statesman

'A perceptive masterpiece. Elevates the human spirit. A soundtrack to all our lives.' – Dr Rock (Little Richard's biographer)

'Like most people who have got it right, Clayton is able to see the music in a social context, and his stories, varied and wide-ranging, from encounters with blues, folk, jazz and rock in England, Mississippi and Europe, to his interviewing the owner of the Batley Variety Club are entertaining, witty, enlightening and obviously true. You couldn't ask for much more.' – Paul Vernon, fRoots

'A very beautiful, brave book.' – David Suff, Fledg'ling Records

'I'm surprised there aren't more books like this – gentle, thoughtful rambles through beaten up record collections and musical memories of people who have lived ordinary lives. Ian Clayton has written a history of rock and roll that pulls up a chair and bends your ear, remembering school holidays spent in back bedrooms listening to vinyl, and meandering hours in pubs with friends and accompanying strangers pulling bits of pop apart. Try his journey to find out about the last hours of blues singer Bessie Smith or the epilogue about his late daughter, Billie Holliday Clayton. Here, his mission to marry music and meaning moves up a few mesmerising notches.' – Jude Rogers, Word

'A treasure of a book.' – Morley Observer

'I couldn't put it down. Any music fan worth his salt will feel an affinity with Ian Clayton. *Bringing It All Back Home* is one of the best books I've read in years.' – Ken Smith, Red Lick Records

'This personal meditation on music and its relation to family, place and the past that never really goes away might seem like an echo returned. A lifelong music obsessive, man of the people Clayton wanders and philosophises through India, Germany and Mississippi and on to the Batley Variety Club, examining the universal and the particular to a soundtrack of blues, folk, punk and world music. Even the dreadful tragedy told in the final chapter doesn't prevent his conclusions being full of wisdom and humanity.' – Ian Harrison, Mojo

'Clayton's writing makes music his. His book is chiefly concerned to what music does to you, not how music is made or what it says about its creators or what it stands for. It's a good book, if not a flawless one; a book about the difference between sentiment and deep feeling; about escape and facing up; about how the function of music to a certain kind of listener is to map his world, both inside and out. *Bringing It All Back Home* is an account, as they say on television, of a personal journey. It's in the economic, social and cultural shift that took place during the course of Clayton's post-post-war lifetime – from the life of the mines to Jimi Hendrix in a giant step – that you get to see the real value and, ultimately, the point of popular music as it was constituted during that period. Clayton doesn't explicate this point; it's implicit in his yarns. You begin to get a sense from his story of how 'taste' during that period was more than a fetish of bourgeois individualism; that it was an important tool in the remaking of English society for the better. And no, I'm not joking.' – Nick Coleman, The Independent On Sunday

'Ian Clayton has much to say and he says it so well. We need original eyes to look at the North in these days of extraordinary change. Ian's are among the regions most perceptive and humane.' – Martin Wainwright, The Guardian.

'Ian Clayton has an uncanny ear for voices and *Bringing It All Back Home* is full of voices. It's an enthralling journey through Yorkshire's backstreets via San Francisco and America's Deep South, with an accompanying soundtrack featuring everyone from Bessie Smith to Richard Hawley. It is a book full of love.' – Chris Bond, Yorkshire Post

'The literary equivalent of a great evening in the pub…He loves music and writes about it rather wonderfully. Even more he loves the people who make it. His book is an endearing homage to them.' – Songlines.

'An insightful, funny, very moving autobiography and cultural history, combined with the best music listening list on the planet.' – No Masters Co Operative.

'This is not an autobiography in the strictest sense of the term, neither is it a straightforward book of musical appreciation or criticism. Combine the two and you are still only two-thirds of the way there, *Bringing It All Back Home* has that secret ingredient – that takes a book out of the run-of-the-mill and makes it that little bit different and special.' – David Ward, Pontefract and Castleford Express

'What a beautiful book. It's a rare gift to be able to take those people, journeys, stories, tunes and feelings and to put them into my head.' – Andrew Edwards, BBC Radio Leeds

'One of the most moving books I've ever read.' – The Link

'At first it's a lovely book and then an astonishing one.' – Rony Robinson, BBC Radio Sheffield

'Ian Clayton is a man who loves his music and loves to tell a story. His book is the product of both passions…a compulsively readable heart warming and heartbreaking account of a Yorkshire life.' – Ned Thacker, BBC TV Look North

'Hear a snatch of a record and you're transported back to a place and time that's stayed tucked away for years. Ian Clayton has countless such musical markers in his life. He picks his way entertainingly and eccentrically from one to another in *Bringing It All Back Home,* an amiable, ambling autobiography of sorts packed with encounters and anecdotes. Ian loves people and their stories. The warmth of his personality shines through this book.' – Mike Priestley, Bradford Telegrah &Argus

'An intimate and original memoir which combines rollicking humour and heartbreak in equal measure. It made me seek out some of my CD collection which had been silent for a decade and rediscover forgotten treasures.' – James Nash, Northern Exposure

'This book vividly conjures up the sounds and textures, as well as the sights, smells and tastes of life in the late 20th century. It is a cultural compendium that will make you laugh out loud and cry.' – Gillian Moore, Head of Contemporary Culture, Southbank Centre

'On every page Ian's consummate skill as a storyteller shines through. With each line he writes he has a way of drawing you into his world. A wonderful read.' – Christine Talbot, ITV Yorkshire

'Great stories, very warmly written and proof if ever it was needed, that good music and the core of life are inseperable.' – Mike Heneghan, Mute Records

Bringing It All Back Home
Ian Clayton

route

First published by Route
PO Box 167, Pontefract, WF8 4WW
info@route-online.com
www.route-online.com

ISBN (13): 978-1-901927-35-1
ISBN (10): 1-901927-35-0

Acknowledgements:
Pat on the back and ruffle of the hair to Pam Oxley for typing,
Roger Green, Susana Galán, Manuel Lafuente, Oliver Mantel, and
Anthony Cropper for commenting on early drafts. Emma Smith
for proofreading. Jane Hickson for taking time to listen. Kevin
Reynolds and Steve Truelove for photography on the hardback
version and Andy Campbell for design of the same. Ian Anderson
and Rich Wilson for the artwork on the paperback. Bob Preedy
for permission to quote from his book about Batley Variety Club,
Live Like a Lord. Ian and Isabel Daley for the idea. Mrs McMurry
for recording Elmore James.

Cover Design, Art Direction and Photography
made in The Designers Republic
www.thedesignersrepublic.com

A catalogue for this book is available from the British Library

Written by hand and set in Garamond

Printed in the UK by CPI Bookmarque, Croydon, CR0 4TD

Route is supported by Arts Council England

For my partner Heather Parkinson,
our son Edward and our beautiful Billie

Contents

For the Record
Collecting and Hoarding

Bringing It All Back Home
Knowing and Sharing

Foreword

What is this you have in your hands? Too wide-ranging to be a simple autobiography, that's for sure.

Imagine a magical roller coaster that unfurled beyond the confines of the fairground, looping and winding and soaring around time barriers, oceans and continents through every kind of weather 'til you realise it's mobius-looped its way back to the familiar patch of the original fairground. Imagine the ride! Hovering here (a moment to adjust the binoculars) then momentarily gliding too fast to focus steadily but still always dizzily vivid.

Now imagine it's a book. That, dear reader, is the book you have in your hands. And thanks Ian, for allowing us glimpses of Heather, Edward and the eternally untarnished innocence of little Billie Holiday.

Robert Wyatt

'At home he feels like a tourist
He fills his head with culture
He gives himself an ulcer.'

Gang of Four

'The purpose of music is to elevate
the spirit and inspire. Not to help
push some product down your
throat. It puts you in tune with
your own existence. For me
(music) is deep reality, someone
who's telling me where he's been
that I haven't and what it's like
there – somebody whose life I can
feel.'

Bob Dylan

Got That...Not Got That

Having and Wanting

Subterranean, Homesick and Blue

Everything reminds me of something. I have filled my house and my head with things; books, records, paintings, stories; souvenirs that have no meaning except to me. Sometimes I think my house is my head and my head has become my house.

I want to make a map that charts a journey from a back street in the Yorkshire coalfields to the Mississippi Delta, to the Ganges Valley, to a jazz bar in Germany and back home again, to Featherstone where I belong.

I have a recurring dream. I am trying to get out of Featherstone. Someone has built a barbed wire fence. I leap over the fence. As I land on the other side, a hand holds up the bottom strand and beckons me to come back in again. I crawl through the wet grass back under the wire.

In my dream I could be Steve McQueen revving a motorbike. More often I'm his mate, the little guy who, after a period in the cooler, goes mad and gets shot in the back while trying to climb the barbed wire and is never seen again until he turns up playing a pastry chef in *Crossroads*.

When I was a boy I admired an enamelled sign that was fixed high on a wall at the bottom of Station Lane. On the enamelled sign was a white pointing finger and the motto, 'To the Station'. I liked that. In later years I clutched a copy of the Rolling Stones live album *Get Yer Ya-Ya's Out* close to me as I came home from a record shop called the Kiosk. I played a track on it over and over. It was an old Robert Johnson song called 'Love in Vain':

'Well I followed her to the station
With a suitcase in my hand...
The blue light was my blues
The red light was my mind.'

That song reminded me of the sign which is now long gone. When I close my eyes and dream, I can still see it.

I have spent a lot of time following signs out of my home town. And another part of my life trying to get back in again. Bob Dylan was the first man to pull me out of here and my gran and grandad had a bigger pull to draw me back. The Anti-Nazi League and punk rock offered a tunnel out, but when the miners' strike collapsed that tunnel, I burrowed like a mole blindly back again. Marc Bolan, T-Bone Walker, Van Morrison, Dusty Springfield and a musician called Taj Mahal have all given me a leg up over the fence and spun me round at thirty-three and a third revolutions. My Auntie Alice, a pub called the Top House and a fearsome prop forward called Vince Farrar who played for the famous Featherstone Rovers have all knocked the stylus right out of the groove.

There's a book called *The Recording Angel: Music, Records and Culture from Aristotle to Zappa* by a man called Evan Eisenberg. It's a book about music as a thing, a commodity to consume. There is a chapter in it about a man called Clarence who lives in absolute poverty, pisses in a bucket, shits in the public library toilets and has a collection of nearly a million records. Clarence keeps his records in broken fridges, in ovens he no longer cooks in and under, as well as on, his bed. His shoes slob off his swollen feet and his neck is torn through shaving in cold water, yet he has an encyclopedic knowledge of the George and Ira Gershwin recordings on the Brunswick label. I've no desire to be a Clarence but at various times I have wanted to have a hairstyle like Marc Bolan, play blues harp like Jimmy Reed and sing like Joe Cocker. When I grew my hair long I looked like Joe Cocker. I quickly realised that I would be better off being a listener to music, a collector of records. And we all collect records. The records then become a soundtrack to our lives. Records are about escaping, finding out, searching and planning routes. Of course for most of us the records we gather never bring us anywhere near the people who make them. Records are just 'things' that we end up hoarding. But records can be more than 'things'.

My journey to find music and words started in a house full of arguments and unhappiness. The maps I made to find music that made me happy have taken me on an odyssey to find out what the music was before it became a thing to collect. I really don't think I'm much nearer to what inspired the music in the first place, perhaps just a bit wiser and it's been a good adventure. And sometimes, as they say, 'Putting up the tent can be finer than the circus'.

Sometime in the middle of the 1980s, an old man who I don't know goes into Riverside second-hand record shop at York with a carrier bag full of Billie Holiday LPs. He's decided to transfer all of his collection onto tape and listen to them in future on a portable cassette player that he's bought for his old people's council flat that he's just moved into. I spend thirty-odd quid on a handful of old Verve label recordings that Billie made in the autumn years of her career. As the stylus works its way through the dust and fluff it begins to reveal a voice that the poet Philip Larkin once described as a scorched newspaper. I know all about scorched newspapers. People who know how to draw up coal fires scorch newspapers. As the dust and fluff are further raked away something else begins to be revealed. A breathy, tender, haunting thing that is Ben Webster's saxophone. I go back to Riverside Records and find that the old man I didn't know has sold some Ben Webster records as well. Webster collaborated. Through him I discover Art Tatum, Oscar Peterson, Jimmy Witherspoon, Buck Clayton. I find that he spent the last ten years of his life in Denmark and Holland. I search for the stuff he recorded with Danes and Dutchmen. A new road out of Featherstone opens up.

Heather and me spent the first few years of our partnership travelling. I suppose it's fitting then that one night on an adventure to Prague, in a scruffy little apartment with a three-quarter sized bed, we decided to start our family. Heather became pregnant in the autumn of 1995. When she went for the first scan after thirteen weeks, the nurse operating the sonar machine told her she was expecting twins. They wouldn't tell us at Pontefract Hospital what sex the twins were. We both dreamed it would be a boy and girl. In May of 1996 our dreams came true. Edward and Billie were born on 9th May. May is a good month for blues singers' birthdays. Robert Johnson was born on the 8th, Little Walter, Bumble Bee Slim, T-Bone Walker and Blind Willie McTell were all born in May. We named Edward after my grandad who spent a lot of his life labouring underground at the pit, and Billie after the greatest jazz singer ever to draw breath. When I told the registrar at Pontefract Town Hall that I wanted to call my little girl Billie Holiday Clayton, she shoved her glasses back to the bridge of her nose, let out a sigh and said, 'I see'.

We thought that because I had chosen Edward's name, Heather should have the choice for Billie. She told me that she liked 'boy' sounding names for girls and suggested 'Stevie' after the poet Stevie Smith. Heather's favourite poem at the time was 'Not Waving But Drowning'. Stevie Smith had been born in De La Pole Avenue at Hull. I told Heather that I equated 'De La Pole' with a psychiatric hospital of that name. Eventually Heather came to 'Billie' and I added the 'Holiday' bit.

Within minutes of being born Billie Holiday and Edward Clayton went to the incubators. Heather went to sleep and the midwife said to me, 'Get off home, you're no use here now.'

I came home and cooked a celebratory fried breakfast. The egg I cracked into the pan was a double yolker. I hadn't had an egg with a double yolk since my dad kept hens on the allotment and I haven't had one since.

Edward and Billie have their own rooms. Edward plays his piano in what he calls 'The Music Room'. Billie plays with her dolls in our library. Edward anchors me to my home town. Sometimes I think he is my grandad. I can see my grandad in his chocolate eyes. Billie looks like my granny, she moves like my granny, she even sings like my granny. She loves travelling. She wants to see the world.

I sit in my kitchen following signs, making maps, drawing lines to the world beyond my home town.

The Louder You Scream

'The best stories start anywhere.' This is Chenjerai Hove, a Zimbabwean writer who is touring Yorkshire. He is delivering words of wisdom like a paper boy pushing the *Evening Post* through letter boxes. 'But I think you know that already don't you?' I think I do. It's just that nobody has ever said it to me before. We are sitting in an old Tetley Bitter pub called The Wrens, which stands on a corner opposite the Grand Theatre in Leeds. Comedians and singers from the music hall days look down on us from frames on the wall, stained brown with years of nicotine and beer fumes. 'My wife's feet are in a very bad condition.' I think that Chenjerai is about to tell a joke, but his face tells a different story. 'She has visited many shoe shops here in England and she keeps buying shoes that don't fit her.' I stifle a little laugh. 'The shoes that she buys are not suitable for this journey.'

Chenjerai Hove reaches into his carrier bag. The bag says 'Freeman, Hardy and Willis' on it. He takes out his latest book. It is called *Bones*. I ask him if he will write a message in it for me. He already has his pen out of his jacket pocket and writes: 'For Ian. The world was in words before it was flesh. My love C. Hove.'

Bones is published by Heinemann in its African writers' series. It is about the oppressed and voiceless people of this world struggling to say something. It's not an easy book to read even though it has just a hundred and thirteen pages.

When I get it home I read it in a couple of sittings. It's inside me somewhere now. When I want to find this story all I see are fragments.

Twenty-five years before I came here, in another Tetley pub, this time the Blackmoor Head in Pontefract near where I live, I'm listening to a drunken old piano player called Angus. He plays a skewed version of 'Blaze Away' followed by an even more twisted take on 'God Bless the Child'. He tells me that in the 1950s he saw Billie Holiday sing after hours in a bar at Wakefield. I believe him. Angus continues, gently playing a series of abstracted chords and letting slip his homespun pearls. 'Good ale and music', 'a warm fire to your arse', 'comfortable shoes and a clean place to shit'. He lifts his fingers from the keys and closes the piano lid. He then drains his pint pot and belches into a jacket pocket full of bookmaker's pens. I take the pearls home on the number 70 bus. I am a magpie. I have been a magpie since my story began. I collect things that old men and women say. I gather images from plays and films that I have seen. I pull together sounds, songs, poems and ditties. I can't wait to fly home with them. I want to bring all these things back home.

My gran came back from Blackpool with an Acker Bilk outfit for me. It comprised of a striped waistcoat, a bowler hat, a plastic clarinet, which my grandad declared was Hong Kong made, and a stick-on goatee beard. I had to play along to Acker's tune 'Stranger on the Shore' every time it came on the wireless. These performances didn't last for long because our Tony shoved the clarinet down a storm drain at the

26

bottom of the street. This dates my first musical memory. My first visual memory appears as frozen milk bottles with the cream pushing up the foil tops. This would have been the freezing winter of 1962/63, the time of Bob Dylan's first visit to England when he appeared in the BBC film *Madhouse on Castle Street.*

I live in my own madhouse. My father can't keep down a regular job. My grandad, my mother's father, can't stand my dad and threatens to give him a 'bloody good hiding' most days. My mother shouts and cries a lot and spends lengths of time squeezing almost invisible spots in a mirror. My gran believes my parents should never have married. They met at the seaside when my mother was working as a teenage chambermaid and my dad was spinning girls round on the fairground waltzers. 'The louder you scream the faster we go, girls.' My mother screamed for him the loudest. One day they arrived back from the seaside holding hands. They told my grandparents that my mother was pregnant with me. My grandad gave my dad a bloody good hiding and told them to get married. My gran washed a caseful of my father's stinking shirts.

I never got close to either of my parents. My dad was useless at playing football, cheated at draughts and didn't know the answers to any questions. My mother made herself beautiful, but never got taken anywhere. They never went to pubs, except on holiday, never had a meal in a restaurant, never visited a museum or art gallery, never read a book and mainly listened to music because it was on the wireless. I never heard either of them make a critical judgement on anything apart from each other. My dad's answer to my mother's unhappiness was to buy her a bigger television and a whistling canary in a cage. Their solution to our unhappiness was to tell us to get to bed. I had a lot of fights at school and in the street outside our house. I didn't cry much. Though there is one moment burnt into my memory. It would be the summer of 1964. I know it because I started my first school day at Girnhill Lane Infants with my foot heavily bandaged. My mother took my brother Tony and me to a paddling pool in the Valley Gardens at Pontefract. She had a hospital appointment and the hospital was next to the gardens. The water in the paddling pool was black filthy, but I paddled. Someone had thrown a bottle into the pool. I stood on the broken bottom of the bottle and it stuck to the underside of my foot. Blood came to the top of the mucky water. I cried. My mother swept me out of the water and held me close to her. She was wearing a suede coat with a sheepskin collar. I pressed myself into that collar as she ran to the hospital. My mother cuddled me as the doctor stitched my foot. I have frozen that moment like a photo in an old handbag. I show the little scar to my own children today.

As an eight-year-old boy I collect football cards, the ones that come in packets of pink bubblegum. I found this collection of cards recently. They were bound by a perishing rubber band that was wrapped twice around them sometime between The Beatles disbanding and 'Ride a White Swan' getting played over and over at the St Thomas Church Hall Christmas party. I am the fastest schoolyard flicker and dealer of football cards who ever lived. I slide these cards from one hand to the other while a circle of schoolfriends intone a playground mantra. 'Got that…Got that…Not got that…Swap yer that!' When Alan Ball is transferred from Blackpool to Everton in real life for the then unheard of sum of £100,000, he goes from my arse pocket into Stephen Brightmore's in the blink of an eye.

In this collection George Eastham of Stoke City vies with Bobby Tambling of Chelsea. Willie Morgan is a product of Burnley's youth scheme. Ernie Hunt is on his way to Coventry City and another Coventry Ernie, Ernie Machin, is recovering from a broken leg. Len Badger is a Sheffield United hero, the improbably named Ian Storey-Moore is at Nottingham Forest and Peter Knowles, the brother of 'Nice One Cyril' Knowles, is a clever midfielder at Wolverhampton Wanderers, who is described as a good prospect for the forthcoming World Cup in Mexico.

The Move become the first group to be played on Radio One singing 'Flowers in the Rain'. On this day I am pushing a wheelbarrow around the new council estate selling cabbages out of my dad's allotment. There is a man who always buys more than he needs and gives me more money than he can afford. He has a dog and shouts, 'Get under, Satan' at it. Less than twenty years from this time he will be on strike from his job at the pit. Within five years of the strike finishing he will be so drunk that he won't know who he is any more. When he dies through liver failure everyone who gets drunk at his funeral tea will say what a good man he was. There is another man, a huge man who rides a racing bike like a circus bear. He will come to the end of his life drinking twenty pints a day and growling like a wounded animal. He will stare hard at anyone who comes within five yards of where he stands at the corner of the bar in the Working Men's Club. On this day he ruffles my hair, pays for a cabbage and says, 'Go steady with that barrow, love.'

There are no flowers in our allotment. Only vegetables and a lot of stones and pieces of wood and old rolls of lino and carpet. When my wheelbarrow is empty I push it back and stand it by some sacks in the shed that my dad calls his 'cabin'. On the back of the cabin door is a magazine photograph of Les Kellett, the Saturday afternoon wrestler. He is wearing striped trunks and wrestling boots. He crouches on one knee and stares out of the picture. He looks like the podgy farmer that he probably was. His face is a slightly wizened mask. My dad looks a bit like Les Kellett. He sits in his cabin drinking cold tea out of a brown-stained tin cup and leafs through a collection of nude girl magazines that he keeps under the pile of sacks. These magazines have been swapped many times with other blokes on the allotment site. Most of them have had their edges eaten by mice.

My dad likes the music of The Platters, The Ink Spots, Al Bowlly and Al Jolson. He claims his hero is Mario Lanza and he tells me that Mario Lanza died through eating too much rich food. My dad says that the water left over when you boil a cabbage is the finest thing a man can drink. He drinks a pint of it every time we have cabbage and puts some on his face. When he was a young man he thought he was Gene Vincent. Before he looked like Les Kellett, he looked a bit like Gene Vincent. When he worked on the fairgrounds spinning the cars on the waltzers he wore a brown leather jacket and written in studs on the back it said his name, Sid.

Sometimes he sits on the step of his cabin and philosophises.

'We're all animals y'know, lad. We'd eat owt if we were hungry.'

He swills the dregs round in his tin cup and throws them onto the garden.

'Plants like tea. See that mare's tail. That's the most successful plant there ever was. It hasn't altered in twenty million years. When dinosaurs were roaming about the forests were full of that stuff. That's where all the coal comes from. When the forests died down and rotted it made seams of coal. The coal that they're all digging round here comes from forests full of mare's tail.'

He stops talking then and whistles 'Whispering Grass' to himself. Most of the time he spoils thoughtful moments by singing 'Leap Up and Down with Your Knickers in the Air'. It's a song that he's learned from a cabaret group at the social club when we go to our caravan.

Our static caravan is at the seaside near Withernsea. Here I pick up bits of driftwood, old rope, shells and patterned stones, and other things lost at sea. I want to find pieces with words almost washed off them. I don't know why I do it. Do I want to give a home to flotsam and jetsam? Why is it interesting? Is it because I don't want things to be lost? And by finding things and collecting them, do I render them no longer lost? At George Street School I learn from a student teacher that ancient people made fetishes out of coloured stones and twisted tree branches. I make my own collection of these and keep them on a shelf in our bin hole.

Our next door neighbour's son Billy Telford decides when he reaches fourteen that he doesn't want to play at marbles any more. He gives me his collection. I save this collection of coloured potties, steel bollies and glass alleys in a cardboard box that once contained a pair of Stylo Matchmaker football boots.

Next door but two lives Frankie Parr with his auntie. Frankie plays the big bass drum in the Salvation Army band. He gives me his old stamp album. I move from football cards to stamps. It is around this time that I start to get interested in maps. I want to know where Sarawak is. In which part of Africa will I find Togo? I start to bring maps home. Any maps, walkers' maps of the Yorkshire Dales, dog-eared London A to Zs. I draw on my maps. I draw routes that I might one day take. I pore over names like Bechuanaland, Tanganyika, Rwanda and Burundi. This world in words that one day I hoped to flesh out.

In 1971 my mother ran away and left us. My dad said, 'We're going to form a posse, lad.' I said, 'Why?' He said, 'We're going to lasso your mother and bring her home.' The posse set off from Kirkgate Station to track her down. She came back. Not long after this my parents decided to 'give it another go' and bought a house that had seen better days in the back streets of Hull. For the first time since he married my mother, my dad was out of reach of my grandad. For the first time in her married life my mother couldn't open the front door and shout for help. I hated moving to Hull. On the day we left I was eating fruit salad and Carnation cream out of tins at my gran's kitchen table. I threw the cream into my dad's face. He slapped me across the head and told me to get into the lorry. Outside, my father's brother, who already lived at Hull, was grinning and waiting in a pick-up truck full of our furniture. My one memory of that journey is of a sentimental country and western song playing on the truck's radio. It was a song in the charts at the time called 'Nobody's Child'. When the song reached its second chorus my dad and his brother joined in:

'I'm nobody's child, nobody's child
Just like a flower I'm growing wild
No mammy's kisses and no daddy's smile
Nobody wants me, I'm nobody's child.'

They both grinned like Cheshire cats and ruffled my hair.

In Hull I spent my time collecting maps and stamps. The Second World War had only been over for twenty-odd years and Hull, which had been one of this country's worst bombed cities, still had huge areas of ruined buildings. On the Beverley Road was an old cinema called The National. I liked to go there and search through the ruins. There was a record shop between the bowling alley and the Black Bull pub. In the window was the cover of an early Tyrannosaurus Rex LP called *My People Were Fair and Had Sky in Their Hair...But Now They're Content to Wear Stars on Their Brows*. The cover picture showed Marc Bolan with mystical people climbing through his corkscrewed hair. The cover fascinated me. I spent hours with my face pressed against the mucky window of that record shop breathing my own daydreams onto the picture.

Four years after their fresh start in Hull, my mother and father divorced. Their marriage had disintegrated into a series of rows, fights and solicitors' letters. My mother moved out to live with her new man, my father's brother, the one who had grinned in the lorry. My father stayed on at the terraced house in Hull that he had bought with some compensation money he had got after being crushed in the cardboard box factory where he worked. I wrote a letter to my gran and grandad to ask if I might come back to live with them. My brothers and me ended up being shared out. Andrew, the youngest, went with our mother and the new man. Tony, the middle brother, ended up with Auntie Alice and I came back to Gran's. She kept the letter I wrote in a blue-flowered teapot until she died.

From 1975 until I meet my partner, Heather, while dancing to a Sham 69 record, I live in Gran and Grandad's back bedroom. I have a single bed with a pink candlewick bedspread, a wardrobe on top of which is a Dansette record player and a window onto a back yard full of noisy neighbours. It is at this time that I start collecting LP records in earnest, *Let It Bleed*, *Electric Music for Mind and Body*, *Working Man's Dead* all come to share that little back bedroom. My immediate world revolves around an ageing pair of grandparents entering retirement, a boring apprenticeship at an engineering factory and a back yard full of gossip and innuendo. Then, underneath my candlewick bed, is a growing pile of records. Underneath my bed is another world.

Back Yard

Outside of my gran's back door is a small wooden stool and a piece of sandstone as big as a window sill. I can't tell you how long that piece of stone has been there, it just is there. This is one of the unities upon which our back yard, and the stories that are spun there, are built. My gran will tell the story of how she once tried to move it and how she broke her toe when she dropped it, so there it stays. Having told the story of how she failed with the stone, she will follow quickly with her story of how fast she could throw a ton of coal into the coal house. It's not timed in minutes or shovelfuls, but compared to a man. 'I can chuck in a ton of coal as quick as any collier,' she'll tell you. My gran is strong, her arms muscular and she wants to prove it. She also wants to show that she doesn't want her husband to have to dig coal down a pit all day and then do the same at home. A cartoon often repeated in miners' newspapers depicts two men towing their bollocks off down the pit. They are joined by a third who says, 'Your coal's been delivered this morning!'

Our cameras at home never have a flash on them. Most of our family photographs are taken outside of the back door. On birthdays, wedding days, funerals and whenever somebody invests in a new film this is where we all troop out to. Someone always sits on the stool, someone always stands on the stone. My grandad stands at the back because he is the tallest. My gran and Auntie Alice find a clean pinny to put on. The most unbearably poignant photo must have been taken during the early part of the Second World War. My grandad wears his army great coat and his military cap almost falling from the side of his head. He has a kit bag by his side. A small Jack Russell terrier stands at his feet. My mother, aged about three by the look of her, sits impassively on the stool. Another photo taken straight after this shows an empty door hole where my grandad had stood. My mother's face is now turned to the left and the Jack Russell is raised on his hind legs also looking out of the picture. The picture captures an exact moment in our family history; the very second when my grandad left to go to war. My mother didn't see her father for six years after that. When he came home she was nine and wearing pigtails and glasses. She asked my gran, 'Who's that man?'

Our family story unfolds against that back door, my brother Tony nearly always has a stick of some sort in his hand and I'm never without a jam jar full of tadpoles or a half-eaten apple or bun. Andrew, the youngest brother, is usually held up like the Challenge Cup in the arms of a rugby player. There I am wearing a Wrangler jacket and flared jeans in a picture that looks out of place amongst an old handbag full of sepia-toned people in demob suits and aprons. There are the neighbours, three tiny spinster sisters, Hannah, Mabel and Doris Pyatt who get up every morning at four to travel to work in the mills at Bradford, twenty-odd miles away by bus. Here is Stephen Brightmore who reads his books about skinheads. Mr Larkins with whom I sat to listen to the 1966 World Cup Final on a wireless he fetched out into the backs. Here are Margaret and John Frederikson who went to find a new life in Australia, they applied for the government's £10, one-way deal, were turned down, but saved up and went anyway. Next, my best mate Roy Herrington who would always lean over the fence and inquire, 'Is your Ian in?' And then old Johnny Hope who introduced me to his wind-up gramophone with a tin horn and engaged me into a love affair with 'talking machines'.

Johnny Hope and his wife Emily are so old that even my grandad calls them old. Johnny likes to sit on the stool outside of our back door and make up stories about his life. In his pocket he will have a brown egg from the allotments. He will give the egg to the first woman who passes by and sing them a song in a corncrake voice.

'Poor old Johnny's dead
He died last night in bed
Cut his throat on a bar of soap
Poor old Johnny's dead.'

He can recite Featherstone Rovers' teams right back to Edwardian times like prayers. Later I will research his mantra in the newspapers of the day 'In 1906, the Rovers beat Widnes in the second round of the Challenge Cup. Randall, Higson, Jukes, Kellett, Sammy Southall' and on and he's right.

I am the only boy in our street who is allowed to go into Johnny's house. Emily is not well and lies on a leather chaise longue covered in crocheted blankets all day. I show my manners and talk quietly. I also give Johnny the odd Woodbine out of my grandad's packet. The house is filled with potted plants, newspapers, ornaments, pictures, empty milk bottles and dog food tins. There is an old chocolate tin and on its lid is a lady, leaping through the air with a flowing scarf. Johnny tells me that the picture on the tin is his wife Emily. I visualise her as Isadora Duncan, she is dancing with Johnny when they are young to music coming out of the tin horn on his wind-up gramophone.

'Will you play your gramophone for me one day please?'

'I can't lad. It wants a nail.'

'What does it want a nail for?'

'To play the records with. You need a nail or a thorn.'

'They call it a stylus now, Mr Hope.'

'Aye. Well that one wants a nail, lad.' He spits great gobstoppers of phlegm into his crackling fire.

'What do you want to hear that for anyroad? It's no good now.'

'My Auntie Alice says that you can play music on them old gramophones by putting the corner of a photograph into the grooves.'

'Well thy can tell thi Auntie Alice from me that mine wants a nail.'

I don't think I ever got to hear Mr Hope's wind-up gramophone. I can't even picture it now, though I can picture his sideboard, his chair by the fire, his hearth full of ashes, his half-empty milk bottles. Yet it symbolises something special. A relationship between two neighbours eighty years apart. A love of storytelling, of things. I think of all the ghosts that might have been unleashed had I persuaded him to let me play a record with the edge of an old photograph.

The chair I'm sitting on to write these stories came from my gran and grandad's house. It's one of a set of four that

Heather and me rescued from the skip, rubbed the varnish off and painted sky blue. In March of 1938 my gran and grandad furnished their first house at 3 Mafeking Street, Featherstone, on the HP. The book she paid three shillings a week on came to me with all the other signposts and road maps of life passing in an old teapot full of papers when Gran died. The book sets out what they bought; a rexine sofa, twelve oak rods to hold a stair-carpet in place, a fireguard and some oak-leaf patterned oilcloth. When my grandad came back home from the war in 1945, they still owed six pounds three shillings on the book.

I also have my gran's rent books. Between 1938 and 1981, when she moved to the council flat, she never missed paying the weekly rent, except on one memorable occasion at the time of decimalisation. Gran miscalculated the new money and left half a pence short. Instead of telling her, the rent collector, a trilby-wearing solicitor's agent from Leeds, put her ha'penny in arrears. When my grandad got home from the pit he went berserk. The following week my grandad, snoozing on the rexine sofa after a day shift, jumped up to confront the rent man. He told him that if he wanted the ha'penny he would find it up his own arse, because that's where it would be shoved along with the rent book and his trilby if he didn't get out of the house. The rent man, a pathetic creep in brogues and gabardine raincoat, stood trembling and asked, 'Well, Mr Fletcher, I don't think that's very proper behaviour and besides how can I collect the rent if I'm not allowed in?'

'Let me tell thee this once, shithole. In future thy can collect the rent off the stool by the back door and whistle for thi ha'penny.'

For the next ten years various rent men collected the rent from the stool at the back door, none dare enter and the half pence arrears stayed as a permanent feature of the rent book.

If it sounds like a music hall ditty, that's what it probably is. It puts me in mind of the old Gus Elen song, 'If it Wasn't for the 'ouses in Between'.

'Oh it really is a very pretty garden
And Chingford to the eastward could be seen
Wiv a ladder and some glasses
You could see to 'Ackney Marshes
If it wasn't for the 'ouses in between.'

Except this wasn't London. This wasn't London by any stretch of the imagination. But it was music hall. These were the songs I heard at my gran's and at her sister's, my Auntie Alice, ninety two now and still going strong. My grandad had had a piano when he lived at home. No furniture, shoes provided by a charity called 'Boots for the Bairns', tea out of jam jars, but they had a piano. By the time their generation was growing up in the 1930s, music hall had spilled out of the theatres and into the pubs and working men's clubs. They sang fragments of songs and parodies that had been around when their grandparents were young.

'Dickie Di-doh sells fish
Three ha'pence a dish
Don't buy 'em, don't buy 'em
They stink when you fry 'em.'

'Joshua, Joshua,
Sweeter than lemon squash you are.'

My grandad sang that every night to his pint of Tetley's. He joined in when the club turns sang. Even on the more modern stuff in the 1970s when I started drinking. 'Solitaire', 'The Most Beautiful Girl in the World' and 'Feelings'; massive working men's club staples round our way. My gran and Aunt Alice's conversation was dappled with catchphrases from George Formby, Frank Randle and Albert Modley. 'Turned out nice again', 'By, I've supped some ale toneet', 'Eeeh! We're in a worse state than Russia'. Every time I reddened up through embarrassment if someone belched or farted in the house, Auntie Alice would sing in a keening voice:

'You're shy Mary Ellen, you're shy.'

I didn't even think about it at the time. It was just normal household banter. As I've grown I've come to realise that they were just responding to the popular culture of the time by incorporating it into their daily lives. When my grandad mimicked George Formby's dad and sang:

'When Hackenschmidt run second in the Derby last July,
I was standing at the corner of the street.'

or Formby's own:

'With my little stick of Blackpool rock
Along the promenade I go

41

It might be sticky, but I never complain
It's nice to have a nibble of it now and again.'

He was doing exactly what I was doing with my hairbrush when I sang, 'Ground Control to Major Tom.'

When Neil Armstrong became the first man to set foot on the moon I ran into our backs to look up at the sky. Old Johnny Hope was squatting, like old miners do, by his back door and spitting. I went over and said to him, 'Mr Hope, a man has landed on the moon.' He didn't say anything for ages and then just said, 'Oh aye.' I wanted to know why he wasn't excited. He just carried on spitting and staring into space. Eventually he said, 'I think I've seen a rat in my bin hole.'

Tears and Fingerprints

'It's alright going away, but it's always nice to come home again.' My gran and grandad said that every time they went on their holidays. They only ever went to Blackpool. In forty years of marriage they never missed. They always stayed at Mrs Calloway's boarding house at the back of the Tower. My grandad ate three oysters every morning and then went for three pints of Tetley's bitter. My gran's favourite was a vulgar Wigan comedian who had been brought up a few streets away from George Formby. This was Frank Randle; Gran and Grandad saw him every time he appeared at Blackpool Pier shows. Randle belched a lot into the microphone and had the catchphrase that went 'By! I've supped some ale toneet!' which my gran liked to imitate.

My grandad's favourite singer, he said, was Caruso. I don't know how he came to this because he didn't have any records by Caruso in his house. In fact my grandad didn't have any records by anybody in his house because he didn't have a record player. They had a wireless, but the only time I can recall them listening to it was when a programme called *Down Your Way* was on. That and, bizarrely in a town sixty miles from the sea, the shipping forecast. I once heard my grandad singing the Slade song 'Cum on Feel the Noize' in a voice that was a cross between Andy Williams and George Formby. Another time I heard him coming home from the Girnhill Lane Working Men's Club and belting out 'Solitaire' with all his words mixed up:

'Nah! Solitaire's the only game in town
An' ev'ry road it takes me brings me round
When I'm by mysel...it's never going to end
I'm playing Solitai r r r e – ah!'

He stumbled in the front door. My gran had a pot of tea and a meat sandwich waiting for him.

'One of the finest turns I've ever seen, Hilda, that's what was on at that club tonight.'

'Pipe down now then, Eddie. Our Ian's to be up for work in t'morning at seven o'clock.'

'Seven o'clock! He ought to have been like me, up at bloody quarter past four for that pit. Seven o'clock, he dunt know he's born, with his bloody long hair and his patches on his jeans.'

My grandad spent forty years of his daytime life underground. He was a subterranean, a tail-gate ripper at Sharlston pit. He crawled about on all fours getting coal. He told me that this country would always want coal. 'Do you know lad, the coal miners of the world are the finest body of men who ever drew breath.' On his gravestone it says, 'A good and honest collier'.

I grew up at Number 4 Mafeking Street, my grandparents lived at Number 3 and my Auntie Alice at Number 14. This house had no books in it. Actually, there were two books in it. The first was a big New English dictionary bound in maroon coloured leather. My Auntie Alice won it at Sunday school in the 1920s. I still have it. The second was a book called *Better Sight Without Glasses*. My gran bought it to try and improve my mother's eyesight when children started to call her 'specky four-eyes'. My mother's sight was ruined when a boy next door threw a bunch of keys into her face when she was four. I don't know where that book is any more. The first book I treasured was about Emmeline Pankhurst. I was nine. I borrowed it from the local library because I liked the cover and it smelled good. I had to return it. The librarian checked it for tears and fingerprints. She told me to wash my hands next time I wanted to borrow one of her books. I made a promise to myself that one day when I had my own house I would have my own library.

In our house we had a handful of records. The first one I treasured was 'A Hard Day's Night'. I can remember this because my dad worked on the night shift at Lyons cake factory. He stole swiss rolls. When he got the sack he went to work at a wool factory. He stole wool. He was good at nicking wool. So good that most of the women in our street who knitted their families' jumpers knitted them with wool that my dad had nicked. One of the neighbours who fell out with him reported him to the wool factory. My gran and mam sat up all night cutting up wool and feeding it onto the dying embers of the fire. Hard day's night.

The first record I bought with my own money was, depending on who I'm talking to, 'Lola' by The Kinks, 'In the Summertime' by Mungo Jerry, 'Ernie' by Benny Hill, or 'Where Do You Go to My Lovely?' by Peter Sarstedt. For the sake of argument I'll go for 'Those Were the Days' by Mary Hopkin. My friend Stephen Brightmore was the first in our gang to go and see a Leeds United game at Elland Road. He saw them play Vitória Setúbal, a Portuguese team, in the Fairs Cup. He came to school the next day with the TV commentator Brian Moore's autograph on his programme, a yellow, blue and white scarf tied to his wrist and a new song:

'Those were the days my friend
We took the Stretford End.'

Later Brighty bought those slim New English library books, *Suedehead* and *Skinhead*. We sat on his back step reading sections out to each other. After a while the books would automatically fall open at the pages with a sex scene on them. 'He inserted his penis and plunged up and down on her.'

Brighty had the original 1968 version of 'Deborah' by Tyrannosaurus Rex on the Regal Zonophone label. It had a brown paper label. The hole in the centre was blistered and scrawled by being constantly pressed onto the peg in the middle of his record player.

We had a little red memo book. It was my job to take it to Johnson's corner shop every time we wanted a bag of sugar, a quarter of cheese or a couple of eggs. Mrs Johnson or her daughters would write the price in the book, sign it and at the end of the week tot it up when my dad's swiss roll wage arrived. One day in the spring of 1971 I stood listening in the shop to Margaret Johnson, talking to a girl called Jayne Summers. In between blowing bubbles of gum and doodling long-haired boys onto the side of the sweets display case, she said, 'Have you heard T. Rex's new record? It's like really cool y'know.' It was the best sentence I'd ever heard anybody speak. On the Saturday I walked to Pontefract and at Jays record bar in the Market Hall, I bought

'Get it On' by T. Rex. It cost 42 pence, 8/- 5d in old money. Since that day I have never stopped collecting records. Not many weeks have gone by when I haven't bought one.

I shared a cold back bedroom with my two brothers, Tony and Andrew. In the winter-time we wrote messages on the frozen ferns of our window. At night-time we pissed in a white enamel bucket with a blue rim. Sometimes we shit in it. The floor was covered in oilcloth, grey with black and white swirling patterns like a skating rink. I'd seen pictures of Jackson Pollock paintings in a book at George Street School. For a while I told myself that, although my gran had made our bedroom curtains, Jackson Pollock had designed the oilcloth. I propped myself up in bed on my elbow. I listened to the drunken good nights and laughter of people coming home from the Girnhill Lane Working Men's Club and I listened to Radio Luxembourg on an old Bush wireless whose signal flowed in and out like the tide.

The dial on the radio is pleasing to turn. It moves slowly and smoothly and the red line it's attached to visits Athlone, Hilversum, Riga, Rennes, Allouis, Reykjavik, Belgrade. On the short wave I can hear Lisbon and Ankara. I like the far off voices and the static. I even like the pauses in between. In fact I become obsessed with the pauses. In Mr Rhodes's class at George Street School I listen not so much to what I'm being told but to the pauses. I like the general hubbub of a class full of children who live in the streets near me, but I like more the way the sound rises and falls, an accidental climax of noise followed by a lull, then a gentle increase and another fall. The waves coming in and going back out again. In the playground I like the stories about what was on TV last night.

Everyone has seen *Opportunity Knocks, The Benny Hill Show* and *The High Chaparral*. Every story starts with the line 'Did you see?'. My brothers and me are always sent to bed early. If I don't know the ending of this week's *High Chaparral* or *Department S* I make up my own ending. And strangely when I tell the story none of my mates know the difference. Manolito rescues his sister Victoria from rogue Apaches by proving his own skill with a bow and arrow. I have a gang around me hanging on to my version. Sounds from far away. Pauses. Stories with alternative endings. Later when I leave school I find an apprenticeship at a local engineering works. I lie in the bath every night after work and listen to 'Revolution 9' from The Beatles' *White Album*. The track is made up of cut-and-paste sound. Random noise. Radio stations and Lennon's voice intoning over and over again, 'Number nine, number nine, number nine.'

My granny thinks there's something wrong with me. She tells the neighbours about me and 'number nine'. One of the neighbours tells her, 'Our John says he was always a bit strange at school.'

My gran wanted to play the violin. She never got near one. She wanted to write poetry. One day in the 1926 strike – all my family's stories start during miners' strikes and wars – the teacher at her junior school asked if anyone knew a poem. My granny's hand shot up.

'Yes Hilda, come to the front and recite your poem.'

My granny went to the front. Put the corner of her pinafore in her mouth and at great speed said:

'The elephant is a funny bird,
it leaps from bough to bough.
It lays its eggs in a rhubarb tree,
and sings just like a cow.'

Gran rushed to sit back down. The teacher sighed and said,
'That's not poetry, stupid!'
My gran never bothered with poetry much after that.
Later, Gran became the star of the school when she won a
competition to find the girl who looked most like the flying
ace Amy Johnson. Every time Amy Johnson was on the front
page of the newspapers my gran would tour the school
playground mimicking the photo in the papers. Leaning on
an imaginary propeller, removing invisible flying goggles,
tossing a pretend scarf into the breeze. It was the nearest my
granny got to flying.
Billie plays the violin, I hope she will fly. Her ambition for
this year is to take her violin to the Whitby Rowing Club
during folk week and join in with fifty-odd others playing jigs
and reels. Her other ambition is to continue cultivating the
Frida Kahlo look. She has eyebrows that join in the middle
and ever since I told her that Frida Kahlo had joined up
eyebrows she wants to be like her. I have a beautiful photo
of Kahlo that I bought off a Mexican hippy in San
Francisco. It hangs on our living room wall and Billie stands
in front of it like it's a mirror.
Like my gran once did, Billie likes to recite poetry. Her
latest is the 'Lady of Shalott'. Year five at All Saints School
have been doing it and Billie loves it. We found a lovely
version set to music by Loreena McKennitt and Billie took

the CD into school. She said that three girls and one boy cried when they heard it.

I am invited back to George Street School to do poetry and story-telling with some Key Stage Two kids. The rise and fall of children's conversation is still here. The pauses in the teacher's voice are there. But there's something else. And I don't know what it is. It even unnerves me slightly. After lunch the signal becomes clear. As the teacher reads out the register I realise that it's almost exactly the register I knew thirty-odd years ago except that now these are the children of the children I once sat alongside. A complete A to Z a generation apart. And what's more, Mick was picking his nose just like he used to do. Susan and Julie are sitting together and straightening each other's hair. The template is clearly defined, the knitting pattern intact.

I drew maps. My maps always started in Featherstone. Sometimes they ended up in Scotland. In Scotland the places I know I learned from listening to the football results on a Saturday teatime. Alloa and Fife and Stenhousemuir appeared on my maps. I didn't know where they were so I arranged them. Sometimes my maps ended in Africa. In Africa the places I knew I learned from my stamp album. Rwanda-Burundi, Tanganyika, Zanzibar, Belgian Congo. I told myself that when I left school I would draw maps, that I would go to college to study how to draw them for the Ordnance Survey. A few months before I left school a stone fell out of the roof at Sharlston Pit and hit my grandad. After that his epilepsy became more frequent. I never went to Ordnance Survey college.

Never Be the Same Again

We spot the Samaritans tent lit by a couple of paraffin-driven Tilley lamps. Flying about the tent are four huge balloons and at the gap in front of the flaps are three trestle tables. A man with a ginger beard and a woman in a kaftan are resting their bare feet on the table and rocking to and fro on fold-up chairs. A woman in a knitted two-piece wearing a string of pearls comes out of the tent and asks us if she can help us. 'We were wondering if you know where we could get our heads down for the night?' We swing our rolled-up sleeping bags off our shoulders.

'Have you checked out the crash marquees?'

'We didn't know there were any crash marquees. What are they?'

The lady with the string of pearls tells us that some big marquees have been set up for people who want to stay the night, because the festival organisers had already decided there would be no official campsite. 'The best thing you can do is find one of the crash marquees and bed down for the night. There won't be any more trains 'til tomorrow morning because there's been a derailment. I've got a bit of lentil soup left if you want some.' She indicates a blackened casserole pan sitting on a sort of retort stand near a fire. The soup has dried up a bit, but it tastes good, even out of a cardboard cup with wings on. I share out a Crunchie bar. The man with the ginger beard and the kaftan woman move for the first time to take a piece. Kaftan woman says, 'Like cool! Chocolate!' Then she puts her feet back onto the trestle table.

We walk back to the area that the lady with the pearls has pointed to, past a camp fire where a serious looking gang of hippies are nodding their heads in time to a freshly minted bootleg tape of Eric Clapton singing 'Cocaine'. We find the crash marquee. It's big enough to sleep a hundred people in sleeping bags, but there are just two in it. They turn out to be sisters, one is eighteen, the other one is fifteen. They have travelled on a scooter from Ashby-de-la-Zouch. When they went to where they thought they'd left it, the scooter wasn't there.

'I think we'll look somewhere else in the morning. We might find it somewhere else if we try hard enough,' says the older sister.

'Like Carlos Casteneda like,' says Dave my companion on this adventure.

'What?'

'Well, like, Carlos Castaneda says, like, if you look hard enough you can find a car underneath a stone, like.'

'Right on! Really!'

'We left it near a tree,' says little sister.

'What kind of tree?'

'Well, like just a tree, man. With leaves on.'

In the pocket of my ex-army jacket I have a can of Worthington E. I crack it open. I take a sip and offer it round. The sisters take a sip, Dave takes a sip and it comes back to me. Dave has a few crumbs of Lebanese Gold left. He rolls a joint. That gets passed round.

'I can see my scooter if I close my eyes. It's crying.'

'Shit man, we need to like go and find it.'

Little sister lays down. She pulls big sister's coat across her. 'I'm so tired.' Big sister organises the coat so that it covers her as well and cuddles up beside her. Dave and me finish the can and drop the roach into it. It sisses.

Silence.

Five minutes later little sister says in a very tired voice, 'You don't think somebody could have pinched it, do you?'

Dave and me lay down. The zip on my sleeping bag is broken, I wrap it loosely around me, whichever way I turn my back ends up on the damp grass. Dave continually scratches at his beard and mop of tangled hair. No matter how hard I try I cannot get to sleep. I listen to a gang of Hare Krishnas chanting in the crash marquee next door. Somewhere a dog barks. Somewhere else a woman is singing 'Blowin' in the Wind'. It's two o'clock on Sunday July 16, 1978. A few hours before Bob Dylan has taken his last bow after an encore of 'The Times They Are A-Changin'. We are somewhere on the border between Surrey and Hampshire on a disused aerodrome called Blackbushe.

A quarter of a million of us have been brought here over the last couple of days by trains to a station called Fleet from one called Waterloo; trains and the odd scooter. Over one hundred years before we came, the trains of the South Western Railway Company brought thousands of people to a station just a couple of miles down the line from here for a very different festival. This crowd were dressed in the clothes of the 'Fancy-set' for they had come to witness what was probably the most brutal fight ever fought between two men. On a chill April morning in 1860, Tom Sayers, Britain's best bare-fist fighter, fought America's John C. Heenan for two hundred pounds and the title World Champion. In the hours of mayhem and violence that followed Sayers lost the use of his right arm, while Heenan lost an eye. Spectators fought the police and when someone slashed at the rope with a knife, Sayers was saved from being choked on it.

I saw no violence in that crowd of a quarter of a million today. Someone told me later that they'd seen cans thrown near the front of the stage, but they were empty ones.

The journey started back in May at a place called Thwaite Gate on the edge of Leeds. The Leeds busmen had been on strike for a while and their comrades in other bus companies in a show of solidarity had decided to only run services to the city boundary. We took the last bus of the day to Thwaite Gate, full of beer from the Blackmoor Head in Pontefract. Bob Dylan was to play his first British dates since 1966, six nights at Earls Court. Barkers the music shop on The Headrow in Leeds had been chosen as one of the ticket agents. We trudged the three miles from Thwaite Gate into Leeds city centre and arrived just after one in the morning. The queue was already round the block and the shop wasn't opening until nine. Within two hours of the shop opening all the tickets were sold out. Shop assistants came down the line to tell everybody they had to go home. Nobody wanted to move. A woman in an Afghan coat called Acid Annie laid down in The Headrow, kicked off her slippers and screamed, 'But you can't do this, man! I saw him in Manchester at the Free Trade Hall, you can't do this to me.' A policeman told her to put her slippers back on and go back home. She told him she wanted to die right now. I knew Acid Annie, she worked in a chemist's shop in Wakefield. A few weeks later I saw her laid flat out and naked at Blackbushe aerodrome. She had dyed her pubic hair and the hair beneath her armpits with cochineal and painted a sunflower on her belly. Some red-haired children were dancing around her singing 'half a pound of tuppenny rice' and blowing bubbles from a bubble tube.

Such was the demand for tickets at Earls Court that hundreds and thousands of Dylan fans were left disappointed. A rock concert entrepreneur, best known for his parties at Crystal Palace, very quickly got his act together and created 'The Picnic' at Blackbushe. In the meantime Dylan did his six nights at Earls Court and went off to the Zeppelin Field at Nürnberg, to Rotterdam and Paris and then came back to this old airfield near to where the first world title fight had been fought.

Back to Barkers. This time we got tickets.

On the Friday evening before the festival, four of us try to hitch from the place on the A1 where it intersects with the M62. Nobody wants to pick us up. We shouldn't be surprised, we look like medieval minstrels mixed with something out of a spaghetti western. I am wearing cowboy boots, jeans with more patches than original jean, a filthy old army jacket and a leather cowboy hat. *Roots* is a popular television programme at the time. For some reason my mates are calling me 'African George'. Then there's Fuff in a biker's jacket and bowler hat. Dave in his tie-dyed gear and lumberjack's coat, Alf from the chemical factory with hair down to his arse and Max who looks like King Charles with his golden hair in curls. That's if King Charles ever wore Levis. We're cold and the beer is wearing off.

We jump in a taxi to Doncaster station and take the late train down to London. On the way across London we nick a pint of milk apiece from a passing float and join with all the other medieval minstrels, spaghetti westerners, pressed flower-children, longhairs, beardos, weirdos and a man wearing a German Second World War helmet, to find the train for this place called Fleet.

There's a reggae band called Merger playing when we enter the site. It's taken ages to get in because someone thinks we've got forged tickets. A bloke in a cheesecloth frock is telling the security man that he will be sure to faint and possibly die of a broken heart if he can't pass through the gate. A rock band called Lake are next then Graham Parker and The Rumour. Joan Armatrading sings 'Love and Affection' and about fifty of us sit cross-legged holding hands and hum the bass part. Years later when I find out that Joan Armatrading is a staunch Tory Party supporter I try to obliterate that lovely memory, but it won't go. I want to melt my Joan Armatrading LPs into plant pots but I can't. While we're holding hands some little parachutes float down from the sky, attached to them are badges that say 'Street Legal' on them.

During Eric Clapton's set I close my eyes. Too much canned Worthington E, too much Leb Gold. I hear the old Bessie Smith song 'Nobody Knows You When You're Down and Out'. I fall asleep. I hear 'Knockin' on Heaven's Door', I think I've slept too long and am missing Dylan. Then I hear 'Key to the Highway' and realise Clapton's still on. I fall asleep. 'Layla, you've got me on my knees' brings me back to my feet. When Dylan finally comes on he looks an inch or two tall from where we are. He is lit well enough for us to see his top hat. I find out later that he's borrowed it that morning from the commissionaire on his hotel's revolving door. He sings 'Baby Stop Crying', 'Is Your Love in Vain', 'True Love Tends to Forget', all songs from the new album. It's only been out for a month or so, already people know the songs off by heart. Then more familiar songs, 'Girl From the North Country', 'Like a Rolling Stone', 'Simple Twist of Fate', 'Just Like a Woman' and a slow almost blues version of 'I Want You'. The reference books will tell you that the set consisted of thirty-five songs, the longest Dylan concert ever. Then it's over. Trains derail. The Samaritans give out soup. Two girls from Ashby-de-la-Zouch search in vain for a scooter called Gandalph. Dave and me lose Max, Alf and Fuff. Acid Annie shivers and can't find her clothes.

In the crash tent, I can't sleep. Dave is still scratching his beard.

'Did you ever read anything by like, Richard Brautigan?'

'No.'

'He's like this writer from San Francisco. He wrote some poems called *The Pill Versus the Springhill Mining Disaster.*' Dave recites by heart some of the poems.

'Sounds good.'

'Good! Good! This is like the best writer you ever heard, man!'

'Right.'

'There's a book called *The Abortion*. There's a library in it where people can bring books that they've written themselves. *Growing Flowers by Candlelight in Hotel Rooms* is one, *Love Always Beautiful* is another. It's been rejected by publishers over four hundred times.'

'Bert Stevens told me about a book called *Catching Voles in the Outer Hebrides by Moonlight*.'

'Fuck Bert, man.'

In the weeks after Dylan I collect the Picador editions of all the Brautigan books.

When day breaks we roll our sleeping bags up quietly. We're worried that the girls might ask us to help them look for their scooter. As we crawl out of the marquee, older sister says in the sleepiest voice you ever did hear, 'We did something really good here y'know.'

We say, 'Yeah!' Dave pulls two dog-eared paperbacks out of his knapsack. The books are by Michael Moorcock, one is called *The Final Solution*, the other the latest in the Jerry Cornelius series, *Condition of Muzek*; he gives the sisters one each.

In London we find the shop that only tired people coming back from pop festivals can find. It sells smoking paraphernalia, patchouli oil and mats for people who struggle to roll big joints. I buy a copy of *The Rubaiyat of Omar Khayyam* and read it to Dave who sleeps all the way back up on the train. 'Awake, for morning in the bowl of night, hath cast the stone that puts the stars to flight.' In my pocket is a badge I also bought that says 'Legalise Cannabis'. Dave won't let me wear it on my army jacket because 'we'll attract too much attention to ourselves'. We're dishevelled beyond belief, we smell like goats and every other passenger on the train is staring at us and Dave thinks if I wear a badge we'll attract attention to ourselves!

Nearly twenty years later I go to see Dylan again at Stratford-upon-Avon. This time with the photographer Kevin Reynolds and a brand new tent. We make the mistake of deciding to put up the tent after the gig. We see Dylan, Van Morrison and a superb show in a marquee put on by the acid jazz band Galliano. We get so stoned that we can't talk. We spend two hours trying to put up the tent, then finally realise we've been trying to put up a ground sheet. We cut our losses and sleep on the ground. Before we do Kevin takes the reflective red hazard warning triangle out of the boot of his car and erects it next to our heads. 'You never know,' he says, 'some fucker might come by on a motorbike and run us over!'

If you look it up on the internet, you will find the Festival Welfare Report on Blackbushe, written by a woman called Penny Mellor, who was a fieldworker at the time. The report, compiled in the weeks after, talks about the bench seats in the lavatories being too high and getting easily messy. It mentions cold and hungry people wandering around in the middle of the night and about cancelled buses and trains. It says that it became impossible to walk without treading on litter and there were very few problems with drugs.

I got home to my gran and grandad's house. In the weeks and years after, my granny compiled her own report. It consisted of just one sentence. 'Our Ian went to see Bob Dylan and he's never been the same lad since he came home.'

A Seed Doesn't Stay in the Ground Forever

Searching and Finding

When the Train Left the Station

The Elephant and Castle pub has a beautiful façade that advertises in glazed stone a long gone brewery from Boroughbridge. Behind its façade hide off-duty prison officers, on-release prisoners (Wakefield Prison is next door to the station) and people sinking quick 'uns before rushing to catch trains to London, Leeds and Plymouth.

This evening I'm drinking John Smith's Magnet ale. A man behind the bar is brandishing a video of the film *This Sporting Life*, the Lindsay Anderson black and white film about northerners, rugby league, brutality and loveless sex.

'If you want to know anything about fuckin' rugby league, watch this fucker.' Nobody is listening.

All the prison officers in here have beer bellies. Their trousers hang low like holsters and their keys are attached to their belt loops, jingling. I take my pint to a chair. A wizened man steps nimbly out of my way and gently gestures for me to pass, then bows ever so slightly, politely and lightly as I do. When I sit down the wizened man turns and sits down next to me. He says 'Hello' as I take my first swig and I hurry the beer down because I want to be polite and say 'Hello' back. When I do he averts his eyes and begins to drum his fingers on a bacca tin that is decorated with spent matches. I was just starting to think he might be an ex-con when he says, 'I've only got six weeks to do…me. They've started letting me out at weekends.'

'Wakefield?' I ask.

He nods in his slight way. 'Wakefield, Armley, Hull, Manchester. Eleven years, me. Manslaughter. I've got my smokes and half a beer. I take my time, me. Fifteen years I've done, me.'

He speaks like an agitator post on a washing machine. Nervous as well. Eyes all over the place and fingers drumming on his matchstick tin like Buddy Rich.

I tell him, 'I used to teach in Wakefield.' Then I mention a few names.

'I knew him,' he says. 'Clever man, him, got it all up here.' He points his finger at his temple. 'Smokes a pipe.' I nod. 'Got long hair.' I nod again.

It says 'Chris' under a cross on his tin. 'My name's Derek,' and he offers me a wizened hand. 'It's my round,' he says. I have known him for seven minutes.

'I'm in a hostel at the moment. Hostel...fags...beer...I take fish and chips back, I like fish and chips, me. Do you like 'em?'

'I like to smell them.'

'From my cell window I can smell beer brewing.'

Wakefield's old brewery, Clarks, is jammed in between the railway station and the prison.

'I take my fish and chips back and they ask me my number and then tell me to go to bed.'

'Where you from originally?'

'Where am I from originally...Isle of Man, me...Manchester, Armley, Hull...Wakefield. They killed three dogs throwing slates at Manchester. I didn't. Not me. In fact I know I didn't.'

I go to the bar. I buy two more halves. The barman picks up the video, then realises I've already heard him.

When I sit down again, Derek or Chris asks me what is in my pouch. 'Dutch tobacco,' I say. 'It's called Drum.'

'Can I try one?'

'Course you can.'

'Three Castles, I can get that. Samson, Old Holborn, Golden Virginia, St Julian, I can get that. Thiedemans Gul, Drum I can get that if I want, me. I know I can.'

His hands shake like a dog shitting razors. He tears the paper, screws it up and throws it into the ashtray. 'Not often I do that, me.' He takes out a worm of tobacco. 'Must have nipped it with my nail. Not often I do that.' He throws a second Rizla into the ashtray. He tries again and succeeds this time in rolling a cig as thin as a pencil. I smile by way of congratulation. 'Look at them two at the bar rattling their keys. I can't stand them. Shit men. I know them, me.' He nips his fag and then turns his back to me. I don't know what to say.

I have four or five minutes before I have to go for the train. Two of those minutes pass in silence. Derek turns round again.

'I'm nervous because I know you're going to report me for being pissed.'

'No, I'm not. I'm getting ready to go for my train. I'm off to the Cork Jazz Festival.' I know he doesn't believe me.

'I'm alright, me, you know. Got me smokes...me beer.' He rattles his pocket. He shakes my hand. 'Come in here next Saturday, I'll treat you.' I tell him I must go now. I make for the door. He follows me. We stand on the pavement. We look at the station, the brewery, the prison. Derek tells me, 'Last week I asked one of the screws, "How do I get to the station?" He said, "Go out of the front gates, walk up this street, turn left after a hundred yards and you're there." I said, "No. How do I get to the station?" He said, "I've just told you. Out of the front gate. Turn left after a hundred yards and you're there!" He didn't know what I meant. How do I get there? When you've been in prison for as long as I have you don't know how to turn left and right on streets.'

I'm in Cork, Ireland, for the annual Guinness Jazz Festival. I'm with Heather and Paul Noble, a lad from work who's a Smiths fan really but he likes any live music. We're staying on Grosvenor Street in a huge row of decrepit and very seedy Edwardian houses. It costs £3.50 for a bed for the night and £1 for clean sheets. Toilet roll is provided free and you can get a shave in the kitchen by looking into the wing mirror of a lorry that someone has bolted to the wall. The Pogues are blasting out from somebody's cassette player downstairs. They're singing 'A Pair of Brown Eyes' but this is being drowned out by a drunken lunatic singing 'Diamonds on the Soles of My Shoes'. This lunatic is called Danny. He is from Oswaldtwistle, he told us this on the boat over from Holyhead to Dun Laoghaire. He told everybody this, including a quiet Finnish man who was travelling to Cork to see Van Morrison.

'Hey! Beardy, where you from?'

'I am from Finland.'

'Fuckin' Finland! All your javelin throwers are on fuckin' drugs!'

'I'm sorry I didn't understand.'

'Fuckin' javelin throwers, on drugs.'

'Sorry.'

'Fuck…in…jav…lin…throw…ers. I say throw…ers, on…fuck…in…drugs.'

'Oh! I see.'

'And your fuckin' power stations are killing our sheep.'

'I don't know about that.'

'Fuckin' Chernobyl. Haven't you heard of that?'

'This is not in Finland.'

'Course it fuckin' is! Blowing up and killing our sheep!'

The gentle Finnish man goes back to his book. He is reading a dog-eared copy of *Dubliners*.

'Hey. Finnish. Wales looks like Finland. But you can't tell 'cos it's dark. Have a look.'

'Will you please stop poking me with your finger.'

'I'm trying to show you.'

'I see.'

'Can you understand a word I'm saying? I can't understand a word you're saying.'

I prayed Danny from Oswaldtwistle was not going on to Cork.

'I'm off to Cork for the jazz.'

'Oh! Are you?' The Finnish man puts down his book. 'So am I.'

'Trad jazz. That's my stuff, Finland. I don't like that modern shit.'

'I am fond of Van Morrison.'

'Aye, well I like her a bit, but I like the old banjo. Can't beat a bit of the old banjo. Have you seen that film

Deliverance? Good banjo in that you know. Them hillbillies know what they're doing.'

We don't see the Finnish man again after we get off the boat. Not even at the Morrison gig. Danny from Oswaldtwistle seems to be everywhere and never without a drink in his hand.

We take a taxi in the pouring rain and we're dazzled by coloured lights on strings above the roads. We ask the taxi driver why the Christmas lights are up in October.

'Well you see sir, the Cork man is a clever man. The dustbin men have been on strike for six weeks now and the rubbish is piling up around our feet.'

'So!'

'So, 'tis a good idea that they put up the Christmas lights so that the people are looking at the nice colours and not down at the stinking rubbish.'

At the Metropole, Mary Coughlan in a floppy black beret is sizzling. She sings 'Don't Get Around Much Anymore', 'Mama Just Wants to Barrelhouse All Night Long' and tells us to the accompaniment of her band clicking their fingers 'I Wanna Be Seduced'. In between songs she tells us that the Bishop of Galway has taken a dislike to two-piece bathing costumes. After the gig we have a quick chat in the bar. In one hand she has a glass of whiskey, in the other a pint of Guinness.

'Are yous from Newcastle? I once lived with a bunch of guys from Newcastle.' She goes on to say that her first album *Tired and Emotional* was voted record of the week on Capital Radio in London. I tell her that it has become one of my favourite records. It still is now.

'D'yer know until last year I only ever sang songs in the bath. Then one night in the back room of a bar in Galway somebody entered me for a talent competition.'

Danny from Oswaldtwistle arrives. 'Fuckin' lovely Guinness. You don't see many women supping from a pint glass, love!' Mary Coughlan drifts off to join the band. Paul, Heather and me drink up and seek sanctuary in the pouring rain.

Fat Sam's Band are belting out Louis Jordon and Cab Calloway stuff in The Grapevine and Johnny McGuinness and his boys are doing 'Won't You Come Home Bill Bailey' at The Ritz. We shelter in the doorway of a building society. In the window they have a huge poster that says, 'Home Loans and All That Jazz'.

Late night at the Jury's Hotel, Ruby Turner is mining some deep soul stuff. She has been mistakenly introduced as 'Miss Ruby Murray' by the MC, who has also warned us of the hazards of dancing on the tables. Her version of the old Etta James standard 'I'd Rather Go Blind' is belting, though I still think Christine Perfect's version is the best. I go to the lavatory. As I finish peeing I zip up and look to my left. A short, stocky man has come to the stall next to me. I recognise Van Morrison. I can't stop myself from saying, 'Van Morrison! Can I just say how much pleasure you've given me over the years.' And I offer to shake hands. Van Morrison is still pissing. I can feel my face turning red. I quickly pull back my hand. He grunts and doesn't look up. As my old gran would have said, I don't know whether I want a shit or a haircut. Van Morrison shakes and zips up. He goes over to the washbasin. I follow him. I wash my hands in the next basin. He reaches the hand drier before me. It doesn't work. I offer to hit the chromium button for him. He grunts again. I start to say, 'I'm sorry, you must get fed up of people coming up to you in pub...' He turns on his heel. A huge guy who looks like a bodyguard is holding open the lav door. Van Morrison ducks under his arm. I follow. The guy holding the door lets it go and it hits me on the side of the face. I stand there for a minute or two. The door springs open and hits me again, this time smack on the nose. It's Danny from Oswaldtwistle. He looks at my bleeding nose. 'Who's fuckin' done that?'

I blink water out of my eyes.

'This Ruby Murray's good, isn't she?'

The following day we escape from Danny Oswaldtwistle by telling him we're going to Sligo. We then take a bus to Killarney. We check into a hostel called The Four Winds and find ourselves sharing a room with a loud girl from Boston, Massachusetts called Laura. She has a cold sore and is feeling sorry for herself. She's one of those Americans who amuse and appal by turn. There's a quiet Californian girl called Kendall who wears a backpack almost as big as herself and is reading some stuff about Italy, and an Aussie girl called Trish is rubbing surgical spirit into the balls of her feet. That night we all sit round the kitchen table and smoke the world to rights until the dawn breaks.

'Do you have like Hare Krishnas in Europe?' This is Boston.

'Yeah!'

'And in Oz,' says Trish.

'They're really cool people, right?'

'Yeah!'

Pause.

'Do you have like Amish people in Europe? They're really cool as well, right?'

'Yeah! They come from here.'

'Wow! Is that for real? Hey! I thought they came from Philadelphia.'

'Is that where the cheese comes from?'

'Say what?'

'Doesn't matter.'

'OK, that's cool.'

Pause.

'Do you have 7-Up over here? I need 7-Up.'

'What is it?'

'Soda pop.'

'Soda. You only see it in bars. It comes out of siphons.'

'OK, that's cool.'

'You get Coke though, right?'

'Yeah!'

Pause.

'Did you guys get the fallout from Chernobyl?'

'We don't know. There were some newspaper reports about sheep being poisoned on the mountains in Wales.'

'J e e e z z, is that a fact?'

Pause.

'My dad says that these things will happen all the time in Russia in the future. He says that their nuclear power stations are so rusty and old that they will all blow up. One by one. Jeez, wouldn't want to be in Europe when that happens.'

'Why have you come to Europe?'

'Jeez, I'm wicked fuckin' sorry. Shouldn't I have come?'

'We just wondered why that's all.'

'What is this? Pick on the fuckin' Americans time?'

By nine o'clock we're all back round the table for breakfast. A bunch of international stereotypes by cuisine. Trish the Aussie has Vegemite on toast, Kendall the quiet Californian prefers muesli and we pan fry some fresh whiting and butter crusty bread. Laura arrives clutching a can of Coke.

'Do you want any of this, Laura?'

'No thanks I had chicken.'

'What?'

'I bought a Kentucky Fried Chicken last night and I saved some for breakfast.'

'Really?'

'Yeah! Normally I eat cold pizza for breakfast and maybe a beer.'

'Sounds disgusting.'

'Well I'm wicked fuckin' sorry.'

Later in the morning Kendall the quiet Californian comes to see us to wave goodbye. She's setting out for Italy. She wants to apologise for Laura and tell us that not all Americans are like that. We tell her that really we find Laura to be a good laugh. It's just that she doesn't seem to realise it herself. We also invite Kendall to come and stay with us in Featherstone if she gets fed up with Italy. Three weeks later she lands on our doorstep. Kendall spends ten days with us and comes to believe that this rough industrial area of West Yorkshire is one of the arts capitals of Western Europe. By coincidence Wakefield is celebrating its centenary of becoming a city. The local authority have pulled out all the stops to put on their best arts festival ever. We see Adrian Henri's recreation of the Wakefield Mystery Cycle at Pontefract Castle. The world premiere of John Godber's 'Salt of the Earth' at Wakefield Theatre Royal. A bhangra concert at the Unity Hall with the most fantastic Asian buffet in the interval. Jack Hulme's photographs are being displayed at Pontefract Museum and there's great stuff at the Sculpture Park.

'But I thought you said this area was depressed with nothing for people to do?'

As we waved her off to Manchester Airport we didn't have the heart to tell her that things like this only happen once in a blue moon.

'You will come to San Francisco one day won't you?'

'One day!'

At the time we scraped together to pay our £27 a week mortgage, my outgoings on record buying and Heather's bus fares to Leeds University every day.

'One day!'

Kendall shuffled off into the distance. Her big rucksack full of Tetley bitter beer mats and packets of tea.

Heather and me saved up for two years after that and made it to California. We landed in San Francisco just after the 1990 earthquake had cracked rows of houses on the waterfront. We stayed with Kendall in her apartment on Frederick Street. Frederick Street is in the Haight Ashbury district. This is where between 1965 and 1967 a whole generation of kids

73

seemed to turn on, tune in and drop out. By the time we got there over two decades later the fragrance of patchouli oil was still billowing out of the shop doorways. You could buy tie-dyed t-shirts even in the pet food stores and acid casualties were still roaming in the Golden Gate Park. We bought books about Ken Kesey and Augustus Owsley at the Great Expectations bookstore at 1512 Haight Street and psychedelic posters advertising Country Joe and The Fish's appearance at the Avalon Ballroom. We were in our glory pretending to be hippies. Heather wore Indian dresses that she had bought ten years before in the Rattan bazaar in New Delhi and I grew my beard especially for the occasion. On the day before we came back to Featherstone I asked Heather to take a photo of me on the steps of the house where the Grateful Dead once lived. Later on we drove past the house again in Kendall's yellow Cadillac and I told her about the photo. She said the Grateful Dead actually lived next door. When I got home I framed up the photo and gave it a title, 'Ian sitting on the steps of the house next door to the Grateful Dead's'. Sometimes near enough is good enough. Later still, Kendall pointed out Robert Crumb's house, or at least the one he lived in before he moved to France. In the Mission district I listened to Gloria Estefan singing 'I Don't Wanna Lose You Now' in the original Spanish 'Si Voy A Perderte'. It's far more beautiful that way. And I started a love affair with the Seeco recordings of Celia Cruz, after I saw some pot-bellied little Mexican kids kicking oranges in a gutter and dancing to her music outside a record shop.

Taproom

On a boat in the middle of the English Channel, two women from West Africa told me a wonderful proverb, 'When an old man dies, a library burns down'. I believe that to be the truest of proverbs. I've always befriended old men, from Angus a drunken piano player I met in Pontefract in the punk days to Arnold Millard, a puffed up old pirate I knew for ten years.

It's eleven o'clock in the morning and I'm standing near a broken fence at the corner of Green Lane and Mount Pleasant Street. My friend Arnold 'Sooner' Millard lives in a council flat near here. This morning Arnold is talking to Caravan Kev. Outside his little house Kev keeps a broken down jeep and a motor boat under a torn tarpaulin. It's clear from the conversation that Kev and Sooner are having that Arnold has fallen down drunk the previous night outside the little house and Caravan has helped him home to his old folk's flat.

'I don't know what we're going to do with you, Arnold.'

'Hasn't thy ever been poorly?!'

'I didn't know you were poorly, I thought you were drunk.'

'I'm full of bastard catarrh. A Dutchman give me some cough medicine and it made me dizzy.' He spits onto a flap of tarpaulin.

'That medicine smelled like ale to me!'

Arnold's dog, a fat Jack Russell cross, trots up and lifts its leg upside the broken jeep's rusted wheel arch. 'Get home, you twat!' The dog looks at him and goes sniffing under the jeep. 'Get out from under there, Pluto!' Caravan tells Arnold that he's got to get ready to go out and reminds him to take care of himself. Arnold looks over to me. He doesn't say good morning or hello or anything, but reminds me that Pluto is nearly seventeen years old. 'He's nowt but a bastard, but he loves me.'

'Well, you love him don't you?'

'When Sooner got him y'know he fit into a pint pot.' For reasons he never explains, Arnold Millard quite often refers to himself in the third person. It's confusing for those who don't know him well. Sometimes he's Mr Millard, other times Arnold, or Arnie, most usually 'Sooner' and often just 'He'. As in 'He's going to the races on Monday' or 'He's full of bastard catarrh again'. The nickname 'Sooner', depending on who's telling the story, was given to him because he would 'sooner' stop at home than go to work at the pit, or because he would 'sooner' have a pint of beer than a cup of tea, or because 'sooner' or later he would be a famous man.

Pluto comes out from under the rusting jeep and cocks his leg up at the broken fence. 'He was the runt of the litter, they were going to drown him in a rain barrel at the allotments. I fetched him back on a bus in a pint pot with an handle on it.'

He has told me this story a lot of times. He has a photographic memory about every aspect of his life and a story for every occasion; mostly inappropriate, always spewed out in a stream of consciousness, disconnected from the day, the general theme of conversation that's taking place at the time and invariably funny, surreal, ribald and foul-mouthed. Even if you cling tightly to whatever he's just said you can't keep up.

'Les has bought a chalet at Flamborough. It's got a flat roof, I've told him you can go from fuckin' Castleford to fuckin' California and there isn't a flat roof worth a toss. They all leak.'

This morning Arnold is wearing his flat cap and crombie overcoat. Underneath is a green suit that came from the wardrobe department at Yorkshire TV. This suit was last seen being worn by a private eye or maybe it was a detective in a drama series called *Ellington* that only lasted for one run. I gave twenty quid for it. Arnold promised to pay me a pound a week in return. So far he has paid one pound in six months. He's also wearing a silk stars and stripes tie. He tells everyone that he won it in a gambling den after a game of cards with the mayor of New Orleans. It did come from New Orleans, but not from a smoky dive after a poker hand with a cigar-chomping mayor. I bought it in a tacky souvenir shop near Bourbon Street that sold snowstorms in a perspex bubble and those pens that reveal a naked woman when you tip them one way and then the other. His shoes were given to him by the widow of a man who he had worked with at Ackton Hall Pit.

'Dead men's shoes always fit me,' he'll tell you. 'When women ask me what size shoes I take after they've buried their husbands, I tell them "owt between a seven and a ten".'

I remember the story told to me about Sonny Boy Williamson, the great blues harmonica player. He cut all of his shoes with a blade so they fit. Even when he had enough money and bought brand new ones in England, he slit them. 'Shoes always fit where they touch,' says Arnold. He laughs and blows snot out of his nose by pushing his finger against one nostril and then the other.

We start to walk down Green Lane. Everybody we pass says good morning to him. In response he either asks a question or makes a statement. 'How's your Jimmy's leg?' 'I ate them two rashers of bacon you gave me with some piccalilli for my breakfast this morning,' and, 'When I laid down last night I thought the Lord was going to take me.' The lady who lives in the flat below Arnold is struggling to cross the road with heavy carriers full of shopping. He offers to help. 'Let an old man help you, Madam!' He calls younger women 'Miss' and older ones 'Madam'.

'Bugger off, Arnold. Get out of my road!'

He offers a wry wink and sings a parody of the old pop song. 'Knock three times on yer ceiling if yer want me.'

Beer, medicine, sexual innuendo, death, food, wordplay, parody and music and song are his staple diet.

When his neighbour is out of earshot he whispers, 'I could have had her last night…she loves me tha knows!'

At the wall of the old Miners' Welfare Hall, which is now home to a gymnasium, a funeral parlour and a car repair garage, he stops for breath. Most aging miners do this, playing out a ritual of walking, coughing, spitting and leaning on walls to catch breath. It's about two hundred yards from Sooner's flat to the pub's side door. Every day he leans on the broken fence, the Welfare wall and the jamb of the pub door before making a grand entrance. I sit on the wall beside him. He takes off his glasses, breathes a mist on the lenses and wipes them with a spotless linen handkerchief.

'When Miss Cliffe had her shop across the road she gave me a new white hanky for my birthday every year. Her birthday was on the same day as mine.'

Miss Cliffe had a haberdashers shop for most of the twentieth century. Before she died the shop was boarded up and eventually pulled down along with the terraced rows sometime in the late 1970s. The back rooms were full of unsold items dating back to Edwardian times; little boys' sailor suits, ostrich feathers, beaded dresses, buttoned shoes and linen handkerchiefs. A health centre stands where the shop once stood. It's where Sooner goes to see a doctor with a Dutch name for his prescription. I picture it's where Miss Cliffe still sits sewing beads to dresses whilst listening to Caruso on a wind-up Victrola record player.

'Do you know who else's birthday is on the same day as mine?'

'John Major.'

'How do you know?'

'Because sometimes you're like a broken record.'

'Broken record my arse. Tha's reading my mind, pirating me. Tha's like a pirate in my mind!'

Sooner folds his hanky carefully and puts it back into his crombie pocket. He spits behind the wall.

'Always keep a clean handkerchief and a clean lavatory. You can tell a man by his hanky and his pot. Anybody can come to my flat and use my lavatory.'

Pluto trots back up to us. 'Sooner's dog loves him tha knows. Watch him!...smile Pluto...smile.' Pluto bares his teeth and sits on his hind legs. 'See!'

We cross the road to the pub. 'Do you know, when that Welfare was in full swing on a Saturday night, if tha didn't get a fight or a woman there was something wrong with thi.'

The Miners' Welfare dance was known for miles around. In the 1940s and 50s when people still needed coal and miners had money for beer, a local dance band led by Norman Longbottom attracted huge crowds. Cleo Laine and Johnny Dankworth played there and every local youth worth his salt got his first bloodied nose at the top of the stairs that led into the dance hall. Sooner leans on the jamb of the pub door. I look back at the Welfare building and think about Brylcreemed men in their best suits knocking seven bells of shit out of one another while Norman Longbottom takes to the mic to encourage the dancers to move nearer to the stage and away from the bother at the back.

Sooner and me are the first into the pub. Nat King Cole is coming gently from the speakers on the wall. 'Gee it's great after staying out late.' Sooner joins in immediately, 'A…walking my baby back 'ome'. Elizabeth is wiping glasses and putting them back onto shelves.

'Madam barmaid, may I sample a vessel of your finest ale!' Sooner is already into slow-timing mode.

Elizabeth smiles and pulls a pint of Tetley bitter for Arnold and one for me. He picks up the glass, wipes the bottom of it once on a bar towel, then drains the pint pot in one go. He wipes his mouth on the crombie sleeve, belches and announces, 'Didn't even touch the sides.'

'Are you paying for them both, Sooner?'

'Elizabeth! Now come on. I only said I wanted to sample a vessel of your finest ale, not pay for one!'

'Sooner! Are you skint again?'

'Madam. I am as familiar with money this morning as a toad is with feathers.'

I pay for the two pints and one more for Arnold, but tell him I can't afford to do it all day. I can see wheels turning behind Sooner's eyes.

'Elizabeth, do you happen to know if the landlord is available?'

Pete, the landlord, is summoned by an intercom that links the bar to the upstairs room. Sooner sits in his favourite chair. From here he can watch the horse racing on the telly, sing along to songs between races, spot who is coming in through the window as well as request another pint without having to stand up. Peter already has a five-pound note in his hand when he reaches the table. He has a resigned look on his face when he asks, 'Are you boracic on a Friday morning, Mr Millard?' He doesn't wait for an answer that he wouldn't have got anyway, but puts the fiver onto the table in front of Arnie.

'Now landlord. You tell me. What can an old-age pensioner get for a skin diver these days? Can't tha manage a cock an' hen?' Peter grimaces, contorting his face into a smile like Pluto's. He produces a ten-pound note. Arnold takes it and in the same movement scoops up the five. Before Peter can speak Arnold announces, 'Peter! I hope if the Lord takes you before he takes me, that he waves you through the gate and thanks you for being a good-hearted man.'

'You're worth a bob on you are, Arnold,' Peter says and asks Elizabeth to refill the glasses.

By two o'clock Sooner is pissed. He's still wearing his

crombie. His stars and stripes tie is skew-whiffed and the neb of his flat cap is resting on the top of his spectacles. In the time we've been here miners' widows have been in, eaten specially priced dinners, sipped half shandies and gone. Two taxi drivers have finished the early shift and are propping up the bar. A small gang of lads who have no work to go to are playing pool and a man with a walking stick is sitting across the room gazing out of the window.

'Mobility baron him, tha knows!' announces Arnold. 'Never worked a proper day in his life and now he's claiming mobility, he'll end up with one of them shopping scooters next.'

'You can't talk like that, Arnold.'

'Who can't! I know him. I know what he's like. His father was the same when we were down t'pit. Everybody else had finished their stint and he'd be there, "Come on rally round lads." Well he can rally and fuck off for me.' He then bursts into song:

'Now mother she has gone to heaven
And father he works down below.
Be nobody's darling but mine love
Be nobody's darling but mine.'

A catarrhic yodel escapes from somewhere inside him. It is terrible. Like the musical equivalent of phlegm.

The man with the walking stick shouts across. 'Pipe down, Arnie!'

'Why doesn't thy fuck off!'

Elizabeth spins round, one hand under the whisky optic,

another goes onto her hip, she sighs. The lads look up from the pool table and the taxi drivers turn on their bar stools.

Arnold looks from one to the others. 'What?'

Walking stick looks to Elizabeth. 'If it was left to me I'd have him barred.'

Elizabeth leans over the bar. 'No swearing, Arnold!'

'I'm not swearing at you, Madam.' He mutters something under his breath and then shakily stands to face Elizabeth and begins to sing again, this time addressing Elizabeth with pleading eyes and arms outstretched:

'I was scarcely twenty-three,
On my first trip to sea,
When I was shipwrecked off the coast of France.
There, a lady in a boat, dragged me out by the coat,
Then laid me down in the world to rest.
As I lie there at rest, I saw that lady get undressed.
She had the map of England tattooed across her chest.
And further down, to my surprise,
Was the place where Nelson lost his eye.
Land of the Portuguese, was tattooed upon her knees,
She had China and Japan on her thigh.
I was looking for Hong Kong,
When her husband came along.
I let the rest of the world…go by!'

There is a round of applause from the taxi drivers. A hearty laugh from Elizabeth, the pool gang whoop and whistle and walking stick man sups off and, as Arnold would have it, fucks off. One of the pool gang asks if Arnie knows anything by The Rolling Stones. Arnie suggests that Mick Jagger's mother used to stick his lips to the shop window when she went shopping. Another lad asks for 'Smells Like Teen Spirit' by Nirvana, Arnie shouts, 'Never mind fucking Nerve Anna!' Then a third member of the gang asks if he can do 'My Way', the Sid Vicious version. One of the taxi drivers joins in. 'He's never heard of Sid Vicious!'

'How does thy know?'

The taxi driver looks flummoxed. Sooner winks at me, blows a kiss toward Elizabeth, then says, 'I once had his mam!'

A pause and then a Vesuvius of laughter erupts.

'Tha's what?' choruses each one to a man.

'I've told yer!' Arnie pushes the flat cap from the top of his glasses, straightens his tie and takes out his linen handkerchief to dab at the corner of his mouth.

'He was an awkward little bastard was Sid in them days. There's no wonder he ended up like he did.'

Arnold Millard would be the Falstaff to my Prince Hal if we were in a Shakespearean play together. If we travelled to the crossroads in the Mississippi Delta he would be the devil who showed me how to play the guitar. Today he is a drunken old git who tries to get me pissed in the Top House. He is the former merchant seaman who claims he had sex with Sid Vicious's mam in Stoke Newington. I don't believe a word he tells me when he's drunk, but today there is a twinkle in his rogue's eye that says, 'It's true tha knows'.

The Top House truly is a bar of outrageous stories. This is the bar in which Geoff Raybould, another spinner of bizarre yarns told me he'd had a hand in writing Paul Simon's song

'Homeward Bound'. Geoff loved to tell the story of when he was a young train driver in the mid-sixties.

'I was sitting in my cab at Widnes railway station and I saw this little student sitting on his own with a guitar, he looked right miserable. I asked him what he was doing. He said, "I'm just sittin' on this railway station." So I said, "Have you got a ticket?" He said, "Yeh!" I asked him where he was going and he said, "Homeward bound." I told him, "I wish I was!"'

I don't know a man or woman in the Top House who believes Geoff's tale. His answer to all the disbelievers is always the same. 'Well go over to Widnes railway station and you'll see a blue plaque that tells you it's true!'

Geoff once found a dead stag by the side of a railway line. He fetched it back to the depot with him and then had to work out a way of getting it back home. At the time he travelled to and from work on a moped. Undeterred he fastened the stag around him with bungee straps, its chin resting on the top of his crash helmet. The police patrol who eventually stopped him could hardly believe what they'd seen gliding through the early morning mist. A man on a moped with a dead stag as a pillion passenger, its huge antlers flopping back and forward as Geoff went through the gears.

We're joined at the table again by Pete the landlord. He has put a quid into his own jukebox. 'Lay Lady Lay' is followed by 'Copperhead Road' is followed by 'Brown Eyed Girl', then Wilson Pickett's 'Midnight Hour'. Pete has eclectic taste and he has prepared all the music for his jukebox. It is the best jukebox in the district, it compares with the one at the Blackmoor Head in Pontefract in 1978 after the Blackmoor had been the place to be seen for above ten years. Arnold dozes off under his flat cap. Pete puts on the home movie he made of our trip to the southern states of America in 1997.

We'd landed in Atlanta and we had driven the hire car down to Daytona Beach. After a swim and a steak and eggs breakfast we went to sit in a Hells Angels drinking den called The Boot Hill Bar to watch the Harley Davidson Rolling Thunder rally go by. Four days later after a dash across Alabama, Mississippi and a night in New Orleans, we found ourselves standing in front of a jukebox in a wooden plank shack called Granny's Bar and Grill.

Granny's Bar and Grill is in Hempstead, Texas, somewhere on the road between Houston and Austin. The place qualified for that name because it was run by an ancient old lady, it had a fridge full of Budweiser and a huge iron frying pan. There are probably one hundred and twenty selections you can make on this jukebox and between us we recognise about three of the artists, the obvious one is Bob Seger singing 'Like a Rock'. We press for that and there's some pieces by Lydia Mendoza, the singer of Mexican Norteño music, who I recognise from an old Arhoolie record. Her version of 'La Cucuracha' is accompanied by real cockroaches dancing round the pool table. All the rest are Tex-Mex dancing songs. We try potluck. Some Tex-Mex accordions crash in and we suddenly gain the attention of four tough-looking Mexican kids who up to now have been playing doubles at pool and casting us the occasional aggressive look, as though to say, 'What the hell are you lot doing in our bar?' It's the sort of look you get in the taproom of the Top House if you're not from Featherstone, yet there are signs in this bar that you don't get at home. One in the lav says, 'Please shit in the john, not on the floor'.

Travelling with Pete and me on this trip are Cheesey, a former winger with the great Featherstone pub rugby league team Jubilee, and 'High-Arse' Clarkson, a six-foot-four-inch second row forward with their arch rivals Featherstone Miners Welfare. High-Arse takes his opportunity to engage the Mexicans in conversation.

'How does tha go on for a game o'pool in here, kid? Does tha put thee money on t'side o'table or chalk it up on t'board?'

The tough Mexican lads look at one another and hold their cues like baseball bats. They say nothing.

'I say…How's tha go on for a game o'pool?'

The boys ignore 'Arse' and continue playing.

The old lady sensing possible bother comes over.

'Where you guys from?'

'Featherstone,' says High-Arse in an outrageous accent that is three quarters West Yorkshire and the rest his attempt at an American voice. It's a language that probably only seventy-odd people in the world could understand and all of them would be sharing baths after a game of rugby.

'Is that in East Texas?'

'No, love, West Yorkshire!'

'Where's that?'

'England, love.'

'I ain't never been further east than Little Rock.'

'Can you ask these lads if they'll give us a game o'pool.'

The old lady asks. The Mexican boys shrug and set up the

balls. High-Arse tosses up for the break and smacks the balls all over the table. The white leaps over the cushion and hits one of the Mexican lads on the shin. A sharp intake of breath. The lad bends down, picks up the ball and walks over to the table. He places it into the semi-circle and says, 'My friend has two shots now.' Then he laughs. The others laugh. The old Granny laughs and so do we. High-Arse slaps the lad on his back and says, 'Tha'll do for me, old cock!'

A round of Budweiser in here costs ten dollars for the eight of us. Every time we pay at the bar with a ten-dollar bill, the old Granny gives us a dollar for the jukebox. Later, when her son arrives he fries us some shrimp and catfish in the big old iron frying pan and we all sit around dipping our bread into this lovely supper. We fall out into the Texas night air playing air accordion and air violin. The Mexicans drive off in a pick-up truck. We return to the cheap motel that is run by a Korean with a shotgun behind his reception desk.

Next morning Cheesey locks the hire car keys inside the car. We call the nearest garage. Four tough-looking Mexican lads turn up in their pick-up. They're bleary-eyed and laughing beneath their baseball caps. In no time one of them has got us into the car with a twisted piece of wire.

'How much do we owe yer, kid?'

One of the lads reaches up to put his arm on High-Arse's ample shoulder. 'It's alright, old cock,' he says in an accent more outrageous than Arse's attempt to speak American.

We carry on up the road to Austin.

Here we meet Thom the World Poet who welcomes us to the Austin International Poetry Festival. Thom has been a poet since the days in the 1970s when he gave out poems written on cigarette papers to construction workers in his home state of Queensland, Australia. I first met him when he came to recite his poetry at Featherstone Library. By that time he was based in Austin, a radical centre for art, poetry and blues music in America. I took him to look at Featherstone Rovers' ground and we sat in the grandstand and talked about O. Henry and Dylan Thomas and the experimental group Gong with whom he had collaborated for many years. Later I took him to the old pit site and told him stories about miners' strikes down the years and about the day in 1893 when some soldiers came to our town and opened fire on the strikers, killing two and wounding twenty more.

In Austin that evening Thom asks me to get on stage in a bohemian coffee bar full of men and women in berets. He wants me to tell stories about Yorkshire mining communities. I start with the story of how James Duggan and James Gibbs came to be shot dead near the side door of the Top House by the South Staffordshire Light Infantry. I am joined on stage by a thin young woman playing a double bass, she tunes into the rhythm of my story. A mandolin player joins us and then an older man swoops in on alto sax. I get to the bit where a Lee Mitford cartridge passes through the body of an onlooker and a cymbal crashes. The audience join in with a wailing sort of chant. There is a scene in Tony Hancock's film *The Rebel* where he's with a gang of existentialists, one of them says mystically, 'Where am I? I am near,' and Hancock says, 'Washing my feet in a glass of beer.' It feels like one of those moments. Later a construction worker's yellow plastic safety helmet is passed round and people throw in dollar bills.

Arnold begins to stir. He pushes the neb of his cap back from his eyes and makes the sort of tutting noise that drinkers with a mouth like the inside of a canary's cage make when they first wake up. 'Bring some more ale please, landlord.'

'Haven't you had enough, Arnold?'

'A man can never have had enough good ale, landlord, you should know that!'

Peter orders the next round. Arnold belches and then leans forward conspiratorially. 'Did I ever tell you the tale about Harriet de Lyle and Clara Gayle? They were a pair of music hall turns who appeared in this pub afore the First World War.' The thought of a music hall act called Gayle and de Lyle makes me smile.

'What's tha fuckin' laughing at? It's true! They were singing in here one night pissed up and one of them kicked a lamp over and nearly burnt the place down. Landlord then was a man called Thomas Palmer. He tried to have them arrested for singing while pissed up. The bobby who they fetched said they couldn't be that pissed if they could sing and say poetry.' As if to accentuate this he begins to recite a poem that his father had 'composed' during the First World War:

'Twas on the sixth of August lads,
One bright and sunny day.
We landed in the Dardanelles some thousand miles away.
We knew not what before us lie,
But heard the shot and shell
And many a man who lived that day,
Will live no more to tell...'

He continues with an epic tale of how the Munster Fusiliers captured the heights of Chocolate Hill and made the Turks run across their homeland plain. It is stirring stuff. The taxi drivers and young lads playing pool stop taking the piss and listen respectfully. Peter comes back with the beers and carefully places one on a mat in front of Arnie. He swoops it up in one movement:

'I'll raise this glass filled to the brim
To the boys who knew no fear
And when I hear the noise
And clamour of war and din
I'll never forget the Gallipoli lads
And the struggle I was in.'

A round of applause and Arnold takes a bow. One of the taxi drivers asks him if he'd like a whisky to chase his beer.

'Aye!'

'Do you want owt in it?'

'Aye! Another one.'

Introducing Mr B. B. Singh!

Heather and me spent our first summer of love together in the crumby staff quarters behind the Woolacombe Bay Hotel in North Devon. Heather worked as a waitress and I made sandwiches for and carried the cases of the retired colonials and tuppenny ha'penny millionaires who came to stay there. Heather was nearly sacked for fashioning her hair into a blue mohican. We still joke now that she was the first of the mohicans.

The staff quarters were full of dreamers. Along the corridor was an acid casualty from Wales who'd had a bad trip some years before and never quite got things back together again. His job was to fish the rubbish out of the outdoor pool every night and polish shoes that were left out. There was a scouser called Teapot Mick and another one, an emaciated pothead from Huyton, who once set fire to the curtains outside of our room. I chased him to his bed and gave him a good hiding. He laid there with his lighter in his hand crying, 'It wasn't me, la.' Next door to him was a beautiful New Zealand surfer girl who didn't wear clothes in her room. She had more cups of tea brought to her than anybody I've ever known.

Johnny Morrish was next along the corridor. Johnny was one of the coolest people you could wish to meet. He had a battered acoustic guitar and grew his own. He spent the summer listening on his bed to Marianne Faithfull's *Broken English* LP. There was a weirdo who had escaped from somewhere who tried to kill himself in the kitchens by pulling the deep fat fryer onto himself. We didn't know his name. The only thing we knew about him was that he took size fourteen shoes. John Walchester and his girlfriend Sally became close friends. John was from Stoke and liked Swamp Dogg. He's still the only person I know who collects Swamp Dogg records. John and Sally got married and moved to Norfolk. We still maintain the friendship. We last met for a beer on Cromer Pier and tried to fit twenty-five years into an hour and a half.

Towards season's end everybody talked about the travelling they would do in the winter. Heather, me, John and Sally and a dustbin man from Bristol, who drew scenes from *Lord of the Rings*, called Kevin, bought a £27 ticket for the Magic Bus and landed in Athens. We hung around the Acropolis and the markets near Syntagma for a while and then split up. John and Sally went off to the islands. Kevin, Heather and me booked flights to India via Egypt and Pakistan. I was twenty-one, Heather would be nineteen. We'd heard stories from hippies in their thirties, like Johnny Morrish, about trips to India and we would bump into people at festivals and gigs who would tell us that Kashmir is just the best and that Freak Street in Kathmandu is 'the' place. It was time to bring my maps to life. In Karachi we ate a goat that had been running about round the hotel courtyard and in Delhi we got so stoned on the first night that the bed floated out of the room on a lizard's back.

We are staying in the Hotel Kesri in Old Delhi, on a street called Pahar Ganj in the Rattan Bazaar. In our room are three wickerwork beds and a small chest of drawers. The toilet is a communal hole in the floor behind some slatted Wild West saloon doors on the landing. You don't go here unless you really need to. We have a friendly lizard that Kevin the dustbin man has christened 'Copernicus'; it comes out of a hole in the ceiling and crawls down the wall to see us two or three times a day. A notice over Heather's bed says, 'Please refrain from smoking hashish in the room'. We have a balcony on which sit some cane chairs. A pigeon roosts in the eaves above us. Kevin has decided to call this one 'China Street'. This is where we come with our tolah of manali hash to smoke and watch the world go by. A tolah of hash is about as big as your index finger and costs about twenty rupees. Below there are children selling clay pots full of vegetable curry, pineapples and oranges. There are fortune tellers, calendar vendors, ice-water men with tanks in front of their bicycles and old men with lit incense sticks drawing smoke ring patterns. Whole families on scooters swerve to avoid humpbacked cows and tricycle taxis whizz up and down taking European hippies from one café to another.

We have become acquainted with an Indian student called Dik. He heard us talking one day and asked us if we were from Preston. He told us he had relatives in Preston and they spoke English like us. One evening he takes us to what he describes as a 'rock concert'. The concert takes place at the Jesus and Mary College for Girls. We are greeted at the flaps of a filthy marquee held up on bamboo poles by a nun in striped pop socks. She asks us if we are 'ready to rock'. The tent is full of Indian students eager to celebrate the last evening of Rag week. On a makeshift stage, the Maurice Jenkins Experience are tuning up. There are shouts from the crowd: 'Jethro Tull', 'Zappa' and 'The Doors'. The band open up with 'YMCA' and segue straight into a Boney M number. There is a chorus of whistles and boos. The band stop playing and an elderly piano player comes to the mic. 'Please stop being so rude or we will not proceed with the entertainments.' The booing stops. The old man makes his next announcement. 'Please be putting your hands together for guitar legend…Mr B. B. Singh.' A Sikh man with a Fender Stratocaster runs on stage. The band kick straight into 'Jumping Jack Flash' and the audience go wild.

Our student mate Dik joins us back on our balcony. He wants me to give him a pair of black plastic shoes he's seen under my bed. In between leaving the hotel in Devon and setting off for India I hadn't bothered to unpack. This means I have carted across Europe and halfway across Asia a full wine waiter's outfit comprising a cheap white nylon shirt, a velvety bow tie, some black polyester trousers and a pair of black plastic shoes. I have also brought in the side pocket of the rucksack a large yellow enamelled alarm clock with bells on. Dik tells me he will tell me something about myself and give me two books in exchange for the wine waiter's outfit and the clock. After a couple of joints we shake hands and make the exchange. He reaches into his haversack and gives me two books, the first is *Sakoontala* by Kalidsa and the other is a small book of poems by the Bangladeshi writer Rabindranath Tagore. He then totters off into the night spitting red betel juice onto the pavement. I shout after him, 'What was it that you were going to tell me about myself?' He turns round and smiles. 'Your mother's name is Pauline.' The hairs on my body all stand up. 'How could you know that?' He points his index finger to his lips and smiles. He then looks down at the shirt and trousers hanging over his arm and the pair of shoes gripped between his thumb and other fingers and says, 'Be careful on your journey!' We never saw Dik after that.

One day we followed an elephant's arse down the street to a café called Gobhind. On either side of the street are speakers attached to bamboo poles, mainly playing the Hindi film music of Ashe Bhosle and Lata Mengashkar mixed with the occasional speech from Indira Gandhi. A man is slapping a little boy for pissing on a pyramid of oranges he has been building. Inside the Gobhind café, Jimi Hendrix is blasting from the speaker in an upstairs room. We order plates full of curd and sing along, 'There must be some kinda way out of here, said the joker to the thief.' When the song finishes I notice a very dignified and calm looking man on a table opposite. He beckons me to come over. He is wearing scarlet silk clothes, a little cap and Turkish slippers. He has a neat little goatee beard and pince-nez glasses. He puts his fingers together as though to pray, bows very politely and says, 'Hello, my name is Paul Unadcath.' I introduce myself, Heather and Kevin. Paul tells us that he came over to India in the late sixties, that he was one of the first to go on the original hippy trail. He's never been back to England since. 'I sell carpets now,' he says.

'What kind of carpets?'

'Magic ones.'

Paul offers us a Dunhill cigarette each from a silver case. 'You know this is a really cool market, but you should travel up to Nepal and take an apartment in Pokhara before the winter draws in.'

Two days later we take the Assam mail train down the Ganges Valley. It travels through Kanpur, Allahabad and Benares on its way to Mussafapur in the east. There we were to head north to Kathmandu. Between Kanpur and Allahabad we share our peanut shell strewn compartment with a team of office workers. Their spokesman is a little fella who they all call 'Buddha' or 'Three Foot'. He reads our palms and recites ancient Sanskrit poetry. In return they ask us to sing an English folk song. We give a very rough and nicely out of tune version of 'The Fog on the Tyne' and 'On Ilkley Moor Baht 'at'. Watching but not joining in is a hippy who earlier told us he was from Essex. He said he was going to the mountains to breathe fresh air and recover from dysentery that he'd contracted in Sri Lanka.

At midnight we fold down the wooden beds. The last thing I say to Heather before 'Goodnight' is, 'Is your money and passport safe?' She says, 'Yes it's in my green bag and I'm using it as a pillow.'

Just before six in the morning Heather wakes me. The strap of her green bag is tied round her wrist, but the bag is no longer attached. The one thousand pounds she has saved from tips and wages all season at the hotel in Devon has gone, and so has her passport. I threaten to punch everybody on the train. The only man I can't find is the one who wanted to breathe fresh mountain air. As Johnny Rotten said, 'Never trust a hippy!'

We get off the train at a godforsaken hole called Barauni Junction near a village called Beguserai somewhere in the east of India. We report the theft to a couple of bemused policemen in a village cop shop who ask Heather to tell them the name of her father and grandfather and then insist that we go back to Delhi to inform the British Embassy.

On the night before we left for India, Heather and me had a meal in the Oriental Chinese Restaurant in Pontefract with Heather's mother and stepfather Dave. After I polished off an orange plateful of chicken sweet and sour and three pints of Double Diamond I went to the back for a pee. The door in the lav swung open behind me. It was Dave. He pushed me up against the urinal. 'I can't stop thee taking her to India,' he said, 'but if owt fuckin' happens to her I'll knock thi fuckin' head off when tha gets back.' We finished our tinned fruit salad off with looks at one another.

On Platform One at Barauni Junction we wait for the train back down the Ganges Valley to Delhi. Heather sobs and I don't know what to do or say. Next to the seat we're sitting on is a small dog. I stroke it for five minutes before I realise that it's a dead dog. I jump away. As I do I look at Heather. She is still sobbing and I notice that her hair is crawling with lice. I let out a howl and take her by the hand. I run her down the platform screaming for water. As if from nowhere a tap appears. I turn it on and cold water streams out. I wash Heather's hair. A sergeant from the Indian army appears and offers to share some fried fish that he has wrapped in a newspaper. A surreal moment at a desperate time. The Delhi train steams in and we climb aboard.

Heather sobs on and off all the way back to the Hotel Kesri in Old Delhi. We take a room next to the one we had vacated a couple of days before. When Heather drops off to sleep I follow the elephant back to the Gobhind café. Lata Mengashkar still sings from the speakers on the bamboo poles and the old man still guards his pyramid of oranges. In the café Hendrix sings 'All Along the Watchtower' again and Paul Unadcath bows and offers me a seat. I tell him the story. He gives me a piece of paper and tells me to meet him the following morning.

We take a taxi to the address on the paper: 'The Hotel Taj Mahal Intercontinental'. This is one of the finest hotels in the whole of India. Fountains of coloured fragrant water play in the foyer, the floor has mosaic tiles and chandeliers hang from the high ceiling. At reception I ask to be taken to Mr Unadcath's room. A tall Sikh man in a golden sash shows us the way. Paul welcomes us at the door. Under the chromium lid of a tureen he has breakfast waiting. We tuck into eggs, fried bread, tomatoes and sausage and wash it down with a lovely cup of darjeeling.

'I have made an appointment for you at the Embassy and sent a telex to Lloyds Bank in Yorkshire to arrange a re-issue of your stolen travellers cheques. Everything will be fine after today.' Heather smiles.

Later at the Embassy we tell our story and the official assures us that issuing a new passport will be no problem. To this day Heather keeps as a souvenir the passport she was issued with a stamp from the British High Commission in Delhi. At Grindleys Bank near the Connaught Square we were assured that they were in correspondence with Lloyds in Bradford and that replacement travellers cheques would arrive shortly.

That night we plan a big thank you for Paul Unadcath. We

follow the elephant past the speakers on bamboo poles. The man with the oranges is sitting quietly cross-legged. Hendrix blares from upstairs, but Paul Unadcath is nowhere to be seen. The following morning we take another tricycle taxi to the Taj Mahal Intercontinental. I step up to the reception desk.

'May I see Mr Unadcath in room 112a please.' The receptionist looks at me. 'I have no Mr Unadcath here.'

'Did he check out?'

'No sir, you misunderstand me. I have no record of a Mr Unadcath.'

As I write this story more than twenty-five years after it happened I am sitting smoking at my kitchen table. When I close my eyes, I see Paul Unadcath in his scarlet silk with his Turkish slippers. I am listening to a recording by Ravi Shankar and Ali Akhbar Khan, a recording he recommended.

'But you must know him, I had breakfast here with him yesterday!'

'No sir. And what's more, we don't have a room 112a.'

A Sikh man with a golden sash ushers us to the front door.

Born in West Yorkshire

My home town is full of ghosts. It is also a blues town. Like all blues towns Featherstone thrives on shadows and echoes of what once was. There are echoes here that started off as sounds a long time ago. This town is crammed with superstitions and primitive beliefs. From my grandmother I learned that when the thunder and lightning comes you should always open your back door and cover your cutlery with a tea towel. She shouted and bawled if you put new shoes onto a table or attempted to cut your nails on a Friday. Once when I put some green remains of a Christmas tree on the fire she said, 'We might have bad luck now.' Another time when we sat together looking at the patterns in the flames she noticed a piece of soot dangling from the bars of the fire grate and she told me we could expect a letter to arrive. Whenever gypsies came to the door selling pegs, my gran always crossed their palms with silver for fear that they might spit on the step and curse her.

Whenever I fell down and cut my knees or suffered stomach ache, my gran put her hands on the bit that hurt. She said that her granny had taught her that you can heal people who you love with the warmth from your hands. I have carried this on and added my own take on it. Our little Billie doesn't believe in plasters for grazed knees. She always says, 'Daddy put your healing hands on me.' I do and recite a daft little rhyme:

'Healing Hands. Healing Hands. Will you heal this girl.
With a whippy hippy wag and a long tailed bag
Heal this girl with the power in my hand.'

It always works.

Featherstone is where people once came to from the countryside to build a life and a family around coal, bringing a strange dialect with them. Featherstone, like the first two lines of a blues song, likes to repeat itself. Featherstone is the most remote of the blues towns, a long way from the Mississippi Delta, yet if you drew a line between New Orleans and Memphis you might find Featherstone on that line. Somewhere between Rolling Fork where Muddy Waters was born and Clarksdale, the birth town of John Lee Hooker, is Featherstone.

Forging links between northern industrial towns and the Mississippi Delta is something that occurs to me one drunken afternoon in a bar on the edge of Sheffield city centre. The bar is called Fagan's, it's an old-fashioned spit and sawdust place that would have at one time catered for thirsty steel workers downing pints like they were going out of fashion. I find myself in the company of the Sheffield musician Richard Hawley and his manager Graham. Richard Hawley writes the most beautiful modern ballads and sings in a baritone voice that Scott Walker would have been proud of. I first came across Richard when I heard his song 'You Don't Miss Your Water' on an album called *Lowedges*. Richard downs pints of Guinness and I try to keep up on bitter. He likes to tell stories. He is from a musical family. His uncle is the Yorkshire blues guitarist Frank White and his father played in a band. Richard tells of how in the 1960s, his father was about to go on stage at Batley Variety Club. Just before the band are announced his dad decides he needs to pee. He asks a man backstage where the nearest toilet is. The man says, 'Can't tha piss in that sink?' Richard's dad says, 'Well I'm not sure I can piss in a sink.' The backstage hand says, 'What's up with thi? If it's good enough for Shirley Bassey I'm sure it's good enough for thee.' We all laugh like drains and Richard orders another round.

After seven or eight pints Richard asks the landlord to hand him an acoustic guitar. With the encouragement of Graham he plays the sweetest of lullabies. It's called 'Who's Gonna Shoe Your Pretty Little Feet', it's like a spiritual and will appear on the new album *Coles Corner*. Coles Corner is a semi-mythical, but real meeting place in Sheffield. The entrance to an old department store where thousands of Sheffield courting couples have arranged to meet over the years. There is a moment or two at the end of this lullaby when we all let a breath out and ponder. Then Richard says, 'Reight then!', hits a chord and kicks into John Lee Hooker's 'Big Legs Tight Skirt'. He plays the blues like he was born in Rolling Fork, Mississippi. I egg him on by mentioning Charley Patton, Blind Lemon Jefferson, Peg Leg Howell and any other blind, crippled hollerer of the blues I can dredge up from a beer-befuddled memory. Richard retunes his guitar and plays 'Mystery Train', belting out 'Train I ride…it's sixteen coaches long.' After the first verse I clap my hands and shout, 'Little Junior Parker and the Blue Flames.' Richard stops playing, reaches for my hand and kisses my knuckles, it seems not too bizarre in a smoke-filled taproom on the edge of Sheffield city centre. 'Most people would have said fuckin' Elvis Presley,' says Richard. 'Let's have another beer.' At this juncture, if Richard had told me that he was on the lorry that took Ike Turner to Memphis to cut 'Rocket 88' with Jackie Brenston and The Delta Cats, I would easily have believed him.

At the beginning of 2006 I got a text message from Richard. 'Watch *The South Bank Show* tonight. I won!' I watched it. Melvyn Bragg was giving out the annual awards for excellence in the arts. A right old mixture of people had been invited. Tracey Emin was there, Darcy Bussell the ballet dancer was another, the lad who played Harry Potter gave a speech and Eric Sykes, the old comedian, had everyone in fits of laughter. Melvyn Bragg read out the nominations for the award for record of the year. They were Gorillaz for *Demon Days*, Kate Bush for *Aerial*, and Richard Hawley for *Coles Corner*. Jarvis Cocker was invited up to the podium to reveal the winner and present the award. Richard went up to collect his sculptured doorstopper. He looked nervous, rubbed his chin and fingered his nose. He leaned over the microphone and addressed the gathering of arty-fartys. 'I should thank my dad and my grandad and Jarvis here, but I think I'll tell a funny story.' He launched himself into the tale about his dad, the sink and Shirley Bassey at Batley. Held up his award like Bobby Moore, said, 'Thank you' and jumped back into the audience.

My favourite Yorkshire blues man remains relatively unsung. His name is Roy Herrington and he was born just up the road from the Rat Trap Working Men's Club in Featherstone.

Roy collected recordings by J. B. Lenior and Buddy Guy when the rest of the kids at school were into 'Chirpy Chirpy Cheep Cheep'! Roy Herrington is the man who many people in this part of the world must thank for setting them on the road to Bluesville.

I am wearing a cheesecloth shirt, some bottle-green Oxford bags with pockets on the side of each leg and a pair of orange platform shoes. I am on the stage at Batley Variety Club with my friend Roy Herrington and half a dozen pot-bellied rockers who are spinning their wives around. One woman keeps taking a running jump at her partner. She wraps her legs around his back and he tips her right over his head. She rolls down his back and takes another running jump. I put my arm around Chuck Berry's shoulders, his shirt is wringing with the sweat that lathers his back. I'm close enough to see the pencil-thin moustache he's sporting and the wild glint in his eye as he powers his way through 'Johnny B. Goode'. I am ecstatic, this feeling will only ever be equalled when in 1983 I run onto the rugby pitch at Headingley to put my arm round Peter Smith, a heroic loose forward who has just helped Featherstone Rovers to win in the semi-final of the Rugby League Challenge Cup. Back in Batley, Chuck Berry segues into 'Brown-Eyed Handsome Man'. I twirl to the front of the stage trying to jive on my platform shoes.

Memory fuses here. I seem to recall Chuck Berry came on after an escapology act and a man who did Tommy Cooper impressions. I'm not sure any more. I know Chuck did the daft crowd-pleaser 'My Ding-a-Ling', I recall the crowd joining in with gusto and remember thinking that my mother and father would have been the first to sing along.

It's Roy who has organised this trip to pay homage to one of his heroes. He originally wanted us to skive off school for the day and knock on Chuck's dressing room door. I never could skive school and fortunately for me Roy's brother Gary couldn't drive us until he'd finished work at the pit. Roy was determined to get nearer to Chuck Berry and so we launched ourselves at the stage.

Berry moves to his left and my arm slides from his wet back. He plays 'Oh Carol' and then I see Roy doing a kind of Lindy-hop with Chuck's daughter Ingrid, who has been on backing vocals. For a matter of minutes this chips-in-a-basket nightclub is our own personal jook joint.

Roy is from Halton Street. Us Featherstone lads stick together and when we got into our final year at The King's School in Pontefract, Roy and me became close friends. Roy is probably the most naturally gifted musician I have ever known. By the time he was fifteen he could play boogie-woogie like Albert Ammons and guitar like T-Bone Walker. He had in his mam and dad's back bedroom a priceless collection of blues records. J. B. Lenoir on the Chess label, B. B. King's 'Live at The Regal', Elmore James thrashing away on slide guitar on the Fire and Chief recordings and Robert Nighthawk playing live on Maxwell Street. Off Station Lane in Featherstone is another Maxwell Street. It's where the annual visiting fair used to set up on the foothills of the slag heaps. Somehow when we sit in Roy's bedroom listening to Robert Nighthawk, out in his own Maxwell Street, we feel strangely closer because of this. Many years after these back bedroom listening sessions I met the writer and photographer Val Wilmer. She gave me a photo of the blues musician Johnny Embry sitting on a battered chair playing guitar on Maxwell Street, Chicago. A circle joined. I listen to Robert Nighthawk now and airbrush myself into that photo.

In Roy's bedroom we travelled to Chicago on his dad's beetroot beer. Roy's dad George had an allotment. He told us that he grew cabbages as big as armchairs and beetroot from which he fermented a wicked indigo-coloured brew. We listened together and drank and in moonlit streets on my way back down Station Lane to Mafeking Street I spewed purple sick into three different grates.

Roy is asked to give concerts at school with a blues and rock 'n' roll band he's formed. At one of these concerts he walks on stage with a woodcutter's axe over his shoulder. As Christmas approached his mother had asked him what presents he wanted. He asked for a new axe. He meant a Gibson. His mother took him literally. Roy showed no hint of disappointment as he unwrapped a chopper big enough to fell a tree. At concerts he places his wood axe on the piano lid, straps on his old Gibson and kicks off with his own composition 'KSP Boogie' (King's School Pontefract Boogie). Then follows it with B.B.'s 'Sweet Little Angel', Elmore's 'Dust My Broom', T-Bone's 'Stormy Monday', a cracking version of Mayall's 'Looking Back', 'Johnny B. Goode', 'Great Balls of Fire', 'I Saw Her Standing There'. It's a set-list he will return to throughout his career. It's bloody good. It's had them dancing from Pontefract to Estonia. The serious music fans at our school quoted Pink Floyd, the guitar attack of Wishbone Ash, Hendrix, Led Zep *One, Two, Three,*

Runes and *Physical Graffiti*. They'd also quote Roy Herrington. Clapton is God, Herrington has all the best tunes.

On the day we leave school, Roy creates a parting gesture. He customises his blazer. He narrows the lapels and on the back in steel studs writes a message. It says, 'Rock 'n' Roll'.

For a while after leaving school, Roy works as a roof tiler and in the evening plays his blues for beer in the back rooms of Tetley Bitter pubs. The group is now The Stormy Monday Blues Band. Roy on guitar and vocals, Big John Barker who looks like Deep Purple – all of 'em – on bass, Mike Proctor or Mick Grace, a scrapyard owner's son, on drums and a six foot seven inch tall keyboards player called Mark Haddleton.

One night in an upstairs room at the Pack Horse, a pub full of students opposite the University in Leeds, they are joined for a couple of numbers by an electric violin player called Jörge Petersmann. Jörge is a German at the university on an exchange programme. He offers to set up a short tour in the Ruhrgebeit, the industrial north of Germany. Roy doesn't need asking twice. Stormy Monday load up a transit van, drive down to Felixstowe and cross to the Hook of Holland. They take the E30 motorway into Germany and play gigs in Wuppertal, Düsseldorf and Cologne. While the kids back home are dressing up as pirates and eighteenth century dandies and dancing to Culture Club, Spandau Ballet and the Human League, serious young men with beards and women who roll Drum tobacco in middle-class areas of Deutschland are grooving to the King's School Boogie.

Roy and the boys make two more tours to Germany within a year, each one bigger than the last. Roy is paid proper money and falls in love first with Wuppertal and then with a primary school teacher called Ute. In the same season as Featherstone Rovers win the Rugby League Challenge Cup with a team of fearsome coal miners, he leaves his home town and settles in Wuppertal.

Wuppertal is the home of the Pina Bausch Dance Company, the home of the European Free Jazz movement, Peter Brötzmann and Peter Kovald live in this town and Sainkho Namtchylak brings her extraordinary Tuvan overtone singing here. It's where Friedrich Engels did a lot of his early writing. It has Europe's most astonishing feat of transport engineering, the Schweberbahn, a floating monorail system over a hundred years old. It has a vibrant Turkish community living on the side of the valley in a warren of streets full of corner shops and bars where old men play backgammon and drink buzzbag wine. It's also home to intimate smoke-filled bars where you can roll your Drum whilst listening to Fela Kuti, The Rolling Stones, and Okay Temiz.

Okay Temiz is a tremendous Turkish drummer who drums on hand-beaten copper drums. He did an album called *Turkish Folk Jazz* on the Sonet 'Universal Folk Sounds' imprint. The cover of the album features a bare-breasted mythological figure with a swirling veil on her head not unlike the pattern on our bedroom oilcloth. Temiz is accompanied on the album by two musicians; Saffet Gündeger, a Turk, on clarinet and Björn Alke, a Swede, on bass. In more pretentious moments I tell people it's the best album he's ever done. On the sleeve notes Gündeger quotes Coltrane and Charlie Parker and says that he appreciates music from Japan and Tibet. 'All different flowers give a different kind of smell,' he states. They don't write sleeve notes like that any more. Then again.

Roy Herrington has a splendid disregard for prevailing fashion and image. Ever since I have known him he has announced himself in an eccentric way that is part slow-timing and another part subversion. His hair is the colour of apricots. He wears things like his dad's mustard-coloured cardigan done up with brown leather buttons and turquoise flared trousers. When we were kids he would turn up at my gran's back door with a donkey jacket on. In one pocket would be a catering sized packet of salted peanuts, in the other half a pound of cheese. He went through a phase of body-building and would only eat high-protein foods. Roy's knowledge of the blues, both theoretical and practical, is immense. We sit in the front room of his apartment watching Lightning Hopkins videos and with his own acoustic guitar on his lap he plays the runs he's just been watching.

Roy lives in Brunne Strasse, right in the heart of the Turkish community. His local pub is The Hasret, a Turkish pub whose landlord once made the mistake of going back to Ankara to visit his folks and got drafted into the army. Roy lives on the third floor. On the stairs leading up to his flat there is the smell of a different country's cuisine on every landing. The flat below Roy and Ute's is occupied by a Bulgarian weightlifter. He must be a famous Bulgarian weightlifter because on his door is a photocard of himself. The sort of photocard I'd collected as a kid that came with bubble gum; Jeff Astle – West Bromwich Albion, Ian Porterfield – Sunderland, Brian Labone – Everton. The most surreal episodes in my life have unfolded in Roy's front room. I usually needed alcohol or grass to go into silly mode. Roy could do it on sheep's cheese.

One day I'm at Roy's with a heavy cold. I ask him if Ute might know a herbal tea or something that might shift it. Roy makes me a peppermint tea with comfrey leaves in it. I ask if he thinks it will work. He says he hopes so, because they are the only two herbs in his kitchen. He then asks me to think of old wives' cures.

'My gran used to say that if you tie your sweaty socks round your neck it will cure a sore throat.'

'Try it!'

He forces me to tie my socks around my neck.

'Maybe if you tie your trousers round your head it will unblock your nose.'

He says this completely deadpan. He looks exactly like his dad did when he told us about the time when he'd seen a swan trying to land in his allotment but it couldn't because the fog over his garden was so thick even a swan couldn't break through it. Or the time when he'd walked all the way home from the Green Lane Club in his stockinged feet because the shoes he'd been wearing were so comfortable he had slipped them off under the domino table and hadn't realised he hadn't got them on when he came home.

'I've got some Fishermen's Friends somewhere. Maybe if you crush them into a powder and snort them like snuff it'll cure you.'

Roy has seasonal obsessions. Every November when russet apples ripen his mother packs half a dozen and sends them by air-mail from Featherstone to Wuppertal. He's the only blues guitarist in Germany who sits munching russets every November.

For many years through the 1980s and 90s Roy is the hardest gigging blues guitarist in Germany. He plays every bar with a stage, every festival and every hall. He forms a German version of Stormy Monday, this time called The Roy Herrington Band. His rhythm section now consists of two brothers from the Neanderthal, Christoph on bass and Micki, a hard-hitting stick man. Roy and the boys have a B. B. King appetite for live shows, playing two hundred and more gigs a year. They record a series of albums starting with one called *A Change is Coming*. On the sleeve Roy is sitting on something like a milk churn on a railway station platform, his beloved Gibson propped at the side of him. He's wearing a beard, jeans and a knitted cardigan. He's staring directly down the camera lens, his fingers poised to bend strings. On the front of my copy of this record he has written in blue biro, 'Without being pretentious – this is the best platter I've ever made. Love Roy.' The album contains a fabulous workout on Calvin Leavy's 'Cummings Prison Farm'.

Perhaps Roy's best record, because it's live, is the one he records with the 1960s R 'n' B singer Chris Farlowe in Berlin. Farlowe is still known for this chart-topping cover of the Stones' 'Out of Time'. As far as I know he still makes a healthy living on the European blues circuit. The CD is full of good singing and playing, especially on 'The Thrill is Gone' and 'Stormy Monday'. But the best track of all is the nine-minute-long warm-up and introduction. Roy has dispensed with his usual 'KSP Boogie' and gone for another of his own compositions, 'Born in West Yorkshire'. It's a pastiche I suppose of 'Cummings Prison Farm':

'I was born in Missouri,
crossed the line to Arkansas.
I was born in Missouri baby,
crossed the line to Arkansas.
Couldn't get no job nor money,
I got in trouble with the law.
They sent me to prison,
down on Cummings Prison Farm.'

Except in his version Roy sings:

'I was born in West Yorkshire,
son of a coal mining man.
Yeah! I was born in West Yorkshire baby,
son of a coal mining man.
Couldn't get no job,
so I started playing blues on my guitar.'

It's blistering, with roll upon roll of cascading piano and
guitar playing as hot as the back of a shovel used to draw a
fire.

On our table at school there was a lad called Tony
Withington who was a tremendous tennis player, he went on
to play against the French champion Yannick Noah. After
school Tony became a miner, a leading light in the coal strike
who took a degree in law. There was an illustrator and poet
called Jim Harwood who, when I last heard, was organising
cabaret at a greasy little club in Leicester called The Attick.
One year below us was Ian Bevitt who these days is a

director on Coronation Street. I bumped into him at the Liquorice Fair in Pontefract last year. He told me how he had worshipped Roy and still thought of him as better than Clapton.

Twenty-odd years after we jived to him at Batley Variety Club, Chuck Berry is headlining a rock 'n' roll revival tour in Europe. Accompanying him on rhythm guitar on the German leg of the tour is my mate Roy Herrington.

Part-time Punk

Mick Griffiths is sitting in his bedroom practising on the Rickenbacker his mother bought him for his birthday. Mick was born on May Day in 1960. I was born in September 1959; we were in the same year at school all the way from Girnhill Lane Infants. In later years his May Day birthday will become his talisman. The bedroom walls are adorned with posters of The Who. He has the 'Maximum R 'n' B' black and white poster that came as an insert with The Who's *Live At Leeds* album and the landscape photograph of Pete Townshend in a white boiler suit leaping into the air above the heads of the crowd at Woodstock. There is another poster proclaiming, 'Frampton comes alive'. On the floor are scattered the albums we're currently playing to death; Nils Lofgren *Cry Tough*, Gallagher and Lyle *Breakway*, Alex Harvey Band *SAHB Stories*. I'm looking through his window, an old man in a flat cap is pushing a wheelbarrow full of chopped wood and a sack of coal. Two women in their pinnies are standing callin at a gateway, they both have rollers in their hair. A mobile shop that sells paraffin and white pudding basins has just pulled up and the man who drives it is ringing a bell to announce his arrival. We'd been reading about how Pete Townshend slid in the rainwater across the stage at The Who's concert at Charlton Athletic's football ground. It feels like the calm before a storm. And it is. The *New Musical Express* which Mick has delivered every week by Ian

Dransfield's newsagents, has published an article under the headline, 'Don't look over your shoulder. The Sex Pistols are coming'.

One night in the autumn of 1976 we hear John Peel play 'Anarchy in the UK'. Not long after, Johnny Sands sits in the back room of The Windmill pub and slashes and hacks at his grey sports jacket with a pen knife. He then fastens up the gaping holes with some safety pins he's bought from the market. When, a few weeks later, someone smacks him in the nose for being a 'punker' he wipes the blood with his sleeve. I'm working as an apprentice bench fitter at the engineering works in Pontefract. Mick asks me if I can make him a big metal badge with 'MG' on it, to imitate the badge on MG sports cars. I do. It must weigh a pound and a half. My gran gives him an old kilt pin to fasten it to his jacket with.

Looking back now, I can recall vividly the *Daily Mirror* headline 'The Filth and the Fury' the morning after the Pistols' infamous outburst on *The Bill Grundy Show*. Of course I didn't get to see the programme, it was only shown in the London region. I recall even more vividly the videoed first appearance of the Pistols on *Top of the Pops* singing 'Pretty Vacant'. I saw it on my gran's black and white telly that she rented from the DER. My gran and grandad watched it too. My grandad said to my gran, 'Just look at these silly buggers, Hilda. If ever they walked up Station Lane they'd have 'em down.'

It's hard being a punk in Pontefract, even harder in Featherstone. You daren't go to the local pubs, so you stay in your mates' bedrooms and venture to places when you know that other like-minded souls will be there. In Leeds there's the

F Club, in Doncaster The Outlook. We become regulars at The Outlook and see the Flamin' Groovies, The Clash, Sham 69, Slaughter and the Dogs, the Angelic Upstarts. A sensitive poet from London by the name of Patrik Fitzgerald releases a lovely quirky single called 'I've Got a Safety Pin Stuck in my Heart for You'. When he comes to Doncaster Outlook we see him. It turns out to be a memorable night. The number 410 bus from Leeds to Doncaster goes from Pontefract bus station every half-hour. Mick and me have just enough money for the fare and a pint in the White Swan pub across the road. The bus conductor comes upstairs and asks us where we are going. In his best deadpan voice Mick says, 'Nowhere.'

The conductor says, 'Come on smart-arse, I haven't got all day.'

'Alright then, Doncaster.'

The conductor rolls two tickets out of his machine. 'And take your chuffing boots off them seats, decent folk have to sit on them.'

As the bus approaches our stop we repeatedly ring the bell. The conductor charges upstairs and raves at us, 'Ring that fucking bell once more and I'll leather the bastard pair of you.'

We haven't got a ticket for the Club. When we get to The Outlook it seems that every punk in Yorkshire is queuing up to get in. A mass of leather jackets. A garden lawn full of green spiky hair. A trampoline full of stiff-as-a-poker dancers already pogoing. This is what we've come for. We go straight to the front of the queue and tell the doorman that Patrik Fitzgerald is our mate and that he's put us on the guest list.

The doorman shoves us both onto our arses and tells us to 'Fuck off'. We get to our feet. Mick pulls out of his camouflage jacket pocket a crumpled letter he's received last week from Patrik Fitzgerald. 'Dear Mick. I'm pleased you like my record. I'm on tour at the moment. It would be nice to meet you if you want to come and see me. Ask for me at the door.'

Mick tries to show the letter to the doorman. He tells us in a broad growl of a Yorkshire accent to 'Fuck off!' again. Then like a little guardian angel in a beret Patrik Fitzgerald comes to the door. Mick pogoes up and down and says, 'He's here, he's here, ask him.' The doorman turns to the little chap behind him and says, 'These pair of twats say they're on the guest list.' Patrik nods and tells him that we're his friends. The doorman snorts and spits into the street and says, 'Well fuck off in then.'

Patrik can't really remember Mick's fan letter, but tells us that he hopes we enjoy the gig, before toddling off to his dressing room. We enjoy the gig. In the cold night air we have to work out how we're going to get home. It is about fifteen miles from Doncaster to Featherstone. If we're late, we're in trouble. Only a few weeks before I'd been locked out of my gran's house after a Thin Lizzy gig. I slept sitting on the pot of our outside lavatory. We decide that we'll take a taxi and run away once we get to Featherstone. The taxi driver senses the tension as he steers through the darkness of the country lanes towards Pontefract. 'I hope you two can pay for this bugger.' We assure him that we can and pat our trouser pockets. The plan we had made while we waited at the rank was to take the taxi to Station Lane, stop him outside of Dransfield's Newsagents, get out pretending to feel for our wallets then run across the old bus depot yard and leap the wall into George Street School where the driver couldn't follow. Things didn't go to plan. The car pulled up. We started to get out. The driver reached to grab me and I panicked. I slammed the door straight onto my fingers. Mick shouted 'run'. We ran. Across the bus depot yard, the car right behind us. Now, one thing I had warned Mick about earlier was the wall. On the bus depot side the wall is about three and a half feet high. On the school playground side it drops about ten feet. 'Whatever you do, Mick, don't try to jump it in one go. Climb on top of the wall then drop down.' Mick assures me that since he's been in the Territorial Army he's learnt how to fall. We reach the wall. I mount the wall, swivel over on my belly and drop down the other side. Mick doesn't break stride and hurdles it like David Hemery. I hear his ankle crack. Adrenalin and fear bring him to his feet. We make it across the playground and on across the empty Wakefield Road with Mick on one leg leaning on my shoulder. We hide behind the old fire station as the taxi driver goes steaming by, no doubt cursing us for the pair of twats he knows we are. It was a punk rock thing to do.

Two days later Mick is in his bedroom strumming his Rickenbacker and resting his pot on a little stool.

In the spring of 1978 we helped to form a branch of the Anti-Nazi League at a public meeting at Pontefract Town Hall. Paul Foot and Arthur Scargill had come to speak. After that we all became fans of the Tom Robinson Band, bought 'Glad to be Gay' badges and 'Rock Against Racism' t-shirts.

It was round about this time that I got my first passport. For ten years after, customs officials in Europe, Asia and America checked the photo in my passport and wondered why it said 'Glad to be Gay' on the lapel of my old grey ex-airforce overcoat.

In the summer of 1978 we organise a bus to take us from outside the Travellers pub to the first great Rock Against Racism gathering at a park in Hackney. X-Ray Spex are on, as are Steel Pulse, The Clash and the obligatory Tom Robinson Band. We all march from Trafalgar Square through Tower Hamlets. Everybody is blowing whistles and chanting, 'Black and white unite and fight, smash the National Front.' I am wearing my old RAF greatcoat. On the march I am brought to earth with an almighty bump. A policeman sidles up beside me. I stretch my arm out and hug him and say, 'Isn't this great?'

'Is it fuck!' he says and pushes me down to the street. He pulls out his truncheon and says, 'Do you want some of this, dickhead?'

'Not really,' I say.

'Well fucking well behave or you'll get some.'

We are bloodied, but unbowed.

Later on that summer someone organises a Rock Against Racism benefit at Pontefract Town Hall. Topping the bill are the Leeds Marxist intellectual rockers Gang of Four. Bottom of the bill are our local punk band The Thrust, named after a chain of petrol stations. Every punk in Pontefract is present; Johnny Sands in his grey checked sports jacket that he's customised himself with rips, chains and blood, Judy Perrin a fourteen-year-old who looks like Debbie Harry, Pete Simpson who sounds like Johnny Rotten, Little Ivan speeding off his tits, Steph in her PVC trousers. The Gang of Four are great and play songs off what will become their first album *Entertainment*, but there's no doubt about who pleases the crowd most. The Thrust have Mick Griffiths on brand new Rickenbacker, swinging his arm like Pete Townshend, and Pete on vocals. He hangs off the microphone stand like a wounded scarecrow and spits out his songs with mighty venom:

'I'm a victim of the system, a proper little twat
I'm an ordinary member of society, society, so...ciety!'

'I'm standing on the factory floor
Don't think I can take any more.'

And the immortal 'Northern Town'.

'You're living in a northern town.
Pit stacks t'only scenery you've got.'

After the success at the Rock Against Racism gig at the Town Hall, The Thrust and its band of followers decide to take punk attitude to the wider community. Somehow they're booked to play at the village hall in Badsworth. This is a village of toffs and self-made millionaires in the countryside between Doncaster and Pontefract. It is where the local fox hunt meets on Boxing Day. The village hall has a rota for flower arranging and hosts local farmers' whist drives. The last place on earth that would host a band with songs like 'Fed Up' and 'Society' in its repertoire. We arrive in a mixture of battered Ford Capris and Transit vans. Bert Stevens turns up on a Triumph Tiger complete with pisspot crash helmet. We'd been there two minutes when the police arrive. Someone has reported 'youths acting very strangely' in the village telephone box. Andy Smith is arrested for spraying 'The Clash' inside the red kiosk. A man in a huge sheepskin coat arrives and tells the two policeman attending that 'we all want our bloody heads knocking together'. Someone tells us this is Cyril Knowles, the former Tottenham Hotspur player. From out of the huddle comes a large green gob of phlegm. It lands on Cyril Knowles' sheepskin coat front. Cyril Knowles tells the coppers that he wants these scum out of the village. We are herded inside the village hall. The Thrust are 'tuning up'. This is a novelty, they've never done that before. Pete Simpson scrawks 'One, two, three, four' and The Thrust crash into 'Northern Town' and all hell breaks loose; wicker furniture is thrown into the air, Johnny Sands dives onto the first copper through the door and wrestles him to the floor. Bert catches somebody's elbow in the teeth and I get whacked over the back of the head with a truncheon. We're herded back out of the village hall and are abused by some local farm labourers who've come to look at a bloke with a blue mohican hairstyle and a lass with her tits sticking through two holes in a bin liner. The Thrust have segued beautifully into a thrashing version of the Tottenham fans' song 'Nice One Cyril' before the plugs are pulled. Heather told me later that all twenty-odd of us tried to pile into Dave Hoggs' Reliant Robin to escape.

A year after this The Thrust will complete their first and only EP. It contains four songs, 'Fed Up', 'Reality', 'Society' and 'Northern Town'. It is destined to become an icon of its time. John Peel plays it on his late-night show and we all rush home from the pub to listen.

In the bogs at Pontefract Town Hall I talk to the drummer with Gang of Four, Hugo Burnham. 'What do you think to The Thrust then?' He tells me that he thinks they 'seem to have a lot of energy', that they ought to 'harness their aggression'.

Gang of Four go on to release easily the best album of the punk years after *Never Mind the Bollocks*. The Thrust implode within months. Mick Griffiths works now at Pinderfields Hospital and tirelessly for the trade union Unison. He has put up twice as prospective parliamentary candidate for the Socialist Labour Party. Pete Simpson, I'm told, works in childcare.

I could never claim to have been a proper punk rocker. You can't be a proper punk rocker if you sneak off to see B. B. King when you should have been at an Angelic Upstarts gig. But I was then, and still am now, a great fan of the Sex Pistols.

I still hold dear three picture-sleeve singles. 'Anarchy in the UK' has a sleeve that features a safety pin sticking through a Union Jack. This is the French Barclay Records version that was imported in large quantities after the original record on EMI had been withdrawn. We all bought our copy at a stall on Pontefract outdoor market that mainly sold Peters and Lee records. 'God Save the Queen', the version finally released on Virgin records, has the famous navy blue and silver sleeve; a portrait of the Queen with Jamie Reed's blackmail letter cut-ups across her eyes and mouth. Curiously the Virgin logo on the back of the sleeve is still the hippy-dippy one that you would more likely find on the sleeve of a Mike Oldfield album. The third is 'Pretty Vacant', also on Virgin. A grey sleeve, on the front it features a smashed mirror in a frame. On the back are two buses with the destination boards accentuated. One board says 'Boredom'. The other says 'Nowhere'.

Southern Comfort at the Back Door

When I call for my mate, Sean Tomlinson, I knock on his back door. Sean's mam and dad dwell in the kitchen. The front room is kept for best. One day in 1979 I knock and his dad answers. Sean is out, but I can wait for him if I would like to. Sean's dad, Tom Tomlinson, is a gentleman of the old school. He works as a high school librarian and likes to make jewellery from precious stones he collects. His walls in the kitchen, staircase and best room are lined with books. He likes to read poetry. Today, when he shows me to a chair he has in his hand a copy of the brand new Oxford University Press edition of D. J. Enright's *A Faust Book*. He picks up the kettle, puts the book onto the table open at the page he's reading and asks, 'Do you want a cup of tea?' I pick up the book.

'I bought this the other week. What do you think about it?' I ask.

Tom, kettle poised in mid-air, looks at me. He says nothing. He turns to the stove and then looks back at me, taking in my roughly patched jeans, Southern Comfort t-shirt and scuffed trainers. 'You bought that book!'

'Yes. I'm interested to know more about people who make a pact with the devil.'

Tom takes a more serious squint at me. This time looking me in the eye.

'What about the wordplay?'

'Sorry?'

'The wordplay. All that stuff about Drol Dog, Lord God, Every Dog and God having its day.'

'The Devil appearing as a black dog. A poodle!'

'That's it!'

'I don't know. I think I need to read it more. I probably need to have somebody like you pointing things out to me.'

'No you don't.'

'I don't?'

'No. Not that book anyhow. It's not very good. Do you know Seamus Heaney?'

'I know some of his stuff.'

'Do you? What do you know?'

I knew he'd ask me that. I hesitate. He waits. The watched kettle doesn't boil. 'I've read one in a book called *Death of a Naturalist* that I like, it's called "Blackberry Picking".'

'Why do you like that one?'

'Cos I used to go blackberry picking with my grandad near the railway line and it reminds me of that.' I blurt this out and immediately feel very uncool. I must be as red as my Southern Comfort t-shirt.

'That's as good a reason as any. Tell me a line from it.'

I feel as daft as a school kid. 'There's a part where he describes a can of blackberries he's picked as "a plateful of eyes". I like that bit.'

'Who else do you like?'

'I like the First World War poets. Siegfried Sassoon. Wilfred Owen.'

'Dulce et Decorum est.'

'Eh?'

'Why do you like them?'

'Because I've got my Auntie Alice's Uncle Fred's First World War diary and I'm trying to fill in the bits he missed. He just mentions a place called Bull Run and he pencils in every time he had a bath. He only had about five baths.'

I feel myself reddening up again. I'm talking ten to the dozen. Part trying to show off, part trying to hide naivety. 'I treasure that diary and my grandad's medals from the second war. I used to polish them every Sunday with Dura-Glit.'

'You won't go far wrong with Heaney.'

Sean comes in. He's been welding underneath his Hillman Avenger.

'Now then!'

'You didn't tell me your mate was interested in poetry.'

'He likes reading books.'

Sean Tomlinson steps out of his green boiler suit that has the signs of welders' hot sparks up the front and puts a toe to kick off his rigger boots. Tom Tomlinson pours out the tea.

'What's all this about selling your soul to the devil then?'

Sean looks at me and his dad. He's been hard at it all morning and is wondering, 'What the bloody hell have these two been talking about?'

Sean's dad says, 'Oh! I'm just interested in this idea of bargaining with a bad man. Like Robert Johnson at the crossroads.'

I see this as an opportunity to get back at Tom in a friendly way for the poetry examination. So I say, 'You like blues music as well then I take it?' Now I look Tom in the eye. 'I love the blues. Do you?'

'Josh White. I'm fond of him and Big Bill Broonzy. I saw him.'

'You saw Big Bill Broonzy? Where? When?'

'I saw him in Castleford in 1956.'

Gobsmacked again. Castleford is a pit town just three miles down the road. At that time I would never have believed that a Mississippi Delta bluesman could have played in Castleford.

'Yes, son. At the Cosy Cinema in Glasshoughton to be precise.'

The Cosy Cinema was a tiny fleapit on a row of coal miners' terraced houses that closed down in the 1960s. Since then it's been a clothing factory called Castletex where everybody's sister and auntie works.

'He played there on Saturday night when he was staying in Leeds with Bob Barclay from the Yorkshire Jazz Band. They say he did that gig for a bottle of whisky.'

'And you saw him?'

'I did.'

Epiphany. A road to Damascus moment. Up to press, all my dreams and fantasies have taken place in remote corners of my mind, on the far reaching margins of my maps. This brings it all home. If Big Bill Broonzy played in Castleford then the maps I draw can have roads coming back as well.

'You've heard what they say about the devil having all the best tunes, Ian. Well he's got the whisky as well. Do you want some sugar in that tea?'

Tom died a couple of years later while I was on the Isle of Skye trying to make sense out of a journal I'd kept in India the year before. I should have gone to his funeral. It's something I regret not doing to this day.

One World

One day not long after his first or second tour of Germany, back before he moved over permanently, Roy Herrington comes to our flat in Station Lane. We haven't been living here long after returning from a three-month trip to India and a winter on the Isle of Skye. Roy sits on one of the chairs donated by Auntie Alice. He's nervously plucking peanuts out of his pocket and chewing them quickly. I can tell he wants to ask something, but he doesn't know where to start.

Then he begins. 'If some friends of mine came over from Germany do you think you might be able to put some of 'em up?' At that time Heather and me have no money, one mattress, about three sets of knives and forks, two pans and three or four plates from different dinner services. We are occupying one room of the flat which we have decorated with wall hangings from India and some tatty old posters from Athena that have fifty or more drawing pin holes in them and six layers of sellotape in the corners. We're not geared up for visitors yet, but there is a big empty bedroom. 'Well I suppose if they bring their own sleeping bags and bedrolls and are prepared to muck in we could manage three people. When are they coming?'

Roy takes another handful of peanuts out of his pocket and throws them into his mouth. 'Well!' – he starts a lot of sentences with 'Well!' – 'They're actually outside in a Volkswagen Camper.' Outside on Station Lane in the camper van were eight people; Jürgen Bredebusch and his wife Barbara. Ute, who ten years hence will become Roy's wife, Mick, who will become his drummer, Jörge the electric fiddle player, Thomas a ragtime pianist and his girlfriend, and Peter Kaufmann, a world traveller who ends up driving taxis around the Reeperbahn in Hamburg. They have all been to see Roy play on his tours of the Ruhrgebeit and become big fans. I don't know what he has told them about where he's from or how big his house is. I do know that Roy lives in a two-up, two-down terrace with an extension and that his brother and sister are still at home and that with all the musical equipment and records, there's probably only enough room in his back bedroom for one small other person.

Jürgen, Barbara and Ute roll out their camping mats and blow-up beds in our empty room and between us, Roy and me find accommodation for the others. And so begins an informal twin town arrangement between Wuppertal and Featherstone. Jürgen Bredebusch, his brother Völker and Peter Kaufmann and their ever-widening network of friends have been over here to stay about thirty times since and us and our gang have been over to Germany almost as many times in twenty-odd years. It is a partnerstadt arrangement that exists entirely on the goodwill and comradeship of an extended circle of friends, most of whom are music fans or musicians themselves, all of whom who are prepared to 'rough' it a bit.

One of the most touching gifts Heather and me were presented with came on the second visit by Jürgen, this time with his brother Völker. They brought us a set of six Rostfrei knives, forks and spoons, a blue enamelled casserole dish and a rack to hang wet towels on. 'Practical people them

Germans,' as my grandad once said, 'I've nowt against them.' In terms of upbringing and background we've not a lot in common. Most of the Germans are middle-class. Most of our dads and grandads worked in the pits and though Jürgen and Völker's grandad worked in a pit near Dortmund, Barbara Kaiser's grandad owned one.

The towns of course have nothing in common. Featherstone is the former pit town which since 1985 when the pit shut down has been struggling with unemployment and attempting to find a new identity for itself. A lot of the jobs for people without qualifications – and there's a good few of them – are minimum wage and warehouse work driving forklift trucks. Wuppertal has an opera house, scores of independent book shops, restaurants from every nation. It has a university campus and that miracle of engineering; the Schweberbahn. Proud residents of Wuppertal will tell you that in over a hundred years it has a completely accident-free record. Except, as Peter Kowald, the improvising bass player, once told me in Jetta's bar, an after-hours den for jazzers, it's not exactly true. On the fiftieth or was it the seventy-fifth anniversary, so proud were the Wuppertalers of their safety record on the monorail system they decided to take a baby elephant up in the train. The baby elephant was named 'Tuffi', advertising for a local yoghurt firm. When the train doors glided open, Tuffi the elephant jumped out and landed thirty feet below in the River Wupper. Luckily the baby elephant proved to be tough enough and survived. The incident has been known ever since as 'Tuffi's Wuppersprung'. Featherstone has rows and rows of red-brick houses which once were home to thousands of miners. It has a famous rugby league team, Featherstone Rovers. In 1983 Rovers reached Wembley and were to play Hull, a millionaire club. Against all the odds, the Rovers with ten miners from the same colliery in their thirteen, triumphed. Jürgen stood on the terraces with me. He still talks about it today. 'Mighty Hull knocked down by a Feather.' He quotes the headline on the back of *The Observer* newspaper from the day after. In Berlin just before they knocked down the wall I once saw sprayed in foot-high navy blue letters, 'Featherstone Rovers 14 Hull 12'. I fantasise that that piece of wall was hacked out by some other underdog who now displays it on his dresser somewhere in East Berlin.

So what do Jürgen, me, Völker, Peter Kaufmann, Ute and Barbara talk about? Music. Jürgen loves Joe Cocker, he works as a steel buyer in a big rolling mill somewhere near Solingen and makes a connection to Sheffield, Cocker's home town. He also collects records by a now forgotten English one-man blues band called Duster Bennett. When I travel beside him in his car he likes to sing along to Duster Bennett's version of the old Jimmy Reed song 'Bright Lights Big City'. Jürgen's car is worth a mention. He drives a big Ford, the sort favoured by Turkish bar owners and shopkeepers, the 'gastarbeiters' of northern Germany. His mates nickname it the Ford 'Ankara'. Jürgen also loves the recordings of Taj Mahal and in his smoother late-night moments, Al Jarreau and Boz Scaggs. Peter played tea-chest bass in a politically active skiffle group and has connections to the anarcho-leftist pirate radio station operators around the Hafen Strasse in Hamburg. This is a wonderful area of graffiti artists, Lebanese restaurants and bars that only close for an hour a day so that they can swill them out. Peter supports the famous anarchist soccer team St Pauli, who against all the odds made it to the German Premier Division and proudly flew their skull and cross bones flags at Bayern Munich and Borussia Dortmund and other grounds of the elite. Once, I walked in the Reeperbahn area with Peter and he showed me the Star Club and the other places where The Beatles played. It was a great thrill. He also showed me a little shop like a newsagents and said, 'It's one of the richest businesses in this area.' When I asked why he said, 'It sells batteries for vibrators,' and gave me a huge wink. Peter lives in a communal farmhouse on the outskirts of the city. More recently it has been a famous brothel. One day Heather and me are given a tour of the premises. Many of the rooms have yet to be decorated. In one the walls are covered in PVC, in another there are shackles bolted to the walls. In yet another area there are scythes, ropes and saw-blades. 'What on earth are they for?' says Heather, wondering what possible perverse uses could be made of these. 'Gardening store!' says Peter, another big wink.

The twinning agreement had its first culture clash one Sunday morning after a late night of drinking Konig's Pils and German Hock. Jürgen and the gang always bring crates of German supermarket beer when they visit Featherstone. I was woken at eleven in the morning by a loud knocking on the front door. I looked through the blind to see Auntie Alice whacking our front door with her umbrella. Just as I looked down, Auntie Alice looked up. 'I can see you, you bugger. What sort of house is this when you're still in bed at eleven o'clock on a morning?'

'Wait there, Auntie Alice, I'll come down.'

Auntie Alice walked into the flat and surveyed the remains of last night's do. Half-eaten plates of spaghetti, folded empty cans, glasses with lipstick traces and ashtrays full to the top. 'You want to get some housework done in here, it smells like a poke o'devils.'

'Do you want a cup of tea? Take your coat off.'

'Aye and make sure you wash the cups properly! I'll leave it on, thank you.'

I put the kettle on and from the bathroom next to the kitchen I heard the lavatory flush. I prayed it wasn't Barbara in the bathroom. Barbara rarely bothered to put any clothes on when she went for her first pee on a morning.

I rushed back into the living room. I was too late. Auntie Alice was sitting on the edge of the sofa with her handbag clutched to her. Standing less than two yards away was Barbara. Five foot ten inches tall, bleary-eyed and completely naked.

'Do you want to introduce us?' said Barbara.

'Er, yes. Erm. This is Barbara, Auntie Alice. Barbara this is Auntie Alice.'

Barbara said, 'I am very pleased to meet you Alice,' and then strolled off to the back bedroom cool as you like.

Auntie Alice pulled her handbag even closer to her chest and fastened her coat up. Even cooler than Barbara's cool German way, Auntie Alice said, 'I didn't know you were running a bloody knocking shop!'

I first meet Völker one evening in a bar called The Optimum. He is guest harp blower with a blues band that Jörge

Petersmann has got together called Black Cat Bone. Völker is Jürgen's younger brother. He is about my age, similar height and built like a brick shithouse. He has some right shoulders on him, through years of training to be in the German butterfly swimming team. If only Germany hadn't withdrawn from the Moscow Olympics in 1980 he might have built a career as a swimmer. Völker took up joinery and music promotion. He has organised tours in Europe for artists who he's a fan of, Eddi Reader being one, but mainly his hero John Martyn. Völker is a walking encyclopaedia of English folk rock, blues, jazz and Bob Dylan. At the last count I think he had over four hundred John Martyn live bootlegs on tape. Völker grew up in that peculiarly German 1970s tradition of political activism, street theatre and impromptu gig organising.

In his beer-drinking heyday Völker was unstoppable, the most drunken sessions I have ever been on have been with Völker. Once in Poland we drank so much vodka that it took us three days to come round. Völker drives a big black Dodge van. Inside it is decorated with beer mats from Tetley's and Sam Smith's. On a trip to Sam Smith's brewery we drank eight pints in one hour in the hospitality bar and then he ordered another round for good measure when we got into the Angel and White Horse, the brewery tap. Völker is such a regular visitor to Featherstone that he and his wife Michaela make it their base. Northern England is their favourite holiday destination.

On one trip Völker decides that we should go and visit John Martyn; at that time he was living in Roberton in an old church with one bell. Later John Martyn will name one of the best of his latter day albums *The Church with One Bell*. We arrive outside his house in Roberton in the Scottish borders in the black Dodge. John's tough looking henchman Archie is there to greet us. 'Ullo Völker.' He pronounces the 'V' like a guttural Scottish 'V' rather than the softer 'F' as in 'folk' the way the Germans do. It is two o'clock in the afternoon and John hasn't got up yet. We sit in the kitchen round a big table drinking tea. John stirs and lumbers down the staircase like a bear, one with a sore head. He opens the fridge door, takes out a bottle of vodka and has a huge swig. I've seen people do that with milk or mineral water, but never vodka. He sits at the table, eyes me up and down and then says, 'Are ye staying for a few days then, Völker?' The hard 'V' sound again.

'No, we want to go up to Edinburgh to see Alan.'

'Fuck him! Stay here and we'll have a party. Who's your friend?'

Völker introduces me. 'This is Ian from Yorkshire.'

John goes into a stream of consciousness monologue in a very passable Yorkshire accent that stereotypes the type of Yorkshireman that I try not to be. 'Giz a fuckin' curry Abdul and make it snappy. By gum I could eat a scabby fuckin' donkey. Bring us plenty o' them chapattis we' it. By, fuck my old boots. Turned out nice again. Can y'hear me, Mother? Eeeh! By gum.'

I don't know what to say. So I laugh.

'By fuckin' hell Abdul look sharp wi' that curry!'

In 1976 I bought John Martyn's *One World* album from Celia's record shop in Castleford. I thought at the time and still do that it's a beautiful record. Even the title 'One World' is lovely and twenty-odd years in front of its time. Now I'm sitting round his kitchen table and he's taking the piss out of me. Later in the day we end up in a pub in the next village. We down a few halves with chasers. John continues with his 'Fuckin' curry Abdul' monologue and at one point kicks me on the shin. I go to hit him back and get pulled up by henchman Archie who says, 'I would nae do that, son.' Back in the Dodge on the road to Edinburgh Völker says, 'John can be like that sometimes.' I still buy John Martyn records. I even have a special section on my record shelves for them. His version of the Portishead song 'Glory Box' was on repeat on my CD player for many weeks.

Völker Bredebusch is a real one-off. Had he been born in Featherstone he would be the sort of man who would be described as a character. Featherstone, though, might as well have been where he's from, he's slept in my back bedroom more times than I have.

We were once in the Jubilee pub, a rough and ready boozer on the Wakefield Road. In 1988 they still had '2, 4, 6, 8 Motorway' on the jukebox. Ziggy Saunders, an ex-miner who had his ear bitten off in a fight and still wears a ring in the bit of a lobe that's left, comes up to Völker and me. 'Now then Ian, how're yer going on? Who's this fella? I haven't seen him before.' Ziggy asks the question without even looking at Völker.

'This is Völker, a good friend of mine.'

'Völker! That's not a name.'

'Well that's what he's called.'

'He's got some grand shoulders on him...where's tha from then Völker?'

'I'm sorry.'

'Don't be sorry, old cock. I'm only asking thee where tha's from.'

'I am from Germany.'

'Germany eh?'

Ziggy pauses for just a second or two and then announces, 'Well tha's come a long way for a good pint, old lad!'

The great irony is that Völker will travel a long way for a good pint. We have travelled thousands of miles together in the black Dodge Ram van that's his pride and joy. It's while travelling with Völker that I have discovered music that has taken me to every corner of the globe. In the days it took to drive to Poland and back, we listened to a bootleg tape of songs called *Cheb Khaled – Live au New York*. It's the collection that became *Khaled* when it was officially released, a massive Euro pop / Algerian Rai music fusion that is sung in Arabic but is more rock 'n' roll than the Stones have done for years. Tricky's first album *Maxinquaye* is another album I associate with Völker's van and Massive Attack's *Protection* another. At the Cambridge Festival one year we saw the Blind Boys of Alabama turn a marquee on a grassy East Anglian field into a southern states gospel tabernacle. Völker set his Sony walkman to record and left it running in his pocket. The resultant recordings wouldn't test the fidelity of your average hi-fi, but there's some choice conversation on there including Völker's story about John Martyn's folk music friend Hamish Imlach. Apparently Hamish Imlach let out the worst fart ever, on this earth or any other. The room cleared within seconds, three people fainted and many were trampled in the doorway.

Völker has introduced me over time to a Dutch blues band called Cuby and the Blizzards, a French rapper called MC Solaar and a host of Polish punk bands including his favourites, Acid Drinkers, who once released a pirate cassette called 'Big Tits'. His knowledge of the British music scene, particularly of 1970s folk rock and experiments in folk undertaken by The Pentangle and Fairport Convention is phenomenal.

In Buckie, a town up on the Moray Firth, we got drunk on whisky and Völker told me that gospel music and therefore soul really originated in Scotland. I knew that Völker's love of Scotland often led him to make great claims, but the idea that James Brown and Al Green's musical ancestry was amongst the clans of the highlands was pushing it a bit. I never thought much more about this until recently when I saw a documentary on BBC4 about a theory propounded by a music professor at Yale University who had once played with Charles Mingus. His theory was that many of the churches in the southern states were Presbyterian Gaelic and it was at these churches where African slaves first heard the 'lining out' songs which featured call and response. Strange as it may be, the first language a lot of the Africans learned in America wasn't English, but Scottish Gaelic. And there was me blaming the whisky in Buckie. On the subject of blame, I have Völker to blame for my guiltiest pleasure, The Carpenters.

In the early seventies when The Carpenters were having all their hits I hated them with a lunatic vengeance. There was a kid at our school called Geoff Morrow who wrote the charts down every week by listening to the wireless on

Tuesday lunchtimes. His charts always seemed to contain a Carpenters song. Völker and me found ourselves eating a curry in 'Uncles', the name we gave to a greasy little café in Pontefract. The conversation ranged around female vocalists. Völker talked about Sandy Denny, Grace Slick and Jacquie McShee. I mentioned Maddy Prior and June Tabor. Out of the blue Völker comes up with Karen Carpenter. He attempted to persuade me that Karen Carpenter was one of the great singers, it was just the material that was lacking.

Back at the flat I told Völker that somewhere there was a scratched old copy of The Carpenters' *Greatest Hits*. I'd bought it from a charity shop in Beverley for twenty pence. At the time I told everybody it was an ironic gesture. Really it was so that I could learn 'They Long to Be Close to You' in sign language. I knew an American student at Bretton Hall called April who said she would teach me. Why the hell I wanted to learn a Carpenters song in sign language I don't know. We sit cross-legged on the fireside rug smoking the Drum that Völker has bought in Belgium. We sing along to the scratchy old record. Strange, but we know the words to all the songs. The scratchy old record has been replaced by a CD version of The Carpenters' *Greatest Hits*. I bought it at Tesco's. I didn't want assistants in record shops smirking at me buying middle of the road music.

At the drop of a hat Völker will jump into the Dodge Ram and drive four hundred miles without blinking. After a pub lunch at the Top House one day we were discussing whether to go for a game of dominoes in the evening or to our favourite Sam Smith's pub at Saxton where you can sit outside and watch the swallows feeding their babies. Völker, out of nowhere says, 'Have you ever been to Ronnie Scott's?' I hadn't. 'Well why don't we go tonight? Annette Peacock is on.' So we do and fortune favours us with tickets on the door. It is one hundred and eighty-two miles from Featherstone to London, I know this because when Featherstone Rovers played Bradford Northern at Wembley in 1973 somebody made a top hat with a signpost on it. We travel one hundred and eighty-two miles to see a very obscure, avant-garde singer dressed in a boiler suit and Elvis belt. It is a surreal evening. It is the first night I meet Robert Wyatt. He is in the audience in high and merry spirit. On impulse I slap him on the back and say, 'Thank you for what you did in the miners' strike.' He thanks me for thanking him. I thank him for his version of 'Shipbuilding'. He thanks me for the kind words.

Three days later Völker says he wants to drive to the Brewery Arts Centre in Kendal to see John Martyn. So we set off again. As we park the Dodge we drop on John Martyn walking back from the shops with a brown paper carrier bag full of vegetables. He says, 'Hello Völker', hard 'V' sound, and appears to have forgotten who I am. After he's gone Völker tells me that John is a great chef and that he likes food as much as he likes booze. Arnold 'Sooner' Millard always used to say, 'If tha wants to be a good drinker, love, tha's got to be a good eater'. John Martyn later performs a magnificent version of 'I Am John Wayne'.

Völker Bredebusch has a little crumpled black and white photograph of his great grandparents. The photo is taken outside of a low peasant cottage somewhere in the mountains of Poland. Völker has an ambition to find that cottage in the village where his forebears were born and take a modern version of that picture. When he's not managing German tours for John Martyn and Eddi Reader, Völker works in a joiner's shop. A big raw-boned Polish lad called Marius works alongside him. Marius smokes West cigarettes one after the other, listens to Warren G. on MTV and is homesick for Szabrze, the pit town in Southern Poland where he was born.

Marius and Völker make a plan. Völker and his brother Jürgen will drive a Mercedes to Szabrze and take Marius home for a few days if he will help them find the little village called Lutomia that holds the key to their ancestry. I tag along for the ride. In some snow-covered uplands in an area the Germans call Schlesian, Marius entertains us with stories about wolves and bears carrying off young children. Through the car window we spot an elderly granny walking in a field with a woodcutter's axe over her shoulder. Marius tells us that she is searching for wolves.

We find the village of Lutomia and in a bar which doubles as a mini-supermarket and petrol station we drink rough vodka with the locals and Völker hands his photo around. An old man claims that he knows the people in the picture and tells us to knock on the door of an old lady about a mile away. Before we leave we are invited to sample something called 'Spiritus'. I believe it is a mixture of raw chemical-grade alcohol and the soft drink Sprite. This and the fresh cold air outside almost fells us like an old dead tree.

The old lady lives in a cottage that is out of a fairy tale. A donkey and a cow live in a lean-to wooden building at the back and there are bunches of drying herbs hanging from the ceiling. She invites us in and offers some more vodka and smoked bacon. When she examines the photo a little tear comes into the corner of her eye. She tells Marius, who translates into German, which is then translated into English for me, that she played with the people in the photo when she was a little girl before the First World War. She then takes us outside and shows us the cottage next door. In the fading Polish winter light we can see that the cottage is the one in the photo. The fruit trees in the front garden have grown, but it's definitely the right place. Völker switches on the Mercedes headlights full beam and sets his camera by its timer. In the full glare we pose, Völker, Jürgen, me, Marius and the old lady. It's a dark photo when it's developed, but it's there. A snapshot across nearly a century of European history.

We leave the old woman with a fistful of Polish zloty and a German Christmas cake wrapped in cellophane and head on to Szabrze. Marius's home town smells like the Featherstone of my childhood. It smells of burning coal and muck. There are slag heaps everywhere and Marius's uncle keeps pigeons in a loft in his back yard. Szabrze has something that we don't have at home. As well as the usual statues to politicians they have statues to famous coal miners. We spend three days here drinking vodka, eating Vietnamese food – for some reason Szabrze is full of Vietnamese restaurants – and listening to Polish punk bands.

On the way back to Germany we cross the border into the Czech Republic and visit Prague. Jürgen stops the car and plants his feet firmly onto the Czech earth just after customs.

'When I was a teenager,' he announces, 'I sat on the tramlines in Wuppertal to protest at the Russian tanks. I never thought that one day I would drive a Mercedes here.'

Got My Mojo Working

Prince Keeyama, the Chicken Man, King of Bourbon Street, Miracle of the French Quarter and Master of Martial Arts is sitting outside a shop called 'House of Voodoo' surveying upper Rampart Street from a tattered deckchair, like my grandad surveyed the beach at Blackpool. He starts to tell his stories.

'The chicken is wise and alert. He'll run and run. He wiser than an owl. He give you energy and knowledge. If you bite his head off, he give you knowledge too.'

Prince Keeyama, the Chicken Man, wears a leather Stetson with a petrified snake on it. He's the sort of man who doesn't look out of place with a dead snake on his hat. He wants to show me around his shop. He wants me to buy some souvenirs. I buy a voodoo doll for five dollars and some John the Conqueror root because I've heard of John the Conqueror root from an old Muddy Waters song and I've always wondered what it was. The Chicken Man says a blessing over it. I feel as though I've got my Mojo working now. Chicken Man then breaks the spell by offering to sell me half a dozen voodoo glass ashtrays at a knock-down price. Later in the day I am walking in Bourbon Street when the Chicken Man rides up on a red mountain bike. He throws me a packet of three voodoo condoms.

'What's that for?'

'To protect you from the Booga-Booga.'

'How did you find me so easily?'

He points to the dead snake on his hat. 'Psychic,' he says and his eyes mist over all mysteriously.

Further on down Bourbon Street a man in a pair of flared polyester trousers is carrying a ten-foot tall plastic cross on his back. A red neon light on the cross beam proclaims that, 'Drug takers, drunkards and effeminate homosexuals are sinners'. Near to him outside a sidewalk café some young men tottering on high heels are squeezed into tight leather minidresses.

Earlier in the day me and Kevin Reynolds and Fuff, who once tried to hitchhike to see Bob Dylan with me, have been into Record Ron's shop on Decatur Street. Record Ron runs one of the greatest second-hand record shops in the world. He sold me a signed photograph of Professor Longhair playing his piano, a Sonny Boy Williamson 78 on the Trumpet label and a T-Bone Walker 78 on Comet with 'West Side Baby' on it. He tells us that we shouldn't leave New Orleans without paying a visit to Cosimo Matassa who these days runs a corner grocery shop off Bourbon Street. Cosimo Matassa is the great record producer who worked with everybody who was anybody back at the birth of rock 'n' roll.

Mr Matassa appears from behind a stack of tinned peas in his shop. He is a small, plumpish fellow with a smile like your uncle. I know that he worked on the early recordings by Little Richard so I ask him if he wouldn't mind talking to us about that time. Mr Matassa smiles his uncle smile and puts his arm on my shoulder and then sighs. It is the sigh of an old man who has been asked too many times to talk about the past.

'You see son, when you get into your sixties a lot of self-examination takes place. You need to have a sense of history and in New Orleans the music gives you that. It's not just in the fabric of the place, but it is the very fabric of the place. It's in the parties, the christenings, the weddings, the funerals and parades.'

He starts to take tins of soup out of a box and place them onto the shelves, blowing off dust and wiping them with a dishcloth as he goes. I want him to stop what he's doing and tell me his stories. I want to know just how wild Little Richard really was, I want him to tell me about Fats Domino, I want him to take me to the place where Buddy Bolden's cornet could be heard eleven miles from on a clear night. Mr Matassa carries on blowing dust off his tinned veg. Kevin asks him if he wouldn't mind having his photo taken outside of his shop. We move outside. Kevin snaps a couple of frames.

'Well thank you for dropping by, boys. Y'awl take care now.'

'Is that it?' I'm thinking. 'Is this what happens when you reach the top of the holy mountain? The wise old sage poses for a couple of pictures and goes back into his shop?'

'What about Little Richard, Mr Matassa?'

'I was what they called in those days a record engineer. When I recorded Little Richard he was a man completely driven on emotion. He thrived on human urges, something kinda rare now. You know son, that guy has been rich and poor five times.' Mr Matassa has one foot in his shop holding the door, another foot barely on the sidewalk.

A few years after this doorstep conversation I found myself in a similar situation with Little Richard's biographer, Charles White. Charles White is another avuncular man with white hair. An Irishman who works as a chiropodist in Scarborough. I stood at the bottom of the steps leading up to his surgery. I told him that his book about Little Richard was the best rock 'n' roll biography I'd ever read.

'Thank you, son.'

I love the part in the book where Bumps Blackwell talks about Little Richard recording 'Tutti Frutti' for Specialty Records at Mr Matassa's studios. He describes a young woman songwriter called Dorothy La Bostrie who went on to write the greatest opening to a rock 'n' roll song ever. 'She was so thin she looked like six o'clock.' This woman was only twenty-one, had a house full of kids and no husband. She was asked to take a Little Richard ditty that was full of lewd lyrics and turn it into something palatable enough for 1950s teenagers and their mams and dads. This she did. She brought the lyrics over to Little Richard at the piano. Cosimo Matassa set his Ampex tapes rolling.

'Awop-bop-a-loo-mop-alop-bam-boom. Got a girl name Sue, she knows just what to do.'

Charles White looks at me. 'That's right young fella, that's what happened.' Then he went up the stairs to examine someone's feet.

Mr Matassa, by way of taking his final bow, leaves us with this: 'Y'know, Little Richard had a kind of experience that soldiers have in shell holes during wars. He took off all his gold and threw it into the sea.'

For the rest of the day I wonder about the journey Mr Matassa has made from recording 'Tutti Frutti' to his corner shop. In the evening we hire a car and set off out of New Orleans up Highway 61. We're headed for Memphis. The car radio provides our soundtrack. Without touching the dial we move through gospel, jazz, soul and, the deeper we get into Mississippi, the blues. We pass a green town boundary sign that says 'Rolling Fork'. I recognise this as the birthplace of Muddy Waters. All out of the car for a photo next to the sign. When we find the ancient wooden shack on the plantation that was once Muddy Waters' home there's another photo opportunity. For a reason I'll never fathom, we decide to juggle walnuts outside of Muddy's house while we're having the photo taken. Sometimes when I look at that picture now I'm troubled with thoughts about it being disrespectful. It's a good job we didn't let Fuff have a piss up the side of the wall like he was going to. Pissing on Muddy's log cabin, now that would have been a scandal.

One Saturday night in September of 1937, Bessie Smith, the Empress of the Blues, was being driven down this very highway to Clarksdale after a singing engagement in Memphis. It was a warm night, Bessie had the window down and her elbow on the sill. Before he had the chance to brake, Bessie's chauffeur Richard Morgan hit a truck belonging to the 'U-Needa Biscuit' company on the side where Bessie sat. Her left arm was all but severed, the nerves and tendons hanging down like telegraph wires. There are a lot of stories about what happened next. Some will tell you that Richard Morgan was drunk and had misjudged the distance between his own car and the parked-up truck, others that Morgan walked ten miles into Clarksdale to fetch an ambulance. A myth that still persists today is that Bessie fell victim to southern racism even at death's door when she was refused admission to a whites-only hospital. Bessie's own son believed that a white doctor who happened on the scene of the crash wouldn't take Bessie to hospital in his car because he didn't want it to get messed up with blood. There will be truth and myth in all of these stories.

The most reliable account I've read is in Chris Albertson's book *Bessie*. According to Albertson, Bessie Smith's car crashed into a truck, that may or may not have been from the 'U-Needa Biscuit' company, in the early hours of the morning about ten miles north of Clarksdale. Richard Morgan, Bessie's chauffeur, had wanted to stay in Memphis playing cards, Bessie had insisted on moving on to Clarksdale. They argued, but Richard Morgan finally agreed to drive. They spent two hours travelling in silence, neither wanting to talk to the other. The road was dark and narrow, Morgan was falling to sleep at the wheel. Distance and proximity are hard to judge at three o'clock in the morning. Suddenly the biscuit truck is in front of them. Within a few minutes of the crash, another car is on the scene. Dr Hugh Smith and his friend Henry Broughton are on their way to do a spot of night fishing. They find Richard Morgan wandering in the road disorientated and Bessie Smith bleeding to death. As they find clean handkerchiefs to wrap around Bessie's arm, the headlights of another car appear. This car smashes straight into their vehicle and the wreckage nearly hits everybody else. In this car are a young white couple who have been out partying all night. Police and ambulances arrive. The white couple are taken off to a white hospital and Bessie is taken in a second ambulance to the Afro-American Hospital on Sunflower Avenue, Clarksdale. Could this be how the rumours about Bessie being refused admission to a white hospital started? It would be true to say that in the 1930s in the American south, an ambulance from a white hospital would be certain to pick up a white injured person first. Bessie Smith died through shock and loss of blood at 11.30 a.m. September 26, 1937 at the hospital on Sunflower Avenue.

We drive into Clarksdale with Bessie Smith on our minds. Clarksdale is also the home town of Ike Turner, John Lee Hooker, Earl Hooker. It's near here where Robert Johnson went to the crossroads to sell his soul. All this in a town that's round about the same size as Featherstone.

We find a bar, buy a Bud apiece and chat to some tough-looking white lads who are playing pool. Kevin and me have heard that the hospital where Bessie died is now a hotel called the Riverside and it has a few rooms to let for hardy blues travellers. We mention this to one of the pool players.

'Wooaaah! You don't wanna go down there boys, them niggers'll shoot ya!' The pool players laugh loudly and clap each other with a high five.

Fuff looks at Kevin and me, shrugs his shoulders, holds his hands out palms forward and says, 'Told yer!' Then he looks at the pool players, 'I told 'em'.

We book into a very cheap, very crusty motel and determine that we won't be put off by a bunch of redneck pool players and that tomorrow morning we will visit Sunflower Avenue.

Next morning we do. We walk right up to the front door of the Riverside Hotel, formerly the Afro-American Hospital, and knock. The door is answered by a polite young black man called Frank.

'Is it alright to come in please? We'd like to look at the place where Bessie Smith died.' Frank steps to one side and waves us in. He tells us that Mrs Z. L. Hill is sitting in her chair in the parlour. She likes to meet guys from England.

Mrs Z. L. Hill is probably in her eighties, she is sitting with a crocheted blanket across her knees. Over the back of her chair is a *Superman II* curtain. Before we can say anything Mrs Hill dives headlong into a sort of mantra.

'Boys, I knew Ike Turner when he was in his mama's belly. When he met Tina I made spaghetti for them at three o'clock in the morning when they got home from a gig.'

We sit in awe. Transfixed.

'It's all about poverty and slavery. You know about slavery don't you? Sometimes them mothers went to work and there was no milk in the house.'

'Did you know Bessie Smith, Mrs Hill?'

'Bessie Smith. Sure I knew Bessie Smith, she died down that corridor.' She points a wickedly crooked finger down a dimly lit corridor. 'Bessie always wore them fine dresses. She sang about when the levee broke and turned all the water loose. All them people was up in the trees yelling and hollering, "Save me, save me!".' Then like a corncrake she starts to sing:

'If I could holler like a mountain jack
I'd go up on the river and call my baby back.'

The telephone rings. Mrs Hill picks it up and places her gnarled old hand over the mouthpiece. "'Scuse me boys, this'll be John Lee Hooker, he phones me from California regular.'

This is turning into a piece of theatre.

'Do you boys like tomatoes?' Mrs Hill puts the phone down. 'It was just a guy selling tomatoes.' She then bids us to come nearer to her. We do. She whispers. 'See that key on the nail there. Well that's the key to the room where Bessie died. Go ahead, take the key and let yourselves in to the room.' We do as we're bid. I turn the key in the lock and push open the door. In the room is an old washstand, a stool and a bed. I sit on the bed while Kevin takes a photo. It is a sweltering hot day outside. In this room it is freezing. Cold enough to see your breath. Kevin and me hesitate to tell each other that we feel 'spooked'. We lock the door and replace the key on its nail. Mrs Hill insists that we should go look at her porch before we leave. The porch is filled with rotten cane furniture and dying potted geraniums. As we turn to come back down the corridor we notice a huge poster of Boy George. Mrs Z. L. Hill shares a similar passion to my grandmother. My gran never missed *Top of the Pops* when 'Do You Really Want to Hurt Me' was in the charts.

Before we move on from Clarksdale there are two things we want to do. We want to visit Wade Walton's barbershop, an institution in the Delta and we want to visit the bar again and tell the pool players that we've been to the Riverside and had a lovely time.

Wade Walton runs a tiny barbershop that has become a focal point for blues music travellers, it's known throughout the Delta as a place to meet, exchange gossip and learn. Kevin and me go in and sit on some steel-backed chairs. In the queue before us is an elderly black man and a young Danish blues fan who looks as though he needs a serious haircut. In the chair is a fat man having a shave. Wade Walton doesn't look up from his shaving.

'We were talking about Ike Turner,' says the Danish man. 'You know he drove up from Clarksdale to Memphis to record "Rocket 88" and some people say that was the birth of rock 'n' roll.'

I did know that. I also knew how they got the reverb. The guys piled all their gear onto one truck and halfway up the road one of the speakers fell off and got broken. They stuffed the speaker with paper and when they came to record that's how they got that sound.

Wade Walton takes the apron from around the fat man and slaps his chin. The Dane steps up to take the chair, but Wade shakes his head and points to the elderly man. The little old fella moves to the barber's chair and Wade starts to cut his hair. When he's finished he announces that he's had enough for today and if we need a haircut, we should come back tomorrow.

In the bar, the same gang are playing pool. We tell them that we didn't get shot.

'You were lucky then! Where you guys going next?'

We say that we want to get to Memphis. We're going to stay in the Peabody Hotel and visit Elvis's house at Gracelands.

One of the pool players says, 'I was there one time. I got so damned drunk on Beale Street that I saw Elvis in the bar. Shit! I am drunk! Then I saw another Elvis and another one and in the bathroom I saw another. Too many god-damned Elvises. There was men Elvises, women Elvises and some you weren't too sure about Elvises. God damn!'

Elvis Has Left the Auditorium

When Jim Clark the racing driver died at Hockenheim in the spring of 1968, I sat watching the announcement on *Grandstand* and felt a wet tear in the corner of my eye. I don't know why. I can't stand cars never mind motor racing.

People can tell you their life story by remembering where they were when famous people died. I don't know if this started with J. F. Kennedy, but it's a beginning. When his brother Robert was shot I heard it on the wireless in Mabel Pyatt's house. I was waiting for her to take out a pan of stewed neck of lamb and pearl barley so I could have a bowlful.

I think I can do it with musicians and pop stars. When Bolan's car crashed into the tree on Barnes Common I was working at the engineering factory in Pontefract, filing the rough edges off bottle mould castings. I ended up there after I told the careers adviser I wanted to draw maps. The careers officer told me that there wasn't a lot of call for map-making in Yorkshire these days. When I asked him why he joked that even the remotest corners had been charted, even places like Featherstone were mapped. 'I live in Featherstone!' I said and stared him out. He shuffled his papers and said, 'Well, er, um, do you like drawing then?' I carried on staring at him. I have made it my lifelong mission to stare in insolent silence at people who take the piss out of where I'm from.

'There's an engineering factory here in Pontefract who want someone to train as a draughtsman.'

'I'd better have that then.'

He gave me a card to take to Werneth Engineering. I got an interview which consisted of them showing me round the works, introducing me to Miss Morgan, the secretary 'who knows where everything is' and asking me to express one eighth as a decimal.

'.125.'

'Can you start on Monday?'

Training to be a draughtsman meant a lot of scraping swarth from under the lathes, sweeping round the bench-fitter's feet and filing the sharp edges off moulds. I had to go to night school. I was more interested in nightclubs and building my collection of Bob Dylan, Beatles and Stones LPs.

I was flat-out pissed in a nightclub in Scarborough when the DJ announced that Keith Moon had died. When Elvis went I don't know where I was, strange really because I can recall Charlie Chaplin dying and a baby giraffe at London Zoo and they went round about the same time. Years later I was nearly thrown out of Elvis's house at Gracelands for laughing and joking with my mate Kevin Reynolds about how fat Elvis was. The tour guide became very insulted and aggressive at the same time and said, 'Elvis was never more than two hundred and forty pounds.' I think Kevin said, 'Well that's fucking fat enough in my book!'

I was once commissioned to edit a book of reminiscences about Elvis on the occasion of the Royal Festival Hall's 'Everything Elvis' exhibition. This was curated by a woman from Alabama called Joni Mabe who had collected literally everything Elvis. There were Las Vegas capes with jewels sewn on them, guitars, shoes, magazines, thousands of snapshots, karate suits, record sleeves and no end of newspaper cuttings under perspex. One cutting was from the *National Enquirer*. It was a story about an Elvis Presley tribe who had been discovered in the jungle. The tribe all had quiffs, wore sequinned belts and sang 'Rock-a-Hula Baby'. Joni Mabe also had a wart which had been removed from Elvis that she kept in a test tube full of embalming fluid and some toenail clippings wrapped in cotton wool, also in a test tube. I had to ask her just how she knew that they were really Elvis Presley's toenail clippings. She looked at me aghast, as though I'd chucked a stone at her. 'Well you can't be sure can you?' I asked. She drew a deep breath and let out a loud southern drawl. 'Excuse me, Mister…but do you really think that Elvis would allow anybody else to cut their toenails in his Jungle Room at Gracelands?' Joni Mabe then told me that she'd been feeling around on the rug in the Jungle Room near one of the sofas when she found the clippings. A splendid image that.

Kirsty MacColl's death upset me. I loved her song, 'There's a Guy Works Down the Chip Shop Swears He's Elvis'. I also loved the story of her old man, Ewan MacColl. His autobiography, *Journeyman*, is a permanent book beside my bed. A dealer in books on folk and folklore who I buy from told me how when Ewan died, his wife, the celebrated American singer, Peggy Seeger, invited bids for his huge library of books. I never thought any more about it until one day my little lad Edward was looking at a book called *Come All Ye Bold Miners*, a collection of songs from the coalfields, because he wanted to learn the words to Blaydon Races. He lifted the fly leaf and said, 'Daddy, who's Ewan MacColl?' When I came to look I found Ewan MacColl's little bookplate hidden beneath the cover. It was a proud possession to start with.

When I heard about John Entwistle dying it saddened me mainly because I had been in his house with him only a few months before sharing a glass, and a laugh. He signed my *Live at Leeds* LP cover for me. It's up there with Ewan MacColl's bookplate, Joe Cocker's message saying, 'Keep on Rocking' on the sleeve of my *Mad Dogs and Englishmen* LP sleeve, and the signatures of the whole of Ladysmith Black Mambazo in terms of importance to my collection.

Nusrat Fateh Ali Khan, the Pakistani ghazal singer had a voice that went right through me. A bloke in a restaurant in Bradford called The Kashmir put me on to him. He gave me a cassette of a live concert in Paris. Then I saw him in the green fields at Glastonbury. He was magnificent. After Glastonbury I saw a snapshot of him pinned to the wall at the back of the till in a curry house in Pontefract, next to one of Imran Khan. The owner told me that he'd been in there for a meal. A story in the Big Bill Broonzy at Castleford mould. A Punjabi taxi driver in New York told me that Nusrat Fateh Ali Khan had died, not long before Princess Diana. Another taxi driver there, this time from Nigeria, told me that Fela Kuti had gone to heaven.

When John Lennon died I believe that I was the last person on earth to get to know. Heather and me were on the Deharadun Express train from Delhi to Bombay. We shared a compartment with two men and a woman from Lebanon. They were in India to escape the bombs in Beirut. They had a tiny baby with them called Radha. One of the men, who called himself 'Lebanese', talked to me about The Beatles. He knew every single Beatles song off by heart. We sang every one we could bring to mind between Jaipur and Maharashtra. When we got to 'Hey Jude', it seemed as though the whole of the train joined in with the 'La, la, la, lalalala'. I didn't know that my friend was exorcising his thoughts on John Lennon. I said, 'I've only heard a little bit of the new *Double Fantasy* album before I came here. I hope Lennon does a tour. I'd love to see him.' 'Lebanese' looked at me as though I was daft.

'Haven't you heard?'

'Heard what?'

'John Lennon was killed the other week.'

Everybody who'd been singing 'Hey Jude' seemed to look at me. I didn't know what to do. It's one of those times when you think you might have to pull the communication cord and stop the train.

I climbed out of the train window and heaved myself onto the roof of the moving train. I sat cross-legged on top of the carriage for what might have been fifty miles. A man crawled over to me and asked me if he could comb my hair. He produced a plastic comb with at least a dozen teeth missing. I told him to fuck off. 'Don't you know John Lennon's dead!'

A long time after this I was commissioned to edit the memoirs of the jazz photographer Terry Cryer. Terry had taken pictures of everybody in his time; Coleman Hawkins, Ella Fitzgerald, Big Bill Broonzy, Muddy Waters. In Paris once he even shared the back seat of a taxi with Billie Holiday. Terry told me a wonderful story about Ken Colyer, the New Orleans-inspired trumpeter from Great Yarmouth who only ever played in the authentic style of the Delta. Colyer was playing a set in a Soho club and a man at the front was noisily eating a packet of crisps. The trumpeter stood it for so long and then stopped playing, walked over to the man with the packet of Golden Wonders and said, 'I am playing music born out of centuries of pain and suffering and all you can do is eat fucking crisps. If you don't stop I'll stick that bag of crisps right up your arse!' This story reminded me of the man with the broken comb nattering me as I took in the news about John Lennon. I swapped the story with Terry. Terry had known Lennon and was still a good friend of Paul McCartney. He took the story in, nodded and said, 'What you have to realise young man is that there are some people in this world who haven't got the manners they were born with!'

When the train stopped at Bombay the first thing I did was to buy a black Kashmiran shawl. I wrapped it round me.

Months after, back in Yorkshire, I was in a gents' lavatory at the Blackmoor pub in Pontefract, a Hells Angel came upside of me. He said, 'I like yer poncho, man.' I told him I had bought it at the time I heard John Lennon had been shot.

'Where were you?'

'On a train in India.'

He looked at me and said, 'Yeah right!'

Beats Working

Looking and Listening

A Musical Education

It's teatime, I'm eating chips and beans on my knee. The phone rings.

'Hello, my name is Alison Roden, I work for Opera North. We're currently working on a large-scale community opera and we wondered if you might like to join us and work on the libretto.'

There is a story that goes round some of my friends when they want to tease me that has it that I said, 'If tha can enlighten me as to what a libretto is, love, I might be interested.'

It's the sort of story that starts because you set it off yourself as a misplaced joke and it sticks. What I really said was probably forgotten by the time I put the phone down and went back to a tea tray full of cold chips and beans.

Three days after the phone call, Alison Roden and the opera's director Stephen Langridge come to see me. They are looking for someone to involve writers from 'the community' to contribute stories that will then form the libretto for an opera to be performed as a promenade piece through the grounds at the University of Leeds.

I am just off the back of a well-received project I did in collaboration with Age Concern. I travelled on a converted single-decker bus across West and South Yorkshire. The bus stopped in lay-bys and car parks near old folks' homes and sheltered housing places. Elderly locals were encouraged to board the bus for a cup of tea and a bourbon biscuit and to tell stories. The theme of the stories was 'Attitudes to contemporary issues'. We compiled the stories into a little book.

Stephen, Alison and me sip tea from mugs and flick through the book. We hit on a story told to me by a lovely old lass who always wears a red coat and red leather boots. She discussed homosexuality and declared, 'We had gays in our day you know. But they weren't like the gays you get now. They were proper gays.'

Stephen and Alison nearly choke on their tea laughing. Less than an hour after meeting them I am offered the job of leading a team of a dozen writers on the opera project. I am to work every Saturday and Sunday at Leeds University and sleep in the spare bedroom at Alison's house. Up to that point I have never seen a live opera performance, neither have I heard a recorded one.

The writing team are an eccentric bunch. There is an elderly Jamaican lady who tells great ghost stories about home to a reggae pulse. She also tells a weird tale of how she had a vision of her journey by ship to England when her grandmother dropped an egg into a glass of water. There is another lady who wants to write a satire on the antiseptic nature of the modern world and pens the first verse of a song that will ultimately appear in the finished piece.

'I love the smell of Izal in the morning
I crave the heady scent of Parazone.'

There's a student who spends most of his time in the workshop sleeping and another man who wants to protest about the amount of concrete in Leeds. I haven't the heart to tell him that for years previous to coming here I have been responsible as a building site labourer for pouring a lot of that concrete onto the open spaces of the city centre.

The poet Carol Ann Duffy joins us for a weekend in the workshop and insists that she must be allowed to smoke whilst working. The smoking does her good and she turns out to be the inspiration we need. In the two days she stays we write up a framework for what the opera should be about.

In the summer of 1990, while England are losing on penalties to Germany in the World Cup semi-final, we open with *The Last Great Northern Hippo Show* at the University of Leeds, right outside the refectory where The Who recorded *Live at Leeds*. The opera is nearly three hours long and involves hundreds of citizens. Music is composed by the head of the university's music department. Lead singer is Tim Yealland, a lovely man who, when he's not singing, creates abstract oil paintings.

The story starts with the finding of some prehistoric hippopotamus bones when workers are digging the foundations of Armley Jail. The bones, being liberated, come to life and the rejuvenated hippo embarks on a journey through the history of Leeds, meeting sundry characters on the way. Tim plays a professor of fossils who wants to keep the hippo for his own collection. There's a woman called 'Woodbine Lizzie' based on a real Leeds character who once tramped the streets of Leeds cadging cigarettes and a man called 'Chick Duggan' who sold *Old Moore's Almanac* on street corners, telling futures for a shilling. The chorus march around with placards emblazoned with slogans 'Fresh Air', 'Green Spaces' and 'No More Concrete'.

The *Yorkshire Post* send their opera reviewer. He writes that, 'This was not so much an opera as a left wing demonstration.'

For me it's a right old eye-opener onto the world of community arts and performance. I also get to see for free three operas at the Grand Theatre starting with Verdi's *Jerusalem* where I am thrown by the audience behaviour. At the time I wrote a weekly column for the Featherstone Rovers match-day programme. In my notes for the game against St Helens I put that I had never heard such hissing and booing since Vince Farrar had been disallowed a try against Whitehaven.

Stephen and me became firm friends and collaborators after that. He encouraged me to seek more work in music theatre and I joined him on some projects with big cultural institutions all over the country.

We worked in Wormwood Scrubs Prison alongside the composer Mark Anthony Turnage and at Maidstone Prison with musicians from the London Sinfonietta. At Maidstone we met a prison welfare officer who wanted to join the project because he had been a professional musician before he became a welfare officer. It turned out that he had been the drummer for a while in the early seventies group Chicory Tip. Me and six or seven of the lads serving time greeted him every morning after that with a rendition of 'Son of My Father'.

Some of the most rewarding work we did was at a hospital in Putney for people with head injuries. Working with Tim Yealland again we did a performance based on the tales of the Arabian Knights alongside patients suffering illnesses like multiple sclerosis or from the effects of horrendous accidents.

In Snape at the Benjamin Britten School we worked with musicians and carers and took the music we made into a home to work with Alzheimer's sufferers.

One day I turn up late for a meeting for people who work on creative projects in prisons, at the Arts Council in Birmingham. Throughout the first session a woman I don't know smiles and waves to me from the other side of the oval table. At the coffee break the lady introduces herself as Gillian Moore and tells me that she knows a lot about my work. Gillian is head of education at London Sinfonietta and in years to come will set up some of the best music and writing projects I have ever worked on.

We start our collaboration in Wakefield Prison. In a room full of tough guys who are anxious not to reveal anything at all about themselves we talk about growing up and our experiences of music. Within an hour I have encouraged them to tell stories about their grannies and Gillian has got them playing a Samba on a variety of Latin percussion instruments. Through Gillian I get to work with Trevor Wishart, see a performance of the work of Iannis Xenakis at Scunthorpe Baths, meet Luciano Berio and work at a drug rehabilitation place in Kingston-upon-Thames with a full Indonesian Gamelan set up. I also find myself working at a summer school in High Wycombe for the National Youth

Orchestra with, amongst others, the jazz-playing Mondesir Brothers.

Stephen Langridge and Gillian Moore have taught me more about the power music has to bring people together than anybody else I know.

Local Interest

When my grandad told me that I should never work down the pit, he never really told me what else I might do. Well, what he actually said was, 'If I ever see thee near that pit I'll give thee a bloody good hiding!' When I asked him what he thought I ought to do he said, 'Read books, lad!' I used the maroon leather-bound dictionary that my Auntie Alice won for occasional reference and even read extracts from *Better Sight Without Glasses*, my word hoard improved dramatically. I got a bollocking at the age of sixteen for knowing too many 'posh' words and I have never had to wear spectacles. Then there was my maps. And where did they get me?

I worked in an engineering factory before fleeing to Cornwall to scrape dried ravioli from pans in hotel kitchens. I laboured with a shovel on building sites for a while. I did a stint in an old-fashioned maltsters where they still used wooden implements. In desperation I took an office job in a factory that made mining equipment. It was a time office and I gave out cards to lathe and milling machine operators. These cards told them how long each task should take. I dream sometimes that I still work in that time office and that I'm late for work.

One November on the cliff tops near Bridlington I found myself in a deep trench. Bert Stevens, who told me about a book called *Catching Voles in the Outer Hebrides by Moonlight*, was working alongside me. We were digging the footings for a new coastguard house and trying to connect a temporary sewage line to a manhole. The wind was blowing sleet over from the North Sea, rivulets of water and sludge were running down the side of the trench and my hands were so cold they were sticking to the ceramic nine-inch diameter pipe. Bert was behind me levering the pipes with a crowbar and cursing our luck. The manhole was full of shit, piss and lavatory paper. We were both hung-over after a session in the Kings Arms the night before and we'd had a horrible breakfast of blackened fried egg and beans on toast in an out-of-season guest house on Marshall Avenue. I stood up, turned to Bert and said, 'I don't want to do this job any more.' Bert didn't move. He just stood there with his crowbar in his hands and looked me straight in the eye. 'Be a fuckin' writer then. You're always telling people you can write!' I didn't throw my shovel down at that minute and pick up a pen, but the seed that Bert planted in that trench that morning did grow. The coastguard house got finished without us. We came back home on Bert's Honda on an icy road over the Wolds. When I thawed out I sat at our dining table and wrote some short stories. Some years later two of these stories were accepted by Radio Four. Round about the same time I start to work as a community book publisher at Yorkshire Art Circus.

I met a man called Julius Hogben. Julius is the only man I know apart from me who has read the works of Cunninghame Graham. Graham was an adventurer from the Scottish aristocracy who became a radical early socialist MP and rode to the Houses of Parliament on a horse he'd bought in Argentina. Julius lived near Queens Park Rangers' ground in London and worked as an editor at BBC TV. He had been on holiday in Tenerife or somewhere at the same time as Barbara Bredebusch, just after she parted from Jürgen. Barbara invited him to spend some time in Featherstone with us, one Easter. Julius came and was pleased to find that Cunninghame Graham and Keir Hardie had visited our local pub at the time of the Featherstone Massacre. Ever since then Julius has written entertaining letters. They're always on the back of old birthday cards and adverts from magazines. It was Julius who introduced me to Ray Hough. Ray is a director at BBC Television and we came up with a proposal to make a half-hour documentary for BBC2 about community arts in Yorkshire. The programme features the work of the Yorkshire Art Circus and assorted characters who have found work through it; Harry Malkin organising his first exhibition on the South Bank, Mick Wilson the Barnsley pointillist winning the South Yorkshire Open Painting competition with his first framed work and assorted elderly ladies pegging clip rugs. The programme went down very well. I ended up working with Ray and the BBC on a further four documentaries. We would sit in pubs writing rough outline scripts on the back of peeled beer mats, then I'd stand in front of the camera and he'd coax the words on the beer mats out of me.

One of these films was a piece of work that I'm very proud of. I had been working at Wakefield Prison every Thursday evening for two years, helping seven or eight long-term prisoners to write poetry and stories. Most of the poems ended up as sentimental letters to loved ones. Ray thought it might be a good idea to put on an opera at Wakefield Prison. We would invite musicians and singers from Opera North and Stephen Langridge, the director I'd worked with on the Leeds opera, and devise and perform a piece put on by volunteer prisoners. Ray put the idea to Alan Yentob, who was then controller of BBC2. The idea went through and would become a forty-five minute special on *The Late Show*. We made the programme over a three-week period, it became the 'Wakefield Jailhouse Opera'. *The Independent* newspaper reviewed the programme in their 'Last Night's TV' slot. The reviewer said, 'Though you wouldn't want the results of the prisoners' efforts on your CD player, it was a wholly unpretentious experience. Even if one of the prisoners did manage to squeeze in the word "Paradigm". *The Late Show's* kind of a guy.'

I didn't work much for the BBC after that, but it wasn't long before I was asked to present on Yorkshire Television. I have been there for the last twelve years. I still keep in touch with Ray. We recommend CDs to each other as we always have done. It was me who first put Ray on to Algerian Rai music and particularly the recordings of Cheb Khaled. He has danced wildly to a song called 'Ya Loulid' at parties ever since. I introduced him to a Leeds band called The Wedding Present. He tells me that their first album *George Best* is still one of his favourites. In return Ray put me onto some great jazz, he used to take me to the Sunday lunchtime sessions at The Bull at Barnes, just down the road from where Marc Bolan crashed his mini. He also heard Joss Stone before anybody else. We went round telling everybody and then before you know it, she's the best thing since Aretha Franklin. It's a bugger when that happens.

Ray tells a story about when he first applied for a job producing at the BBC. He was interviewed by a panel of old school-tie types. The first question was, 'What does your father do Raymond?' Ray told them he was a painter. 'Oh! Really? Would I know his work?' Ray told them that his dad had painted a lot of window frames in his time, so they might do!

Yorkshire Television wanted me to present regional programmes about 'things of local interest'. I was worried when they offered me the work that I would be stereotyped as a professional Yorkshireman. I remember saying to Ned Thacker, the producer who was to look after me, 'You only want me so that you can have a laugh at my dialect. It won't be long before you have me going to Barnsley market, eating black pudding and tripe and stroking passing whippets!' Ned shrugged his shoulders and told me not to be so daft. My first day's filming was at Selby interviewing a lovely man called Howard who sold towels and played George Formby songs on his ukulele in his spare time. The second day's filming was at Barnsley market where I was to sample various black puddings and tripe. I tried the traditional black pudding, the continental black pudding ('wi' garlic in it' as the man said), some flat tripe, honeycomb tripe and pigs bag. The man in the white coat behind the counter then fetched out a long pink tubular thing that shimmered in the camera light.

'What's that then?'

'This,' he said with undisguised glee, 'is weasun.'

'And what's that when it's at home?'

'It's the cow's oesophagus!'

'Yes!' I said, 'I thought it might be the cow's oesophagus.'

I took a bite and looked straight into the camera. 'Lovely! A little bit salty for my liking, but nevertheless…lovely.' I spat some chewed bits out when the camera moved off me.

The programme went out and was very popular. It signalled the start of a whole series with me trawling around the open-air markets of the north sampling local delicacies.

About six or seven weeks after my visit to Barnsley market I was in that town again, doing a story with the sculptor Graham Ibbeson who had sculpted Eric Morecambe doing the 'Bring Me Sunshine' dance for Morecambe seafront. A lad of about fourteen with his baseball cap on back to front came sidling up to me. He took my coat sleeve and said, 'Ay up! It's thee in' it?' I said, 'Aye it's me!'

'Aye, I know, I've seen thee on t'telly.'

'Do you like my programmes?'

He thought for a bit and said, 'No! Tha's crap!'

'Charming!'

'But mi dad likes thee. He watches all thi programmes.' He thought a bit more and then said, 'And thy eats black pudding dunt tha?'

'I do.'

'And thy eats tripe!'

'I do.'

'And thy eats weasun.'

'I do.'

'Does thy know what weasun is?'

'I do actually, it's the cow's oesophagus.'

'Aye, well that's what they tell thee!'

I said, 'Go on then clever clogs, what is it?'

He snorted, spat and then said, 'Pig's cock!'

I may have been the only TV presenter to have eaten pig's cock for the cameras.

It hasn't all been tripe, pig's cock and visits to Barnsley market. One day I happened to mention to a young researcher called Stuart Ramsey that my mother had seen Cliff Richard and the Shadows at the Crescent Cinema in Pontefract. Stuart hadn't realised that before the days of video and bands playing stadium gigs they actually came to see you. And that there were people in small towns the length and breadth of Britain who had stories to tell about bands who later became world famous. Stuart was a brilliant researcher and within weeks he had found people who told stories about Jimi Hendrix, Buddy Holly and the Crickets, Louis Armstrong, The Who, the Sex Pistols and the time when The Beatles were regular visitors to Doncaster. We created a series of programmes called 'I Was There'; it ran for just one package of three half-hour programmes.

Precious Moments

There's a café on the A645 road between Wakefield and Pontefract called The Redbeck; it's known to lorry drivers, bikers and people walking home pissed up in the middle of the night who need a fried breakfast. It has no lock on its door. Since it opened in 1963 it has never closed, not even Christmas Day. Sometime in the late 1970s, the Three Degrees brought the sound of Philadelphia to Wakefield Theatre Club. Around three o'clock in the morning the manager of the club brought the girls, still in wigs, make-up and spangly dresses, for a breakfast special here. Perhaps one day the music hall of fame might erect a blue plaque on The Redbeck's wall recording the event. Ooooh! Aaah! Aaaah! Ooooh! Precious moments.

If you make a link between a twenty-four-hour transport café in the middle of what was once the Yorkshire coalfield and three American singers in high heels and wigs, the possibilities for forging links must be endless. What other strange bedfellows might you bring together?

Johnny Cash is on tour. Heather, Kevin Reynolds and me travel by stretch limo to see him in Doncaster at a place called The Dome. The Dome is Doncaster's attempt to drag itself into the twenty-first-century leisure industry. It's a bitterly cold winter night and it's been snowing for three days. The previous night Johnny, June Carter and the band have been playing across the Pennines in Manchester. A big crowd of local people have assembled in the auditorium to be told over the PA that the band bus has been held up in the blizzards on the M62, but they hope to get the show started within an hour. We twiddle our thumbs and wonder if Russ the Bus, our limo driver, will charge extra waiting time.

The band appear. Johnny Cash strolls out with guitar strapped to his back, follow spotlight glaring. At the beginning of every gig he has ever done he introduces himself with the immortal line, 'Hello, my name's Johnny Cash.' On this night he says, 'Mighty pleased to be here,' he pauses, his thoughts somewhere in a northern English blizzard, 'with all you good people of Don...chester. My name's Johnny Cash.' The band kick straight into 'Folsom Prison Blues'. By the time Johnny gets to the line about 'shooting a man in Reno' the good folk of Doncaster have forgiven the man in black for misusing the name of their town. Rock fans here are rightly proud of the role their town has played in popular music history.

I'm standing outside the Odeon Cinema in Doncaster with a woman called Vanessa Sutcliffe, who is a producer for Yorkshire TV's regional programmes department, a Glaswegian cameraman called Jim Hammill and a sound recordist called Gareth Hall. Gareth is a great rock music fan who once texted me from Glastonbury's backstage area to say, 'Guess where I am'. For months he has been trying to persuade me that Queens of the Stone Age are the best band that the world has ever known. Before that he had burned me all the Spiritualised and Radiohead CDs.

The man I'm waiting for outside of the cinema in

179

Doncaster is called Phil Battye. He's a likeable lad in his early fifties. We ask him to stand in the Odeon doorway, the camera starts to roll and I pretend to approach him for the first time. 'Hello. I'm looking for Phil Battye.'

'That's me!'

'Oh! Hello Phil. I understand you can tell me something about a certain day in 1963.'

'Would that be the tenth of December? A Tuesday?'

'Yes. The day The Beatles played the Doncaster Gaumont.'

'That's right. Me and my mate Ron Mitchenson were standing just down here.'

He points to a road by the side of the cinema and the camera follows his finger. 'It was just before the concert started and this whole area was packed with screaming girls. I never actually saw The Beatles arrive, but I know they were smuggled in, inside of an *Evening News* van.'

Inside, Dave Wright, who still works at the cinema, stands beside the spotlight up in the projection room. He tells us that he feels proud that all those years ago he caught The Beatles in his spotlight. Later he shows us backstage and finds some old microphone stands and an old mic. He thinks they may be the ones that were put out for bands back in the sixties. They might even be the very ones The Beatles used.

Opposite the Gaumont Cinema is the Regent Hotel. It's owned by the same family who had it when The Beatles stayed there. I sit in the bedroom which John Lennon and Paul McCartney had shared. Mike Longworth served tea to a couple of bleary-eyed Beatles on the morning after the Gaumont gig. He reminisces about that morning. 'After I gave them their tea I asked them for their autographs. They told me that they would leave all four autographs for me before they left. Which they did. But the best part of all was going to school later on. In the school playground all my mates formed a circle round me. "Guess who I've been serving tea to this morning?"'

Mike's mother Peggy tells me that The Beatles were like every mother's son. 'They stayed in their bedrooms most of the time, laid about strumming guitars. They were immaculate, mind. They even cleaned their own shoes. Their shoes were perfect. Every mother looks at shoes.' After The Beatles left, gangs of girls came and asked Peggy and other members of staff if they might buy the sheets that The Beatles had slept in. In the end Peggy would tell them, 'No love, The Beatles wouldn't stay in a small hotel like this. Go and try that big place down the road!'

I suppose most people who are interested in music have a Beatles anecdote to relate. Somebody always knows somebody who knew somebody, who knew Ringo's uncle. And like Elvis, the stories multiply tenfold as the distance between their heydays and now increases.

My mate Bill Covington actually played on the same bill as The Beatles and was managed by Brian Epstein. Bill is a drummer and when he was a teenager he was in a band called The Rustiks (they were West Country boys from the Plymouth area). In 1964 The Rustiks won a talent competition and were taken on by NEMS, Epstein's company. Within weeks of signing they were on tour with The Beatles and Sounds Incorporated. They released one single, a song called 'Not the Loving Kind' and when it didn't do anything, The Rustiks became a footnote at the bottom of the dustbin of rock 'n' roll history. Before Epstein dropped them though, they did get to party with The Beatles. It was Christmas in the year of the release of *Rubber Soul.* Epstein had just published his autobiography, *A Cellarful of Noise.* Even he had already forgotten his new protégés. In his book he recalled signing a band called 'The Ruskies'. At the party John Lennon teased Bill. He told him that when he'd read about 'The Ruskies' it had given him and Paul McCartney an idea. He said, 'Me and Paul are thinking about writing a comedy song about four dancers from the Bolshoi Ballet who defect to form a rock band.' Bill got pissed up at that party and later braved himself to tell Lennon that he was his hero and that he thought his song 'Michelle' was beautiful. Lennon pushed Bill to one side, went off to mingle with the other guests and over his shoulder tossed, 'Paul wrote that one.' It was Bill's one and only dalliance with John Lennon. The Rustiks were not completely forgotten. Donovan mentions in his autobiography *The Hurdy-Gurdy Man* that when he first appeared on *Ready Steady Go* he lined up alongside Gene Pitney, Marianne Faithfull, Adam Faith and The Rustiks. At the time Donovan was trying to imitate Woody Guthrie. He had a slogan on his guitar that said 'This machine kills' and wore a Cap Breton fisherman's hat. Somebody nicked the fisherman's hat from his dressing room.

These days Bill proudly shows a small collection of black and white Beatles photographs that he took himself during the Sounds Incorporated tour. As to what happened to Donovan's cap, that may remain one of the great rock 'n' roll mysteries.

The Beatles played Doncaster five times in all. Betty Pearson's husband was the manager at St James Swimming Baths. We take our camera up onto the swimming baths balcony and Betty sits with a sheaf of her poetry to hand.

'In the winter-time the council would cover the pool with a sprung maple dance floor. We had great concerts here.'

'Can you remember The Beatles coming?'

'Oh, yes! I was here when they arrived. They'd been down in London making a record in the morning. They looked tired out. I asked them if they would like a slipper bath. They all said yes. I don't think they all got in the same bath though the slipper baths were easily big enough.'

Betty is itching to read a poem she composed at the time. I ask her if she would like to read. She smiles shyly and takes a breath:

'The floor was springing up and down
Like a giant trampoline
The mirror ball scattering magic hues
Of red and blue and green
Over balcony, walls and floor
Over each dancing pair
Then from the stage comes ringing
She loves you yeah! yeah! yeah!'

I ask Phil Battye, 'So when the *Evening Post* van smuggled The Beatles in, did you go in to find your seat?'

'Oh, no! I didn't see the concert,' says Phil, 'I had to be in bed by half past eight in them days!'

After Bill Covington moved on from The Rustiks he joined a band called The StaggerLees, who were big on the northern club circuit. Greasborough WMC near Rotherham was the biggest and most successful of working men's clubs. One night the club booked Jayne Mansfield. She had developed a bizarre act involving innuendo, ukulele playing and Shakespearian quotes. Bill bumped into Jayne Mansfield in a backstage passageway. 'For about two minutes,' he will tell you, 'I was alone with Jayne Mansfield. And do you know what she said to me? She said, "I'd love to kiss you honey, but I've just washed my hair!"'

What a Wonderful World

On the tarmac at Leeds Bradford Airport I interview Stuart Owen who had been a baggage handler here back in 1967 when Louis Armstrong flew in to undertake a two-week residency at Batley Variety Club. He tells me about the day Louis Armstrong touched down.

'There was a little lad called Enrico Tomasso and his dad Ernie. Enrico played his trumpet and his dad played the clarinet. Louis Armstrong came down the stairs of the aeroplane and when he heard the music he cocked his ear over to listen. He seemed to be thrilled by it.'

'What did you think about it at the time then?'

'Well I was just a baggage handler. The plane came to rest on stand six and then this little, genuine, dapper fella came down and this seven-year-old lad was there for him. It was a lovely moment. Leeds Bradford Airport was called Yeadon Airfield in them times. We didn't get many international celebrities coming through.'

I tell Stuart that there is an old New Orleans song called 'I Walk on Gilded Splinters' and that forever more he will be able to tell people that he once walked in the gilded footsteps of the legendary Louis Armstrong and he says, 'Aye and I unloaded his cases an' all.'

We set up an interview with Bernard Hinchcliffe at the Batley Variety Club, which these days is called The Frontier Club. It's a disco and cabaret bar now. Bernard was the booking agent for the Variety Club. He reminisces about the old days, tales come thick and fast about Morecambe and Wise and Shirley Bassey.

'We wanted to bring an international superstar to Batley. Mr Corrigan who owned the club and me went over to New York to meet Louis Armstrong's agent, a man called Mr Joe Glaser.'

Joe Glaser, according to Stuart Nicholson, Billie Holiday's biographer, was 'a man about town'. He was a brothel owner, on the margins of the organised crime world and wasn't averse to adopting the manner and swagger of the B-movie hood. Glaser's mother owned the Sunset Café on 35th Street, a place where Louis Armstrong had enjoyed great success in the 1920s. In the middle of the 1930s Louis Armstrong returned disillusioned after a long tour to England and the continent. At this point Glaser bought his contract and managed him continuously until 1969. Also on Glaser's roster were Billie Holiday, Roy Eldridge, Lionel Hampton, Benny Carter, some of the greatest names in the history of jazz.

Obviously Glaser had never heard of Batley or its Variety Club. But according to Bernard Hinchcliffe word had slowly been drifting to America about this terrific little club in the north of England that now had over sixty thousand members. A deal was struck to bring Armstrong over in 1968. By sheer coincidence and with great timing for Batley Variety Club, Armstrong's song 'What a Wonderful World' went to number one in the hit parade right at the time of his residency.

James Corrigan, a son of the fairgrounds, had long

dreamed of opening a world-class entertainment venue in the north of England. His model was the supermarkets that were springing up in every town in Yorkshire. If you can buy food cheaply because it's been bought in bulk and piled high, why shouldn't you be able to do the same with entertainment?

James Corrigan was one of the greatest entertainment entrepreneurs of the last century. A man with great vision and practical ability who was completely fearless. He had a knack of bringing even the greatest stars down to earth by refusing to look up at them if they placed themselves on a pedestal of their own making. This was a man who in the early 1970s made an audacious offer to bring Elvis Presley to Britain for the first time. He offered £100,000, an unheard of sum in those days, if Presley would play the Yorkshire mill town of Batley. Colonel Tom Parker, it is claimed, replied, 'Well that will do for the manager, now what about my boy?' Undeterred by big stars and their outrageous demands, Mr Corrigan threatened to introduce interval bingo sessions at his club. Imagine going to see Shirley Bassey or Tom Jones and playing bingo while they towelled down in the dressing room at half-time.

Mr Corrigan came from solid Irish farm-worker stock. His great grandparents escaped the potato famine and travelled first to Liverpool and then to set up a pig farm at Ulleskelf near York. His grandfather Joseph joined a travelling fair and ran a coconut shy and a strongman machine. In the winter he carted coal from a pit in Leeds to sell around the houses of Burley. Joseph was also one of the first to show films on the then new cinematograph machines.

Joseph's second son Joey carried on his father's fairground business and in the summer of 1925, while the family were at the east coast, Joseph Lord, better known as 'Jimmy' Corrigan, was born. Jimmy went into the family business but, while still in his twenties, he emigrated to Toronto. He made a living there selling encyclopaedias and digging worms for fishermen. When he decided to come home in 1958 he landed at Batley railway station with three quid in his pocket.

Jimmy moved into the bingo business at exactly the right time. Old theatres like the Dewsbury Empire were closing down all over the country. With the advent of Independent Television in 1955, it seemed that nobody wanted live theatre any more. Bingo became the in-thing and with little or no regulation, Corrigan and his business partners were raking in the money. Within a couple of years his companies, Corrigan-Ford Enterprises and Mirgalade Ltd, were turning over three quarters of a million. They had twenty-three premises in their portfolio across Yorkshire, some showing films, others playing housey-housey. The mansion and two Rolls-Royces in the drive were not too far away when Corrigan decided on his most dramatic and daring adventure. Entertainment entrepreneurs by the mid 1960s were looking for the next big thing. The theatre was virtually dead, cinemas mortally wounded. The drinkers, diners and dancers of the north demanded something new. The answer was exotic cabaret with chicken and chips in a basket washed down with beer at pub prices. In 1965 the old Embassy Ballroom in Wakefield, after a £20,000 refurbishment, became 'The Kon-Tiki'. On opening night The Dallas Boys entertained a huge crowd who danced, dined and mainly drank the night away. In Greasborough, a village near Rotherham, an old British Legion club was converted into a super-sized 'glamorous' working men's cabaret bar and at Leeds the old Astra Cinema showed its last film *Woman in a Dressing Gown* and re-opened as 'The Ace of Clubs' with meals and dancing from seven until one in the morning and a gaming room for 'Chemin de fer'.

James Corrigan admired these places and wanted to open his own club. One day at the back end of 1966 he found a site on Bradford Road in Batley that had once been that town's sewage treatment works. Within sixteen weeks of buying the site, Corrigan's club, the Batley Variety Club, was built and on Sunday 26 March 1967, fourteen hundred people tucked into scampi and chips and sang along to The Bachelors singing their greatest hits, 'Charmaine', 'Diane' and 'I Believe'. Later that year came Gerry and the Pacemakers, Tony Hancock, the American movie star Jayne Mansfield and Eartha Kitt, who led community singing of 'Ilkley Moor Baht 'at' at Batley railway station.

I become one of the last people to interview James Corrigan, just before his death in December 2000. I travel to an ancient manor house in the Pennines. Mr Corrigan is dressed smartly in an expensive suit and tie. His PA has laid out a huge spread on a polished table. Salmon sandwiches, chicken drumsticks, pork pie and quiche lorraine. Tea is served from a hostess trolley in china cups and saucers. There are two pots for sugar, one contains white cubes, the other demerara granulated. I go for one lump of white and the PA hands me some polished tongs.

'What you need to see is that we were offering value for money,' says Mr Corrigan. He wheezes with ill health, but ignores the pain he's obviously in. He wants to tell his story. He has dignity and a bright pair of eyes.

'I was talking about places like Batley that nobody had heard of. In fact we were drawing up some of the contracts before the first bricks had been laid.'

I ask him to recall some of his early bookings.

'Val Doonican. The Bachelors. You could see them for five shillings. Nobody else was offering that kind of value. Then later we had Shirley Bassey, she was a bit more, I think a couple of quid. Then we captured our big prize, Louis Armstrong. We brought him to Batley from the airport in a chauffeur driven Rolls-Royce.'

Later I'm told a story by a man called Alan Clegg, who was a manager at the club, that the Rolls-Royce stopped outside a derelict old wool mill in the middle of Batley. Children were running around bare-arsed with broken toy prams. A little lad was trying to beat a rat with a stick and another one was chucking bricks at the windows.

'This is the club, Mr Armstrong.'

Louis' face dropped. There was a long pause and then,

'Only kidding.'

Alan says Louis Armstrong's face was a picture.

James Corrigan continues his story. 'Louis Armstrong loved Batley and the people who came to see him loved him too. He spent a good deal of time with them after the show. I remember once he was surrounded by these big burly Yorkshire bitter drinkers wanting autographs, somebody from his team came over to say, "We've got to go now," and he turned round and said, "Leave me alone man, these are my people." He was a lovely person.'

There's some fantastic black and white archive footage from Granada Television's news programme of the time. An interviewer asks Louis Armstrong if he's ever been to Batley before. Armstrong says, 'Well man I played Leeds back in 1932, but I ain't never heard of this place Batley. I don't think they had it in those days.' The newsman asks him to talk about the Yorkshire folk he's encountered. 'All the people are great y'know. We don't shake hands back home. We just say, give me some skin. We been doin' that here. Give me some skin…mop!' The newsman then asks him to describe Batley. Louis thinks only momentarily. 'Batley! Well, Batley is like a human aspirin.' The newsman doesn't know what to say so he repeats, 'A human aspirin?'

'Yep! A human aspirin!' Then he offers one of those huge satchel-mouthed grins.

I wanted to find Enrico Tomasso, the seven-year-old boy who had played at the airport. I track him down at the 100 Club on Oxford Street, London. There in a basement, not a million miles from the basement clubs of Harlem in the days of Joe Glaser, I find him playing trumpet to a packed lunchtime audience. In the break Enrico tells me his story.

'My father had a jazz band, Ernie Tomasso and Friends. I had a jazz band education from an early age. The first Louis Armstrong number I ever heard was "Basin Street Blues". When they asked me to play for him at the airport that's what I played. As Louis came down the steps he heard me blowin' and he came over. He took a shine to me straight away. He did two weeks at Batley and he invited me to come to his dressing room every night. He said, "Don't bring your horn, just come and relax, listen and learn." So I did. When he went back to America I made tapes of me learning to play and sent them to him. He wrote lovely letters back asking about the family and always signed them Satchmo.'

I ask Enrico to explain what attracts him to jazz music. By way of explanation he scat sings the opening bars of 'West End Blues'.

'You see when all the other musicians heard that they went "Like Wow!" I was brought up on the Rolling Stones, but when I heard my first Louis Armstrong record I knew I wanted to be a professional musician. Touch wood I'm earning a living. Life's not bad.'

Enrico picks up his trumpet and blows some air down it. He fingers the valves and then walks back to the stand. As he does I think about Margaret Johnson at our corner shop saying to Jayne Summers, 'Have you heard T. Rex's new record? It's like really cool y'know!' I think about running the two miles back from Pontefract to Mafeking Street in order to play that record on my mam's Dansette. I think about Elmore James singing, 'Got to get up in the morning, believe I'll dust my broom' and how that led me to filling my house with shelves full of blues records, that collect fluff until I blow it off every blue moon. Then I think about first hearing Jimi Hendrix doing 'Voodoo Chile' on a pirate radio station when I lived at Hull and how I've never been the same since.

Young Man Blues

Anybody who thinks about the gritty Yorkshire moorland town of Ilkley will think about the Cow and Calf rocks or the famous old song 'On Ilkley Moor Baht 'at'. Not many will know of this town's connection to Jimi Hendrix, but there are a few people for whom the words Ilkley, Jimi and Hendrix will be forever linked.

This story starts in John Entwistle's mansion in the Cotswolds. Scots Jim, Gareth the sound recordist and heavy rock fan, Vanessa and me are sitting in the pub that Entwistle has built in his own house. It's called the Barracuda Bar and stuffed game fish hang from the ceiling on fishing wires. John Entwistle's American girlfriend tells us that John will be down in a short while. We drink coffee laced with bourbon and wait. John comes downstairs. The interview has been set for ten in the morning by Bob Pridden, who has been The Who's sound engineer for over thirty years. I get the feeling that Bob Pridden hasn't told John that we want to do a telly interview. Perhaps he hasn't heard him, years of The Who at maximum volume have shattered his eardrums. John is very polite, very obliging. We sit him on a tall stool, I sit opposite and in a voice that I hope is loud enough to be heard, but not loud enough to insult anybody, I begin.

'We're doing a series called "I Was There", the idea is to tell the story behind famous gigs that took place in Yorkshire.'

John nods.

'One of the documentaries looks at The Who's *Live at Leeds*.'

John nods again.

'The other one is about when Jimi Hendrix played at Ilkley.'

Another nod.

'We wondered if you might talk a bit about Hendrix, because you knew him quite well, didn't you?'

Nod.

'And then a bit about that night in Leeds.'

I wait for a response.

John smiles.

I wait.

'You're going to have to speak up. I haven't heard a fuckin' word of what you've just said.'

I look at Vanessa for direction. She averts her eye. I look round to Jim, he gives a slight shrug and looks back down his eyepiece. Gareth turns down some dials on his sound kit and moves the boom back.

'You knew Hendrix quite well, didn't you?'

I'm sure Entwistle is now thinking, 'What the fuck is he asking me about Jimi Hendrix for?' But off he goes anyway. 'Yeah! I played with him the first night he came over to England. It was in a place called the Scottish St James. He jammed with us and kept telling me that I was out of tune. He hadn't realised that his guitar was tuned a semi-tone down so he'd been playing in A-flat all night. A few days after that he asked me to be in his band. I told him "No". Then I got a phone call from Noel Redding. Hendrix had told him to ask me what gear I used and that he was to go out and buy the same. It was two Marshall amps and a jazz bass. And that's how the Jimi Hendrix Experience started.'

'Was he the best?' Listen at me. I've got a solid gold opportunity to ask one of rock's greats to talk in depth about the late sixties scene and the best I can come up with is 'Was Hendrix the best?'

'Well he was Page, Townshend and Beck.' Pause, quick afterthought and then, 'With a little bit of Clapton thrown in.'

Ask a silly question.

Two hundred miles north and I'm sitting in the reception area of the Troutbeck Nursing Home in Ilkley. This used to be the Troutbeck Hotel and during the 1960s home to the Giro Club, a blues music venue on wet weekday nights that attracted a handful of hardy fans of Muddy Waters and Jimmy Reed to see people grunting out cover versions of their idols' songs. In early 1967 the lads who ran the club booked a new blues singer just over from America. This was Jimi Hendrix. At the time Hendrix was completely unknown. He had been a minor player in Little Richard's backing group. By the time he was to play Ilkley, 'Hey Joe' was high in the pop charts and Hendrix was massive. To his and his management's credit, Hendrix decided he would still honour all the bookings at little blues clubs dotted across the north of England.

Today I'm joined by Vince Philpotts, Martin Harvey and Peter Dobson, three stalwarts who were at the Giro Club that night.

Vince: 'It was a normal Sunday night really. We'd heard about this new American guitarist who was a bit way out. There must have been three hundred people there.'

Martin: 'The crowd was unbelievable.'

Peter: 'I remember the heat being intense. There was this anticipation y'know. Then the sheer power hit you. "Wow what's that?" as Hendrix laid into his guitar on the first number.'

Vince: 'I think it was at the start of the second number when this guy in a gaberdine raincoat walks in with another uniformed officer. I think they mumbled something about overcrowding.'

The guy in the gaberdine raincoat was Sergeant Tommy Chapman of the West Riding Constabulary. Stuart Ramsay our researcher tracked down now long-since retired Tommy Chapman in the most unusual circumstances. At the same time as researching our series 'I Was There', Stuart was also fixing guests for the live magazine programme 'Tonight'. The guests were the usual mixture of celebrities plugging appearances in regional theatres, celebrity musicians on tour, but no longer in the charts, that sort of thing. Hank Marvin came on, as did Britt Ekland. The Corrs sang regularly before they were famous and Dickie Bird the cricket umpire was always there. On one memorable occasion Steve Harley of Cockney Rebel came to mime to 'Come Up and See Me (Make Me Smile)'. When Jeanette in make-up asked him if he needed powder on his face, he said, 'I'm a fucking rock 'n' roll star dahlin...what do you fink?' Ian Hunter of Mott the Hoople managed to do a live interview by answering 'yes' and 'no' to every question for a full five minutes. One day Stuart gets a call from a man who has just written a book after spending time on a reservation with the Lakota Sioux. It's a beautiful book and the writer wants to tell Christine Talbot, our main presenter, all about it. The writer's name is Serle Chapman. It transpires that Serle Chapman is the son of Sergeant Tommy Chapman, the man in the gaberdine raincoat at Ilkley in 1967. Serle comes and talks about his native American Indian book. Ex-Sergeant Tommy agrees to meet us at the Troutbeck. Vince, Martin and Peter are gobsmacked to shake hands and make small talk with the man who threatened to arrest Jimi Hendrix all those years before.

Tommy tells me, 'I was paying a supervisory visit to the premises. It was something we did to all premises where live music was played. It was said that nine hundred people were assembled. The licensing magistrates would allow a maximum of two hundred and fifty at that particular venue.'

'So what did you do, Mr Chapman?'

'I looked into the ballroom and saw this big crowd. I had to push my way through and then climb up onto the stage. The music was very loud. I walked up to the chap who was playing the guitar and tapped him on his shoulder. I told him to turn down the racket.'

'Was this Jimi Hendrix?'

'I believe that was his name. Yes.'

'What, you went up to Jimi Hendrix and told him to turn down the racket?'

'Yes. And he wouldn't stop playing so I pulled out the plug.'

Vince told me afterwards in a very ironic voice that, 'Hendrix turned up the volume and backed into the speakers to let out a wall of heavy feedback, to the considerable irritation of the police.'

Sergeant Tommy continues, 'I then told everybody that they would have to go home, because fire regulations had been broken and I couldn't possibly allow the concert to take place.'

Apparently there were some ironic boos and hisses, but most of the people behaved themselves, apart from one or two who queued twice to get their money returned on the way out.

The ten-minute film we made about Hendrix live in Ilkley went out one wet Wednesday night. A few days later I got a phone call from a woman called Sheila Lilley. She told me that she had seen and enjoyed the piece on Hendrix, but that the story didn't end with Tommy Chapman shooing everybody through the door. She then told me the extraordinary story of what happened half an hour later. I arranged to meet her for lunch.

To this day the most famous fish and chip shop in the world is one called Harry Ramsden's. It has been an institution in the town of Guiseley, just down the A65 from Ilkley, since the 1920s. It started life as a little wooden hut where old Harry Ramsden prepared his fish and chip suppers. Nowadays it's a big restaurant with chandeliers, fragile little doilies and an organist plays 'Spanish Eyes' to accompany people shaking their vinegar. I meet Sheila Lilley and her husband Dave there and we sit on a wall eating fish and chips out of paper while they recount the story of what happened next on the night of the Hendrix gig.

'We'd got our fish and chips and we were sitting on this wall eating them. We were just wiping the grease off our fingers when I saw this black guy standing waiting in the queue. I nudged Dave. We couldn't believe our eyes. Here was Jimi Hendrix standing in a queue for fish and chips at Harry Ramsden's.'

'Was he still in his stage outfit?'

'Well, he was dressed nothing like anybody else in Guiseley that night.'

'What did you do?'

'I rummaged in my handbag for a pen and went up and asked him for his autograph. He asked me to turn round and he pressed on my back to write his name. He told us that he was sorry he hadn't been able to do the gig.'

Sheila has fetched her souvenir with her. In a frame beneath a photograph of Jimi Hendrix is a scrap of white fish and chip paper, on it it says, 'Love to you. Jimi Hendrix'.

On the day of filming after the cameras stopped rolling I say to Sergeant Tommy Chapman, 'Looking back over the years, don't you feel a bit of a spoilsport?'

Mr Chapman looks aghast at my impertinence. 'I'd heard only a few weeks before that at a concert in America some teenagers had been hurt. I had visions that if a fight started people here could have been badly injured, so I pulled the plug.'

In the Cotswolds, Gareth has told John Entwistle that he plays a bit of bass himself and wonders if he might have a go on one of John's. John Entwistle obliges and plugs it in. I can't remember now what Gareth plays, perhaps something by Queens of the Stone Age. Gareth finishes playing and hands the guitar back to John. I seize the opportunity and ask John if he wouldn't mind playing my favourite bit from *Live at Leeds*, the bass part on 'Young Man Blues'. Bated breath.

'Pardon!'

'Would you mind playing a bit of "Young Man Blues"?'

John crashes into a punk jazz version of the song, walking up and down beneath the barracudas as he plays. It's a moment to treasure, like the day Roy Herrington walked on stage at the King's School with his axe, or the day when I watched John Martyn whack down his vodka bottle from the fridge.

Bob Pridden joins us. Bob is an excitable bald-headed little chap with a photographic memory of the night The Who played Leeds. 'Some people said that *Live at Leeds* wasn't even recorded at Leeds. That it was done in Hull a few nights later. I can tell you that it was definitely done at Leeds, because me and the crew of the mobile unit spent two days setting up for it. I say mobile unit, but there wasn't really such a thing in those days. We actually built an entire studio in the refectory building.'

Live at Leeds was recorded on St Valentine's Night in 1970. Two thousand students turned up. One of them was one of the organisers, John Brisbrowne, who these days has a record shop in Burton-on-Trent. John Brisbrowne told me that he couldn't hear for three days after the gig and he wondered how the band could stand the loudness night after night.

I ask John Entwistle, 'Did you realise when you were

recording it that *Live at Leeds* would become such a benchmark recording?'

'No. No. Not really', he says. 'To be truthful I didn't even know if we were miked up properly.' Bob throws him a playful glance. 'I didn't even hear it until much later. We were in America sitting by a swimming pool in Tanglewood at four o'clock in the morning. Someone brought out a little tape recorder and put the tape in. Keith Moon and me sat and listened to it. We were amazed by what we were playing.'

Bob Pridden joins in. 'It was The Who's best gig ever, and it's an absolutely indispensable live album.'

'And you played Woodstock only a few months before,' I venture.

John gives me a look. 'Yeah! And we were the only ones that got fuckin' paid.'

John Entwistle seems to have had enough talking about the past now. He asks us if we want to stay around and have dinner. We tell him that we'd love to but we have to move on to London because this evening we have an appointment with Julian Temple who worked with the Sex Pistols.

'Pardon!'

'We have to go to London, we're doing a film about the Sex Pistols.'

John Entwistle puts his bass back onto the stand and surveys his collection of stuffed barracuda fish. 'Fuck that!'

Before we leave the mansion in the Cotswolds I ask Bob Pridden if I might nick a couple of plectrums. He gives me an orange one and a lime green one. I give the orange one to my son Edward who for Christmas got a half-size Stratocaster copy. I give the lime green one to Johnny Eagle, a taxi driver and part-time working men's club turn. Johnny Eagle has been plugging away doing sixties covers since the sixties. He is thrilled to bits to be given one of John Entwistle's plectrums. (I don't have the heart to tell him that it might be one of Bob Pridden's.) He tells me that he will use it on one song the next time he plays North Featherstone Club, known locally as 'Top o' t'Knob Club'. On the night of his gig there he phones me to make sure I'm coming. Johnny Eagle doesn't know the chords to 'Young Man Blues' and besides he doesn't think that it would go down too well in the 'Top o' t'Knob' so he has decided to use his plectrum on The Shadows' favourite 'Apache'. And he does. And the girls from Company Travel's taxi office in Station Lane jump up to dance and some of the middle-aged boozers in the corner finger the air. The next time Johnny Eagle takes me to Westgate Station he asks me what I thought to his version of 'Apache'. I tell him I thought it was great, because I did. He says, 'Aye. I could feel the spirit coming through.'

Anarchy in the UK

Julian Temple has locked himself into an edit suite at the top of some rickety wooden stairs somewhere in west London. He is trying to piece together a documentary film about the history of the Sex Pistols. The film will eventually be released as *The Filth and the Fury,* a superb cut-and-paste journey through late seventies British pop music, against a backdrop of the cultural life of this country at the time. I think Julian has agreed to talk to us because we have managed to get him some Yorkshire TV archive footage of the Pistols being interviewed on the regional news programme. Julian worked as an archivist for the Pistols and followed them around with a camera. We are particularly interested in a sequence he filmed on Christmas Day in 1977 at Ivanhoe's Club in Huddersfield.

The gig at Huddersfield has gone down in rock music history. It was one of the few the Sex Pistols were able to play legally after being banned from everywhere, it was also the last gig they were to play on British soil before they went to America, exploded, recorded with Ronnie Biggs and had their bass player arrested for murdering his girlfriend and then die in his sleep after taking heroin. Every punk rocker in the north of England who was born between 1959 and 1963 will tell you that they were at that gig on Christmas Day. It's the punk rock equivalent to the Hull Rugby League Club t-shirt scam. In 1974, Hull, once one of the giants of rugby league, were at a very low ebb near the bottom of the league. One mucky Wednesday night in mid-winter they were to play bottom club Huyton, the laughing stock of rugby league. Just seven hundred and twenty-one people turned up to watch. Some years later when Hull had reawoken from their slumber and were back at the top of the league, an entrepreneurial bright spark had the idea of printing a t-shirt. A simple white shirt with a simple message on the front. 'I was one of the seven hundred and twenty-one.' He sold fifteen thousand. We will probably never know how many punks saw the Sex Pistols at Ivanhoe's. It will be certainly less than saw Hull play Huyton, but I dare bet that far more punks claim to have seen the gig than bought the t-shirt.

In the midst of flickering images on an edit screen of punks pogoing to 'God Save the Queen' and, strangely, footage of a Shakespearian actor as hunchbacked Richard III, Julian Temple tells his story.

'McLaren employed me as a kind of archivist to follow the Pistols around and film whatever they were doing. The gig at Huddersfield was organised in support of striking firemen who were struggling as Christmas approached. I don't believe it was a gimmick.'

'That's hard to believe with Malcolm McLaren involved!' I say.

'Well, I really think the Pistols had a genuine sympathy for the firemen. It was a calm before the storm that blew them away in America.'

Julian Temple's footage is shot on a poor quality camera, something like Super 8, but it is wonderful. It depicts children with 'Never Mind the Bollocks' t-shirts forced over party dresses dancing to Boney M records, while Steve Jones, Paul Cook and Johnny Rotten run around with lumps of cream cake. I'm told later by someone who was there that Sid Vicious was sulking and didn't join in too much with the fun. I'm told later still that he sat on a sink in the dressing room getting a blow-job.

A few days after the London edit-suite interview I arrange to meet Bill Wright. This is the guy who arranged the Ivanhoe's gig. It is a freezing cold day, I turn up in an old man's tweed overcoat and a flat cap that Barbara Kaiser's brother brought me from Germany. He claimed it was the first flat cap to make it out of East Germany when the Berlin wall fell down.

Bill Wright is thrilled to be standing outside of the now derelict Ivanhoe's on a freezing cold day, talking to a man in a flat cap with a strong Yorkshire accent, about one of the landmarks in punk rock history.

'The call came through from Malcolm McLaren. "Would you like to present the Sex Pistols at Huddersfield?" Now I knew that they had been banned from playing everywhere, but when he mentioned the Green Goddesses flying up and down and that we could raise funds for the striking firemen, I thought why not?'

'What was the idea then?'

'That we would have a children's Christmas Party in the afternoon, with sandwiches and cake and competitions to win presents and the Sex Pistols would attend and in the evening we'd put on a full in your face Pistols gig for the local punks.'

'And did it work?'

'You bet! It was just a lovely, genuine, Christmas Day party and everybody involved enjoyed themselves a lot. I think Johnny Rotten had been a playschool leader at one time and he got on really well with the young kids. He was brilliant. I'll never forget him with his big whiffly eyes cutting up slices of cake, with all the youngsters eagerly waiting. It really was lovely. Not so much an anarchic punk gig as a lovely party with jelly and ice cream.'

Our researcher par excellence, Stuart Ramsay, manages to track down three of the kids who were there. Craig Mallinson, now a fireman like his dad, his sister Linzi and brother Dean. We film Craig sliding down the fireman's pole at Halifax Fire Station. He tells us that he won a nice yellow skateboard with red wheels and that it was the only present he got that year. He won it in a dancing competition for the best interpretation of Brotherhood of Man's 'Save Your Kisses for Me'. Linzi his sister says that she'd never heard of the Sex Pistols but it was the best Christmas she's ever had. And Dean says that he wasn't sure what to expect with punk rockers, but found out they are just normal people.

I look at the Julian Temple footage with them. They spot themselves dancing in their 'Bollocks' t-shirts and laugh. I see what Bill Wright means when he describes Johnny Rotten's 'whiffly' eyes and then there's this fantastic bit where the DJ in a strong Yorkshire cum DJ entertainer's voice says, 'Right-o lads and lasses. Let's hear it for t'Sex Pistols. Come on then...'

Craig Mallinson: 'As we came out all these punks were queuing up to get in. I don't know what they must have thought to all these eight and nine-year-olds trooping out of the door. I always smile to myself now when I go round Halifax and Bradford and I see punk rockers in the street and I think to myself, "I've seen the Sex Pistols and you haven't."'

Dean Mallinson: 'Somewhere in Huddersfield there is a little girl who will be in her thirties now and she's sitting on a fortune. One of the prizes the Pistols gave out was a gold disc for one of their records and she very shyly came up to collect it along with a slice of cake.'

The day after the Ivanhoe's gig the Sex Pistols flew out to America and into the storm that, as Julian Temple said, 'blew them away'. The week after the gig the *Huddersfield Examiner* reviewing Christmas Day at Ivanhoe's said, 'Perhaps, Johnny is not so rotten after all.'

That'll Be the Day

I believe it was an old fruit warehouse. It was on Princes Street off Hull's old cobbled marketplace. It was painted in psychedelic patterns in six or seven different shades of Magicote. My mate Pete Rusling and me idled our time away at weekends hanging about round here and told the others at school that we were in the COUM club. We had seen 'COUM Club' painted on the psychedelic wall. Later I found out that this was the commune where Genesis P-Orridge, Cosey Fanni Tutti and other members of what would become the industrial noise pollution group Throbbing Gristle lived after they dropped out of Hull University. Genesis P-Orridge, who won a poetry competition sponsored by Needler's chocolate factory, once came out and said 'Hi' to us. We felt cool.

Pete was a lovely mate. His brother was Paul Alexander Rusling, a famous pirate radio station DJ, whose inspiration washed down onto us. When a lot of the other kids were into the Bay City Rollers and David Cassidy we were talking about Bowie and Mick Ronson. Peter is one of them mates who I am really sad to have lost contact with. The last time I saw him was in 1983 on the top of a Hull Corporation bus on the way to watch Featherstone Rovers play Hull Kingston Rovers in a pre-season friendly. At that time we hadn't seen each other for nearly ten years and there was a lot to cram in in the space of a two-mile bus journey, so we just said 'Hello' and talked about the time I had hung over a railway bridge on the Hull–Barnsley line near his house in Fitzroy Street, with a piece of chalk in my hand. I wrote 'Featherstone Rovers Rule OK'. And the day when we were thrown onto the pavement outside the Haworth Arms for trying to order pints of bitter when we were thirteen. The very pavement where Nick Drake had sat and cried a couple of years before after he found nobody would listen to his sensitive songs in the Haworth Arms folk club.

One day Pete and me were coming back from nicking oranges and apples at the fruit market at Humber Street. I liked going there, because every now and then I bumped into Margaret Johnson's brother Vic who drove a lorry for Sainters Fruiterers in Pontefract and it reminded me of Featherstone. I hated living in Hull. My parents moved there to repair a failing marriage and spent the next three years arguing and fighting. Whenever my mother and father argued in Featherstone my mother would punctuate the row with the same sad refrain, 'I might as well put my head in the bloody gas oven.' By the time we got to Hull she changed the cry to, 'You want to put me in De La Pole.' This was the psychiatric hospital on the outskirts of the city. I once stood behind the stairs door after going to bed listening to my dad's fists hitting my mother in the face. My brother Tony whispered loudly, 'Come back to bed,' but I was frozen to where I was on the third step. When I couldn't stand it any more I burst across the kitchen into the front room and dived on my dad's back, pulling at his hair and punching him. My mother picked up a kettle and whacked him full in the face with it, the spout caught him in the eye. The blood fell all over the white leatherette three-seater settee. They argued about who would pay for it cleaning.

Pete and me, with pockets full of fruit, passed by the ABC Cinema. Outside of the cinema there was a huge queue of screaming Bay City Rollers fans with tartan bags on and nylon scarves tied to their wrists. They were shouting out the names of their favourite Rollers. 'Eric', 'Woody', 'Alan', 'Les'. Pete and me mocked them and laughed all the way back to Fitzroy Street where we coolly played *Hunky Dory*.

Twenty-odd years later I stand outside the boarded up remains of the ABC or 'Regal' as it was properly known. In the drizzle I talk to a Yorkshire TV camera about it being the venue for a great gig by the legendary Buddy Holly. On 19 March 1958 Holly and The Crickets played here on a memorable British tour. I peer with a torch into the derelict remains of the darkened cinema, some pigeons flutter and I imagine.

In an upstairs hall tonight, which is used as a dance school, Yorkshire TV have assembled a Buddy Holly tribute band, the Holly Dayz. Against a backdrop of a rebel confederate flag and a homemade white bedsheet bearing the slogan 'The music lives on with the Holly Dayz' they kick off with 'That'll Be the Day'.

In the audience are Gina Gregory and Chris Hudson who were at the real Buddy Holly gig in 1958 and the also legendary sixties British rocker, Sheffield's own Dave Berry. Gina tells me about swooning to this skinny kid in black-rimmed glasses and how brilliant the gig was after only hearing him previously on the wireless. And how she'd waited for every magazine that came out with a picture of Buddy so she could cut it out and paste it into a scrap book. Chris Hudson remembers the guys in black jackets with white shirts and black bow ties. Dave Berry remembers the Sheffield leg of the tour as a turning point in this life.

'I was just into my teens. Buddy Holly was the first American I'd ever seen. He became a big influence. That guitar sound was something else. After the gig, I bought myself a guitar and learned the three chords I needed.'

Dave Berry went on to become one of the heroes of British rock who had big hits in the sixties and a revival when the punks latched on to him in the late seventies. He is in the record books for having the biggest ever selling single in Holland with 'This Strange Effect'. Some weeks after his appearance on the Buddy Holly feature, he brought his own CD of his hit 'The Crying Game' to the studios of Yorkshire Television and lip-synched to it on a makeshift stage. For the young PAs and operators in the gallery who knew the song from the Neil Jordan film it was a great thrill. For the audience at home – most of whom could remember the sixties – it was a chance to experience real rock 'n' roll nostalgia.

When Rod Stewart was in the charts singing 'It's late September and I really should be back at school', I embarked on a friendship with a schoolteacher who lived in an apartment overlooking Pearson Park, one of the parks that are Hull Corporation's pride and joy. She sat on floor cushions, burned incense and had a mauve lava lamp. I had found her briefcase after she absent-mindedly left it outside on the pavement and returned it to her. She invited me to drink peppermint tea with her once or twice and showed me some poetry she had written, one was about Che Guevara and another was about Sylvia Plath putting her head in the gas oven. I never told her that my mother threatened to do that at least twice a week. I never got to sing that line from Maggie May about 'The morning light really showing your age' to her either. Though I was moving away from school age friends and looking for adult company.

One day I befriended a gang of thirty-something Christian hippies in the most unusual of circumstances. I was exploring a derelict old warehouse off the Beverley Road. In the light streaming through some broken roof slates, I saw a bearded face and the top half of a body. When I approached him I could see the man was fast in a hole. He said he had been collecting wood and had fallen through the floor. I helped him out and because he was limping badly I let him lean on me back to the house he shared with seven or eight others. They fed me. It was the first time I ever had spaghetti bolognese. After dinner, the hippies lit some candles and congregated round a piano to sing spirituals and old hymns.

Hull holds many surreal moments in my memory.

So Lonesome I Could Cry

There's a record producer called Stuart Colman who originated from Harrogate. In the 1980s he produced a lot of the hits for Shakin' Stevens and has gold discs upside the staircase of his new home in Nashville to prove it. He lives next door to Duane Eddy.

I'm touring America with Yorkshire Television doing a series about people from the Yorkshire region who have gone west to make a new life for themselves. I want to meet Stuart because he's currently in the studio with Linda Gail Lewis, Jerry Lee Lewis's sister. I'm laying on a bed in a Holiday Inn on the outskirts of Nashville and I phone him to make a date.

'Can we meet up tomorrow, Stuart?'

'Yeah! Where do you want to meet? Is that a real Yorkshire accent?'

'It's the only one I've got. How about Tootsie's Orchid Lounge?'

'Tootsie's! Well, that's my favourite little honky-tonk. How do you know about Tootsie's?'

I tell him that I have been there a couple of times before. I once did an odyssey to the Ryman Auditorium, home of the Grand Ole Opry and Tootsie's is just round the corner.

'That's right. I'll see you there tomorrow. We'll have a beer.'

Tootsie's is a tiny rough old bar with a stage as big as a beer towel. The walls are covered with sepia-toned photographs that are a hall of fame of everybody who ever sang country music. It's difficult to tell whether the sepia tones are a result of the photographic printing process or nicotine stains engrained over the years. They look as though the walls are built to take them and their faux gilded frames. I order a Coors or something and sit at a little table overlooking the street. Across the way I see a cowboy in full outfit waiting for the pedestrian light to turn green. He's wearing black jeans, Cuban-heeled boots with silver tips on the toes, a leather waistcoat and a black Stetson. He walks with a bow-legged swagger, like the cowboys of my childhood did at the Saturday morning matinee at the Hippodrome on Station Lane, or on *The High Chaparral*. My dad, who liked cowboys would have called him 'Cheyenne Bodie'. My dad called everybody he knew, or in some cases those he didn't know, 'Cheyenne Bodie'. He called the doctor 'Cheyenne Bodie', he called blokes on his allotment site 'Cheyenne Bodie'. The cowboy walks into Ernest Tubbs' record store. I wonder what record he will buy. Then I wonder if Stuart Colman will be a cowboy.

Stuart Colman isn't a cowboy, though he strides through the door with a cowboy cum rock 'n' roll swagger. He tells me that it is his dream to work in Nashville. The best music producers in the world work in Nashville and the best musicians. He says that you can walk into any little honky-tonk in town – he gestures around this one – and pick up a band of the hottest musicians around. He's fixed it for us to do some filming in a studio tomorrow with Linda Gail Lewis. He's also fixed us a table at his favourite pasta restaurant.

On the beer-towel stage a lean Tennessean is going through a repertoire of staple country songs. I offer to put twenty dollars into his tips jar if he will sing us a sad song. He tells me that for twenty dollars he will sing me the saddest song in the world. What would I like?

'Do you know "Lonesome Me"?'

'That ain't a sad song!'

He takes a swig from his bottle and proceeds to play the old Hank Williams song 'I'm So Lonesome I Could Cry'. Everybody in the bar stops talking to listen. The woman behind the bar stops serving and places her elbows on the bar, chin cupped in her hands. It's a piece of theatre I'm sure, but it fetches a tear to my eye. It makes me miss my children so much that I will spend half an hour on a transatlantic phone call as soon as I get near a phone. It makes me miss my childhood. He finishes the song, looks over at our table and says, 'Now that's a sad song!'

Either because of or in spite of his yodelling, Hank Williams was the most poignant of all country singers. He was a pill-popping drunk who regularly fell off the stage in a stupor. He was banned by the Grand Ole Opry who, in the 1940s, wouldn't even let him sing the word 'beer'. On New Year's Day in 1953 he had a big booking in Canton, Ohio. He was to fly from Alabama, but a blizzard grounded his plane. He hired a teenage taxi driver to chauffeur his Cadillac. Posters for that show were all over town with the strapline, 'If the good Lord's willing and the creek don't rise, I'll see you at the Memorial Auditorium, Canton, Ohio, New Year's Day, 1953'. Hank Williams climbed into the back of the Cadillac nursing a bottle of whiskey. Somewhere on the road his driver was pulled for speeding. The highway patrol officer remarked to the young driver that 'the guy in the back looks as though he's dead'. Some hours further on up the road the driver went to shake Hank Williams awake and found that the policeman had been right. Hank was just twenty-nine years old. Robert Johnson having already sold his soul made it to twenty-seven. Jimi Hendrix was also that age when Monika Danneman couldn't rouse him on the day of what could have been Hank Williams' forty-seventh birthday. Janis Joplin took her last dose of heroin at twenty-seven as well.

We drink our beer off and head for the pasta restaurant. The singer in Tootsie's has moved on to another Hank Williams song 'Long Gone Lonesome Blues'. From the walls the frozen images of young country singers stare at us as we walk out the door; Willie Nelson, Kris Kristofferson, Jimmy Rodgers, Loretta Lynn.

The cowboy I spotted earlier comes out of Ernest Tubbs', waits again at the pedestrian light and then heads for the open door at Tootsie's.

In the restaurant Stuart Colman talks about the times he worked with Shakin' Stevens and a band called Pinkerton's Assorted Colours. I only half-listen. I'm replaying in my mind something that happened in Wakefield Prison some years before when making the Jailhouse Opera. The day before dress rehearsal, there was a murder in the prison. One of the inmates on a wing not connected to our project kills another in his cell. The Governor, after advice, decides to let our project run. On the day of the performance, one of the soloists, let's call him Gary, decided that he didn't want to perform his song accompanied by his own guitar that he'd been trying to perfect all week. He says his fingers don't work any more. With encouragement from Ray Hough, Stephen Langridge and me he gave it a go. He played a slightly out of tune guitar to the Kris Kristofferson song made famous by Janis Joplin 'Me and Bobby McGee'. It is the last song he learned before coming into prison. The song that seemed to have kept him going for the nearly twenty years he'd been inside. The refrain 'Freedom's just another word for nothing left to lose' never sounded any sadder. I cried at the end of that performance. When I got home I took out my Kris Kristofferson *Greatest Hits* and played that song about fifteen times one after the other.

In the pasta restaurant I can feel gooseflesh on my arms. I shudder as images of my children, of Gary trying to make his fingers work, of the singer in Tootsie's swirl around on my plate.

Next morning in the studio the drummer is preparing to tune in. He repeatedly hits the bass drum pedal. 'Bap...Bap...Bap...Bap.' Stuart explains that the band he's chosen to work with Linda Gail Lewis are the quickest he's ever seen. They can tune up an entire studio in an hour. Linda Gail arrives. She shakes my hand, 'Well hi to you too, honey!' I say nothing more than, 'Hello Linda, it's nice to meet you,' when she asks, 'Where y'all from?' She has an outrageous Louisianan drawl.

'Yorkshire.'

'Is that near Leeds?'

'Yes, Leeds is in Yorkshire.'

'Yeah! I know. I bin there a few times. I was on Yorkshire Television one time with that laydee Christa Ackroyd.'

I laugh, quite loudly. Linda gives me a look that says, 'What the hell you laughing at?' I have to apologise and tell her that this image I have in my mind of a rock 'n' roll singer from Louisiana standing in a recording studio in Nashville talking about a regional news programme in Yorkshire is a very humorous and surreal one.

Linda takes to the piano and plays some big rolling boogie. She has a song about two trailer-park lovers who win the lottery and take off across America in a Cadillac that she wants to record. The piano breaks in it are superb. I'm convinced that I'm witnessing the making of a worldwide smash hit record. Stuart is more cautious. He tells me that the Nashville establishment are not too keen on piano-driven stuff, much preferring the guitar sounds. He has to find a way of toning down Linda's piano without upsetting her. Meanwhile Linda is banging away with these great rolling chords. In the break I interview Linda for the telly.

'You've got a very strong Louisiana accent.'

'I guess that's right, honey.'

'How does a man from northern England capture that southern states sound?'

'Well, I don't know, honey, I guess you'd have to ask him that!'

She's already fed up with talking and wants to get back to the piano.

'Now you boys, don't forget to come see me when I come back to Yorkshire, y'awl.'

Some time later I hear the final mix of Linda's lottery winners song. The piano is right back in the mix. Not the song I'd been tapping my feet and clapping my hands to at all. Later still Linda Gail Lewis has a fling with Van Morrison and they release a CD called *You Win Again*. On the cover is Van in black Stetson, black shades and a spotted 'kerchief knotted round his ample neck. Linda is leaning towards him with a lovely Louisiana smile on her face. The record is not that good, despite Jools Holland's drooling liner notes, the songs are mainly perfunctory boogies and rock 'n' roll, two big stars going through the motions. There is on it, however, a cracking version of the old Hank Williams song 'Why Don't You Love Me Like You Used to Do?', complete with lots of keening steel guitar.

Linda later told a Sunday newspaper that Van was a considerate lover.

Spinal Tap Room

I have read a story that Ken Kesey likes to tell about the time Allen Ginsberg joined the Merry Pranksters bus trip. This was the psychedelic bus that said 'Further' on its destination board. Everybody was out of their heads on beer or acid and the driver Neal Cassady kicked a broken bottle out of the open bus door. Ginsberg shouted 'Stop the bus!' He then climbed down with a dustpan and brush and started to sweep up the broken glass.

The artist Erika Rushton, who lived in Toxteth, told me that during the riots a family of neighbours looted the local supermarket. When they got to the chilled cabinets they took Blue Band margarine instead of the Lurpak best butter that was next to it. Old habits are hard to break.

Alice Nutter told me that when Chumbawamba were touring the world off the back of 'Tubthumping' they never trashed hotel rooms, because they knew a chambermaid on minimum wage would have to clean up after them.

The only thing I have ever thrown out of a hotel window is a cigarette end, but I suppose I have had my share of rock 'n' roll moments. Along with Fuff, Kevin Reynolds and Les Ponsonby I once threatened to throw an American Marine over the balcony in B. B. King's nightclub on Beale Street in Memphis. We were sat enjoying the band when pieces of ice thrown out of a champagne bucket above started hitting us.

Fuff, followed by me and Les, made nothing more to do than race upstairs to challenge the pissed up gang who were doing it. They turned out to be Marines on leave. Fuff grabbed the first one by the scruff and shouted, 'Tha better stop throwing stuff old cock, else t'next thing ower that balcony is thee!' Whether it was the shock of the aggression or the indecipherable Yorkshire accent that did it we'll never know. The American Marines stopped doing it and even went as far as apologising for their behaviour. Kevin tells me that when we ran upstairs he got talking to some musicians on the next table. They were members of Dire Straits and the Steve Miller Band. He said one of the Dire Straits lads had said, 'Three drunken Yorkshiremen and a gang of Marines, we'd better move, it will be raining Marines any minute now.'

I live for a short while in my late teens on a terraced row called Reams Terrace in Pontefract. It is a two-up, two-down house with an outside lavatory and a cold tap that constantly drips onto the pots and tea leaves in the sink. There is no bathroom. The four of us who live here take weekly baths at friends' houses and pay a shared rent of about eighty pence a week each. Dale whose name is on the rent book is the loveliest of men. He teaches us a lot about sharing, humanity, Loudon Wainwright III and Van Morrison. A dusty, finger-marked copy of *Astral Weeks* stays firmly placed on the record player. A player that long since lost its perspex cover.

Sharing the house with us is Dave who sneaks *Astral Weeks* off the record player every time Dale goes shopping and puts either Lynyrd Skynyrd or *War of the Worlds* on. Dave declares that these two along with Rick Wakeman's LP *The Six Wives of Henry VIII*, an LP that mysteriously melted into a plant pot holder, are the way forward for music. This at a time when The Clash are singing about White Riots and X-Ray Spex are bawling 'Oh Bondage, Up Yours!'. Little Joan, the fourth member of our household, likes Melanie, Joan Baez and patchouli oil. In the summer of 1979 she took herself off to Europe. I last came across her in Syntagma Square market in Athens when somebody stole my sleeping bag and I bought a very cheap and very tacky second-hand one at a stall. Much to my surprise when I pulled my drachma out of my pocket it was Little Joan's little hand that whipped the money out of mine and into her purse.

A guilt trip that I carry from the time at Reams Terrace to this day hit me one Saturday teatime. Dale had spent all afternoon preparing a Chinese meal in the kitchen with the dripping tap. Dale had insisted that we should all be home to eat at no later than five o'clock and that we shouldn't be too pissed. We rolled in at six, worse for wear. I'll never remember what started the row, I just recall the fallout. From a cross-legged sitting position in the little front room we were all calling each other arseholes while pushing noodles and sweet and sour sauce about our plates. I can hardly bring myself to say it but I launched my plateful of food into the air. Real time hung in the air. The food described a perfect slow motion arc just missing the old-fashioned glass lampshade and landed smack on the turntable, food first. Van Morrison had just started the second verse of 'Madame George', Dale's nine minutes, twenty-five seconds of bliss. As the noodles kicked in the stylus jumped to 'The Way Young

Lovers Do' and then to 'Slim Slow Slider' by way of 'Ballerina' before coming to rest on the Warner Brothers label.

'You horrible…wicked…cruel…'

Nearly thirty years on I still feel horrible…wicked…cruel every time I hear 'Madame George', every time *Astral Weeks* is voted the best LP of all time, every time someone asks if Little Joan is still in Greece, every time I see Dale planting sweet williams on his allotment opposite mine, every time I see myself in a pattern of tea leaves in a sink.

I spend my twenty-first birthday in the Marisco Disco, in Woolacombe Bay, North Devon. It is the sort of place that plays Baccara's song 'Yes Sir I Can Boogie', a Devon version of a working men's club for surfers, hotel workers and holidaymakers. Someone has given me a bottle of gin and I'm halfway down it. I lurch up to the DJ and shout, 'Would you mind playing "Honky Tonk Woman"?'

'What!'

'Would you mind playing "Honky Tonk Woman"?'

'It'll take me ages to find it! Will "Wig Wam Bam" by Sweet do?'

'No I want the Stones. I'm twenty-one today.'

'Ladies and gentlemen, we have a twenty-first birthday boy here tonight, can we all sing "Happy Birthday". Rock on!'

'Twat!'

'If I find it will you do a striptease?'

'Aye. Go on then.'

I have another swig out of my bottle. Keith Richards' guitar intro kicks in. 'I met a gin-soakèd barroom queen in Memphis…'

I have another swig and struggle out of my shirt. I then kick off my cowboy boots and start to loosen my belt. I must have looked a right closet. Some chambermaids from the Narracott Grand Hotel start to clap their hands in time to the music and shout, 'Gerrum off, gerrum off.' I throw my belt into the crowd and then take down my jeans and flick them off the end of my foot. I'm not wearing pants. The realisation that I'm standing in the middle of a disco dance floor, naked apart from a pair of odd socks and a gin bottle, hits me. The chambermaids are still clapping and laughing now. The song finishes. The DJ hasn't cued up the next record and I'm still standing there. I don't know where to put myself. Candi Staton launches into 'Young Hearts Run Free'. People start dancing again. I start to crawl between the legs of dancers looking for my jeans and shirt. I never did find my belt.

I'm commissioned to make a documentary film in Belarus. I buy the 'Lonely Planet' guide a few days before I set off. The guidebook advises visitors to take care when eating food that comes from the southern area of the country that has been affected by the fallout from Chernobyl. And strictly forbidden are mushrooms. What the book doesn't tell you is that Belarusians love mushrooms like the Russians love their beetroot and the first thing you'll be offered when you go to someone's house is a plateful of mushrooms. The other thing that the guidebook says is that Belarus is like the piece of forgotten and festering cheese at the back of your fridge. You know that it's there, but you don't really want to go near it.

We want to film a charity worker taking aid to an orphanage near Minsk. The charity people drive over via Poland in an articulated lorry full of new beds and plumbing equipment. We fly in an old Russian aeroplane with formica fold-down tables. The customs take a look at our television equipment and demand twenty thousand dollars as insurance. I approach the chief customs fella and ask, 'Will two hundred Benson and Hedges do?' He waves us through.

Our guide and taxi driver for the week we'll be spending there is called Kyril. He's an ex-army paratrooper built like a brick shit-house. He likes heavy metal and sings 'Smoke on the Water' constantly. For reasons best known to himself, he also likes Smokie and knows most of the words to 'Living Next Door to Alice'. After three days of driving round the Belarusian countryside with Iron Maiden, Saxon, Whitesnake and Deep Purple blasting us, I start to sing George Formby songs.

'She's sixty-six but she looks sixteen
Her friends don't know her
Now her face is clean, she's
Fanlight Fanny, the frowsy nightclub Queen!'

'What a fuck is this?' says Kyril in a thick Eastern European accent.

'George Formby, mate. Haven't you come across him?'

'No. Fuck 'im.'

'Well, he's massive in England at the moment.'

'Fuck you. You pulling my legs! No?'

'No. It's true, Kyril. Big star.'

'I am not fucking believing you. You take a piss of me!'

I laugh and offer him a roll-up.

'Hey Ian! You know who sit in your seat in thees car last week?'

'No.'

'Suzi fucking Quatro!'

'Really?'

Kyril starts to sing, 'When she was sweet sixteen, she was a jukebox queen...'

We join in, 'Down in Devil Gate Drive!'

'Hey! You know it. And do you know I have David Coverdale in this car too. And Lemmy. You know Lemmy?'

'From Motorhead?'

'It is right. Fucking good pisser. He did two bottle vodka every day.'

The orphanage was a tough place to work in. The journeys with Kyril and his heavy metal tapes and stories were a joy. Talk about laughing in the face of adversity.

When I travel in Bill Covington's car he tells his drummer jokes.

'How do you know there's a drummer at your front door?'

'I don't know, Bill,' I lie, 'how do you know there's a drummer at your front door?'

'Knocking gets faster!' He laughs. I laugh. He's told that joke to me fifty times, but we still laugh.

'Famous jazz drummer Buddy Rich gets rushed into hospital. The nurse says, "Are you allergic to anything Mr Rich?" Buddy Rich says, "Only..."'

'Country and Western music!'

'Oh! You've heard it then!'

I don't pick and choose within the different genres of music, I can listen to country just as easy as jazz, blues the same as folk. As Louis Armstrong probably never said, 'All music is folk music, you never heard a horse singing.' I do struggle with the outer limits of the techno scene. I once found myself in the Tresor club in East Berlin. I had gone there to interview a lighting engineer from Bradford called Richard. The Tresor was a labyrinthine cellar, once a rich people's department store where the well-heeled of Berlin stored their wealth in a thousand deposit boxes. During the time of the East German Socialist Republic it had fallen into disrepair. After the Berlin Wall came down the fronts of the deposit boxes were ripped off and now the owners of the techno club had lit candles in them. The music they played in there was the sort you could sandblast your house with. Never have I been as pleased to reach the sanctuary of a fire escape and light up a cig.

Heavy metal I struggle with as well. Alright I have got Led Zep, some MC5 and an Iron Butterfly album lurking on the shelves, but the new wave of heavy metal that struck in the early eighties passed me by.

Strange then that I should befriend one of the great torch bearers of that movement, Graham Oliver, lead guitarist with Saxon, the ultimate new wave of British heavy metal band, or as the aficionados would have it, NWOBHM. Graham is a lovely guy whose main hobby is collecting fine chinaware from Yorkshire's ancient potteries. Graham tells great stories about the extremes of heavy metal life in an accent as broad as mine. Graham lives in Mexborough, a classic South Yorkshire working-class town. He comes to my house to sup Earl Grey tea.

'Do you know, Ian, there was a reight fish and chip shop in Mexboro' in the early seventies. They called it The Hippy Chippy, it was run by a gang of hippies. They burnt incense on top of the frying pans and talked abaht the Guru Maharaji Jai. Hazel O'Connor was one of 'em.'

'What her who had a hit with "Breaking Glass"?'

'Aye and do you know, the week she was in the charts with that, Saxon were on *Top of the Pops* with "Never Surrender" and Tony Capstick was on with that song he did about "The Sheffield Grinder". What's the chances of that? Three acts from one little town all on *Top of the Pops* together. Well Hazel O'Connor wasn't from round here, but she did live at The Hippy Chippy.'

Graham has a great story about Saxon's bass player, Paul 'Fasker' Johnson. Fasker replaced the original Saxon bass player after he dropped out following a world tour.

The band had gone to Hilversum Studios in Holland to record a new album called *Rock the Nations*. Saxon were recording in Studio A and in Studio B was Elton John. Saxon were using a stand-in bass player, but were getting nowhere fast. Someone mentioned that there was a really good bass player who lived near Doncaster. The band flew home for a break and Graham said to 'Biff' Byford, Saxon's flamboyant lead singer, that they ought to try and find the bass player.

'We drove to Ackworth where he lived and knocked on his door. His dad answered and said, "He's not in, lads, he's working in a tyre fitting garage at Featherstone".'

Graham and Biff drove over to Featherstone and when they found the tyre place Fasker was sitting in the back playing his bass guitar.

'We asked him straight out if he'd like to come and join us in the Hilversum Studios. He said, "What wi' Saxon?" We said, Aye!'

Within a few days Fasker had gone over to Liverpool for a passport and a day or two after that he was jamming in a studio next door to Elton John. It was the first time he had been out of the country.

Saxon were working on a piece called 'Party 'Til You Puke'. Elton John walked past the door and said, 'I think it would sound better with a bit of honky-tonk piano on it.' Next thing Elton ordered his roadies to wheel a grand piano from Studio B to Studio A and started jamming with Saxon. He was doing runs like he was on *Yellow Brick Road*. Fasker couldn't get over it. A week before that he had been fitting tyres in Featherstone, now he was jamming with Elton John.

At the time Elton John was having sausage and bacon flown over every day from Fortnum and Mason and he had two cars parked outside the studio because he couldn't decide which one to go back to his hotel in. One was a Bentley, the other an Aston Martin. Fasker said, 'By fucking hell. Tyres on them'll be five hundred pound apiece.'

After that Fasker did two world tours with Saxon. On the first of these tours they were met at LAX Airport in Los Angeles by the American tour managers. Everybody piled on to the tour bus for the forty-mile drive down to Annaheim where the first gig was to take place. The manager leaned over the seat and said, 'Welcome boys. Anything you need before we're all set?' Fasker piped up. 'Aye! I'm fucking famished. Can tha stop at a chip 'oil on t'way!' The tour manager wanted to know if Fasker was speaking English.

Graham is in his fifties now, but still has a penchant for long hair and denim jackets. I ask him if it's true that a lot of the *Spinal Tap* film is based on the antics of Saxon on tour.

'That film makes me shudder,' he says. 'A lot of what you see in that is stuff that I've done. In 1984 Harry Shearer who plays the bass player in the film with the moustache, phoned our management up and asked if he and some scriptwriters could spend some time with Saxon. Three of 'em came and met us at the Birmingham Odeon. Then they went on the tour bus with us every day. I just told them stories about things that had happened to us. Like at Mexborough Grammar School when we were in a band called Son of a Bitch. We always liked to put on a show so we had a dry ice machine with a kettle element in it and a smoke machine that stunk. We were doing a song called "Motorcycle Man" and I ran out on the stage, slipped on some water out of the dry ice machine and fell flat on my arse. The roadies picked me up and I carried on playing. You can see that in the film. That really happened at Mexborough Grammar School, but when anybody asks me these days I tell them that it was at t'Hammersmith Odeon. The guy who picked me up at that gig is called Robbie Price. He's got the top job with Iron Maiden now. He's from Barnsley.'

There's a bit in the *Spinal Tap* film where the band come down onto the stage in a giant pod and they can't get out. Graham claims that this really happened to Bill Nelson of Be Bop Deluxe. Be Bop Deluxe once played at the King's

School in Pontefract. In fact it was the week after Roy Herrington walked on stage with his woodcutter's axe. Graham also recalls the scene in the film where the band get lost under the stage and can't find their way out. 'That actually happened an' all.' He tells how Ozzy Osborne got lost backstage when he was with 'Blizzard of Oz'. 'Imagine that! It seems daft to think now that Ozzy Osborne was once support act for Saxon!'

I ask Graham if he ever heard about the time Jimi Hendrix played Ilkley. He tells me that he once visited Hendrix's dad in Seattle. 'His grandma was upstairs laid on a couch an' all. She was one hundred years old at the time, a full blooded Cherokee Indian. His dad was a right character. I said to him that for Jimi to have all that musical talent he must have got it from somewhere. Jimi's dad said, "I'm musical myself." I said to him, "What do you play?" He said, "The spoons." Can you imagine that? Jimi Hendrix's dad playing the fucking spoons!'

Graham sips some more tea. 'You can always tell it's Twinings. Their Earl Grey is the best there is.' He then takes out of his Farmfoods carrier bag a book about fine Yorkshire pottery. 'Here have a look at this. There's some bloody lovely stuff in here.'

I have a photograph in an old shoebox taken on May Day 1984. The photo features a little sparrow of a fella with a brushy moustache sitting at a Yamaha electric piano, his fingers hovering over the keys. This little sparrow fella is called Janos Szel, he is a friend of Jürgen and Völker who once studied theology at Wuppertal University. Now he is

Pastor at the United Reformed Church of Hungary in Budapest. At Christmas time Janos and Jürgen exchange Christmas cards and phone calls. Jürgen must have joked about what Janos wanted for Christmas and Janos said a Yamaha electric piano. His old pump harmonium in the church had given in after the mice ate the bellows. Jürgen's task was then to work out a way of smuggling an electric piano into Hungary which in those years was still behind an unmelted iron curtain. Four of us decide to make the journey. Jürgen, Völker, Peter from Hamburg who'd once played in the skiffle band, and me. We travel in Jürgen's Ford Ankara. In the boot inside two rucksacks under a case is the electric organ. We decide to cross the border on May Day in the belief that everybody will be either marching up and down or pissed up.

It's a long way down from Wuppertal to Budapest. We break the journey at Stuttgart where we crack open a small barrel of ale at Jürgen's cousin's house. Jürgen's cousin collects owls. I have never seen as many toy owls, pot owls, owl cushion covers and owl tea towels in my life. Halfway down the barrel we do our party pieces. Völker plays the old Little Walter hit 'Juke' on his Hohner harmonica. Peter and Jürgen sing a dreadful version of the old skiffle song 'Paddy Works on the Railway'. I am torn between my corncrake version of 'House of the Rising Sun' and the Cliff Richard number 'Travelling Light'. Inspired by the pot owls I recite 'The Owl and the Pussycat'. Jürgen's cousin is delighted and makes me write it down on a piece of perfumed purple notepaper. She then clips the handwritten note with an owl-shaped alligator clip and fixes it to the kitchen wall.

We continue through Bavaria tanked up on beer heading for the Austrian border. Völker tells his story about Hamish Imlach and the world's greatest fart. Jürgen tells a story about a woman he once saw shitting in a square in Cologne. 'She just lifted up her skirts and shit right in front of the cathedral.' Peter said that he'd seen lots of people shitting on the roadside in Peru.

At the customs between Austria and Hungary we are sober in the light of a morning after a night before. The customs official takes a close look at us and compares our dishevelled appearance to our passport photos. Once in Berlin I had been refused entry to the east because I had a beard but a clean-shaven face on my photo. A clean-shaven face and a Tom Robinson badge. Ever since then I have been paranoid about customs. In Miami, Florida I was asked if I'd flown from Britain to cover the Versace murder. I said, 'Do I look like a man who wanted to write about the Versace murder?' The customs man glared at me. In Pakistan I had a gun pointed at me when I stupidly told the customs I was a writer when it said 'Engineering worker' on my passport.

The Hungarian official waved us through. The electric piano undisturbed. On a cliff top a huge stone eagle peered down at us. In the first town we swerved to avoid some people marching behind a band. Völker wound down the window and shouted, 'Rock and Roll!'

Janos is delighted with his Yamaha electric piano. The photograph taken at the very moment it is plugged in shows it. As a gift in return he takes us to his favourite restaurant. The 'Sipos' is a very traditional Hungarian fish restaurant with really good gypsy musicians playing fiddles and cymbals. We gorge ourselves on carp soup sprinkled with paprika and bottle upon bottle of Bull's Blood wine.

On the way back to Janos's flat Völker says, 'Which side of the Danube are we on? The Buda side or the Pest side?'

Jürgen says, quick as a flash, 'We're all on the pissed side!'

We breakfast on sardine paste on toast and black tea at a little café near a Turkish baths.

A postman with a bag full of letters is already drinking plum brandy. He jabbers away in Hungarian. Roughly translated he is saying, 'I fuck you plums in the arse!' When he realises I am English we have one of those conversations that go:

'Manchester United.'

'Ferenc Puskas!'

'Bobby Charlton!'

'Videoton!'

'Nobby Stee – les! Georgie Best!'

Through Janos, the postman then tells us that if the people don't receive their letters today they'll be very pleased to receive them tomorrow.

Back on the telly I am asked to make a short film with George Evelyn, best known for his Nightmares on Wax record *Smokers Delight*. It's the ultimate late-night chill-out album, written, according to George, in his head on the way home from various raves as the sun came up. I never went to a rave, too busy drinking in taprooms with old blokes who played fives and threes. I decide to talk to George about the streets in Burley where he grew up. George sits on a swivel chair in his cellar studio, takes a pull on a chillum and announces that he needs to think about it. His co-producer Chris Dawkins tells George that he once saw the film about Jimi Hendrix I made in Ilkley and that they can trust me. I tell Chris that the only other musician Dawkins I know is a bluesman called Jimmy Dawkins. Chris tells me that he thinks Jimmy Dawkins is a distant uncle. We embark on a blues journey from this Leeds basement that takes us to the room where Bessie Smith died. George brings his swivel chair to a stop and says, 'Let's do it then, I'll show you where I painted a cricket wicket on a wall at the end of our back yard.' I read in *The Wire* magazine that Harry Smith, the great collector of outsider music, once knocked on the door of the Carter family home. Instead of asking about their mighty musical legacy he asked where they got their patterns for their quilts from. I suppose what I was doing in Leeds was a distant nephew to what Harry was doing. 'Look Ian, this is the painted-on wicket.' George Evelyn seems genuinely surprised that the wicket is still there. We walked round a red-bricked terrace gable-end corner between some mucky wheelie bins. 'See that house there? That's where some students lived and that's where I first tasted broccoli.' He says this without irony.

I still get young third-generation West Indian kids coming up to me in Leeds and telling me how much they enjoyed the George Evelyn film.

The Hippy Chippy, Suzi Quatro's taxi, Bull's Blood wine, fucking plums in the arse, drunken postmen and George Evelyn's taste of broccoli: rock 'n' roll moments to savour.

For the Record

Collecting and Hoarding

Mrs McMurry to the Arctic Monkeys

The decline of the proper record shop upsets me. When I was twelve the records I bought were a three-pence, five-minute bus ride away. Now that shop sells accessories for girls' hairstyling. A visit to Jumbo in Leeds takes me half a day. In London I stand on the pavement and mourn the passing of Doug Dobell's and Ray's Jazz Shop. The return to King's Cross Station isn't the same since Mole on Gray's Inn Road shut up shop. There is a survivor we must give thanks for. JG Windows in Newcastle has been selling music since it came on sheets and cylinders in 1902. My lad Edward follows Newcastle United. On the days when we see home games at St James' Park my credit card takes a beating at JGs. I also give thanks for Red Lick, a mail order company in North Wales, but apart from that it's the local supermarket and I hate myself for it.

My daughter Billie and me are queuing up at the Tesco check-out for people with ten items or less in their basket. In my basket I have some bananas, a packet of Earl Grey, a copy of the *NME* and an Arctic Monkeys CD. The minimum wage lad behind the counter throws his fringe out of his eyes. 'Is this CD for your daughter then?' Before I have the chance to say anything the lad flicks his fringe again and runs the bar code of the *New Musical Express* through the machine. He grins. I grin back and tell him that my daughter doesn't bother with buying CDs because she's got an iPod. On the bus on the way home me and Billie sit on the back seat with our heads together sharing the little earphones on her iPod. We whisper sing the words of 'Life's a Gas' to each other, 'I wanna love you girl like a planet.'

I know that as I gallop down the back straight towards fifty I am the oldest *NME* reader in town and that I really shouldn't be buying CDs by bands whose average age is nineteen. I can't help it. Who should I blame for my addiction? Let's start with a woman who owned a furniture shop in the Mississippi Delta.

In 1950 this woman called Mrs Lillian McMurry who owned the furniture and hardware shop in Jackson, Mississippi, decided to dip a toe in the waters of music recording. She took a group of young black kids into the WRBC radio station and produced a record. 'Every Word of Jesus is True' by the St Andrew's Gospelaires became the first release on Mrs McMurry's label, Trumpet Records. What Mrs McMurry did was astounding. She was a complete novice to recording, but she also lived in a strictly segregated society. As a twenty-eight-year-old white woman, she wouldn't be expected to go anywhere near the places frequented by black people, let alone work alongside a group of black men making a record. Within a year Mrs McMurry decided she wanted to record the blues singers in the area. With her entrepreneurial spirit she knew there was a ready-made market in the Delta for such music. She met up with the living legend of blues harmonica playing, Sonny Boy Williamson and on 4 January 1951 she recorded a session at the Scott Radio Service that resulted in Trumpet 129,

'Eyesight to the Blind'. Sonny Boy on vocal and harmonica, Willie Love on piano and Elmo James on guitar. Eight months later at the same radio station, Mrs McMurry recorded one of the most famous blues recordings of all time. Elmore James walked into the session with a guitar, a bottleneck, Williamson on harmonica and a bass player called Leonard Ware and cut 'Dust My Broom', a reworking of an old Robert Johnson song. A record of such resonance and renown that nearly sixty years on it still sends shivers down the spines of new young blues fans from Jackson, Mississippi, to Dewsbury, West Yorkshire. It is the song that sets me off in search of the blues, the song that set me off on a path of discovery that has meant I've never had enough money to take driving lessons or own a car.

Of course I know nothing of Lillian McMurry when I start collecting and Elmore James is just a name, like Muddy Waters, John Lee Hooker and B. B. King. It's Fleetwood Mac that kick me off. I buy one of those 'Twofer' records. Two records that didn't sell particularly well to start with and then get put together and re-launched as a 'Twofer'. This one is called 'The Original Fleetwood Mac/English Rose'. It has on it some bloody lovely Peter Green compositions and guitar playing and mighty fine slide work from Jeremy Spencer. I read in the *NME Encyclopaedia of Rock* from 1976 that Jeremy Spencer has an obsession with some Delta blues man called Elmore James and investigate a record that Fleetwood Mac recorded in Chicago with surviving members of Elmo's band, J. T. Brown on saxophone, Otis Spann on piano and Walter 'Shaky' Horton on harmonica. It's got 'Madison Blues' on it as well as 'I Can't Hold Out' and 'I'm Worried', all Elmore compositions.

I find Elmore in the most unusual of circumstances. After a boozy night in the Green Dragon at Pontefract, a gang of us decide to spend part of the summer in Cornwall being hippies or beach bums or something like that. We jump into a Transit van. By the time we get to Tewkesbury the beer and the spirit of freedom that sent us on our way is wearing off. Half the gang decide to hitchhike back home. I think three or four of us carry on. We know a barefooted folk singer and a blacksmith from Pontefract who live in adjoining tumbledown tin miners' cottages. We should get a bed for the weekend.

Tommy Palmer the barefoot folk singer moved down to Cornwall sometime in the early 1970s to sing in the back rooms of pubs. He has the powerful and rasping voice of a musician who has more than paid his dues. He picks at the guitar strings with fingers like a clawhammer. He lives with a beautiful blonde woman called Jackie, who reminds me of Joni Mitchell. They live in this little old tin miner's cottage that is all big cushions, patchwork quilts and roof beams held up by an old tree trunk. Next door lives Kirby, a leather-skinned pirate who shoes horses and makes exquisite metal sculpture from bits of scrap. We all drink too much cider and smoke too much dope. We are there in the year that Jackson Browne releases *Runnin' on Empty*. This LP has on it 'Stay', the old Maurice Williams song. We play it over and over on Kirby's stereo. The sleeve on *Runnin' on Empty* has more spliffs rolled on it than any other record, perhaps with the honourable exception of Iron Butterfly's *In a Gadda da Vida* or Jefferson Airplane's *Bless its Pointed Little Head*. The last two tracks on the record segue into each other. First comes 'The

Load Out' and then 'Stay'. Kirby knows exactly the part in the record where Jackson Browne will say 'People stay...just a little bit longer' and extols everybody to 'sssshh!' and listen at that point.

Me and Wes, a car mechanic with a liking for Little Richard and Jerry Lee Lewis, rent a flat in the market town of Wadebridge that's about as big as a shoebox. We christen it 'The Box'. We never remember to pay the rent and on the fourth occasion of rent memory lapse the landlord changes the locks. Wes puts his size ten straight through the front door and says, 'That's what you do to people who change your locks without permission.' We grab our few clothes and go and live in his van for the rest of the summer. That and the living quarters of various hotels up and down the coast.

One day I find myself back in Wadebridge at the Pannier Market. I have bacon and egg in a greasy spoon and then idly thumb through a cardboard box full of LPs that are all priced at a pound. I stop at one with a black and white photo bled out over the full cover. In the top left-hand corner of the sleeve is the serial number Chess 1537. The words picked out in white from the black jacket of the singer say Elmore James – John Brim – Whose Muddy Shoes. Elmore James stares at the camera, unsure, timid perhaps, he holds across his midriff an electric guitar and wraps the massive fingers of his left hand around the neck of the guitar. Beneath his black jacket he wears a white shirt and paisley patterned tie. He has a white handkerchief stuffed into his top pocket. The sleeve of this record mesmerises me. On the back are the original Elmore songs recorded in Chicago in 1953 and 1960 that I know from Fleetwood Mac versions: 'Talk to Me Baby', 'Madison Blues', 'Dust My Broom'. The sleeve note is by Pete Welding, 'Elmore James…Canton Mississippi…January 18, 1918…one of the most influential and widely imitated post-war blues stylists…powerful deeply emotional singer…rough, propulsive, vigorous guitarist…died of heart attack Chicago May 23, 1963.' I was three and a half when he died, eighteen when I found him, in a cardboard box, in a market. It is the best pound I ever spent, the only quid note I had on me. I love that record, it is the one I would run into my burning house to save. It is the record that first turns me on to real blues music.

Through Elmore James I discover Sonny Boy Williamson, Muddy Waters, Jimmy Reed, B. B. King and T-Bone Walker. Through T-Bone Walker I discover that blues can be jazz. I start collecting jazz. Through jazz I discover sounds from outside the western world. Music from Africa, from Asia and parts of Europe that are not even on the dial of my Bush radio. I move on to folk and realise that what some of the singers from Yorkshire are singing about is not that different from what singers from the Delta are singing about. I don't know how many pieces I have in my collection, thousands perhaps, tens of thousands, it all starts with Elmore James and before that T. Rex and then one day I discover Sainkho Namtchylak.

In Wuppertal we always drank on the Marien Strasse. There was a great late-night bar there called Jetta's. At two o'clock in the morning you could listen in there to The Rolling Stones *Exile on Main Street* album or something by Stan Getz or the

Dutch blues band Cuby and the Blizzards. Völker always asked for John Martyn of course, many's the time we've been living on 'Solid Air' in Jetta's. Jürgen liked Al Jarreau's *Live in Berlin* or Jimmy Reed. I have woken up with my hand round a Black Bottle whisky to sing 'Bright Lights Big City' in that bar more than any other. The other late-night regulars in there were the free jazzers Peter Kowald and Peter Brötzmann, legends on the European free jazz scene. Brötzmann makes the kind of records that set your teeth on edge. They always seemed to be surrounded by beautiful Japanese girls. At the time they were recording with Sainkho Namtchylak, an exotic creature from Tuva who wore a vinyl LP as a hat. I never got to know her then. I came to know her through mail order. A mail order record company called Leo Records, run by a Russian ex-pat who once worked for the World Service called Leo Feigin. Leo specialises in the far out, the avant-garde, the downright left field. Where do you go when you've listened to the blues, to jazz, to folk, to global sounds? Further out of course. My next map out of Featherstone took me to Tuva, an independent province between Siberia and Mongolia. The Tuvans are a nomadic people, herding horses across freezing plains. Their indigenous music is overtone, shamanistic singing. The greatest Tuvan overtone singers make two and even three tones simultaneously. This is seriously astonishing music. The first Sainkho CD I buy is called *Letters*, it is a record based on a number of letters sent between Sainkho from an apartment in Moscow and her dad back home in Tuva. It is like nothing you have ever heard.

Sainkho Namtchylak has a gig at a concert hall in the

University complex at York. She appears alongside a Tuvan rock band called 'Yat Kha'. Me and Jane Hickson, my great friend and director of nearly all the documentaries I've worked on, go to see the gig. We have a pub sandwich and then attend the most extraordinary concert I have ever been to. The whole thing opens with a man called Albert Kuvesin growling the lowest note that any living thing has ever made, before Sainkho dances on like a baby bird to twitter, keen and invite us to let the sun shine. I'm led to believe that most Tuvan songs are about beautiful horses. For all I know they could be about pit ponies being brought up out of the mine for their annual run in the fields.

My personal hit parade spans thirty-odd years of record collecting that has cluttered both my house and my head with furniture that doesn't subscribe to any conventional design plan. If I can think of one record that represents the chaos between house and head it's *Shoulder to Shoulder*, an LP by the South Wales Striking Miners Choir and Test Dept. This record came out during the miners' strike in 1985. There are ten tracks on it. The tracks by Test Dept are heavily industrial noise shock things banged out on dustbins and oil drums, but it's the tracks by the striking miners that interest me most. 'Comrades in Arms' is a piece I learned from Grandad. He heard my record of it just before he died, I made a tape for him and he leapt from his snooker-watching chair with fists clenched to let out a raucous version. 'Take Me Home' is just beautiful. It has this tear inducing refrain that goes:

'I remember the face of my father
As he came back home from the mine
He'd laugh and he'd say, that's one more day
And it's good to feel the sunshine.'

Then there's 'Myfanwy', a song of extraordinary poignancy. I once arranged for Arthur Scargill to come and speak at the Central Working Men's Club in Featherstone. The club was packed. Arthur was due to start speaking at half past seven. By twenty-five past there was no sign of him. I was panicking. If three hundred people didn't get to see Arthur it would be my fault. I went outside for a smoke. In a Jaguar at the other side of the road I spotted Arthur. I went over to the car and knocked. Arthur jumped and wound down the window.

'Are you alright, Mr Scargill?'

'Yes. I'm just psyching myself up. Have you heard this music?'

He turned up the volume on his car cassette player. He had been listening to 'Myfanwy' by the South Wales Striking Miners Choir. I looked at him. In the corner of his eyes tears were glistening. He took out a clean hankie, blew his nose and straightened his tie. He then strode into the club to cheers and applause and spoke for nearly two hours on the lessons learned from the shooting of the Featherstone miners. After he'd gone the concert secretary said, 'He's the best turn we've had at this club in the last five years.'

In the twenty years since the miners' strike, my passion has been for the music of Africa. I started visiting a shop called

Sterns at the back of the Post Office Tower in London in the 1980s. It was a shop that had once sold toasters and hairdryers, but kept a boxful of records for Ghanaians and Nigerians who were feeling homesick. I bought *The Indestructible Beat of Soweto* from there, the original one on the Earthworks label, possibly because I'd heard Andy Kershaw playing Mahlathini songs. The LP has got one of those sleeves that I like to be on view, the sort of sleeve that would never work on a CD cover, because it's about defiance, coolness and dancing and needs all the twelve by twelve inches the LP format offers. I bought Hugh Masekela at Sterns, then Kanda Bongo Man, Alpha Blondy, Thomas Mapfumo, Tabu Ley, Salif Keita, and Bibi Den's Tshibayi who did a great dancing record. Even I can dance to 'The Best Ambience'.

I'm on my way to Germany by train. This journey starts at Victoria Station and goes on rail to the channel ferry and by rail again through Holland to Mönchengladbach. Two African girls are struggling to lift cases from the platform onto the train. I offer to help them. They start to giggle. When I try to lift the cases I realise why they are giggling. 'By hellfire, what have you got in here?' They tell me that they have been to Brixton market to buy yards of material to make dresses. Between us we heave four cases onto the train. The carriages are the old-fashioned ones with compartments. We sit together. Sue is from Mali and Ami is from Gambia. They are married to American GIs based near Saarbrücken. Every now and then they travel over to London to buy dress material, records and food. They have a huge loaf of sweet

Jamaican bread which they break pieces off and share. I have a bag full of apples I've fetched from a tree in North Featherstone allotments. Russets. They tell me that they're the best apples they have ever tasted.

I tell the girls that I like the Kora playing of Jali Musa Jawara. You would have thought that I'd thrown one of their cases onto them. 'How do you know about griot music?'

'Well, I don't know a lot about it. But it seems to me that anything that preserves spoken stories and oral history has to be a good thing and I think that's what these singers do.' Sue and Ami slap each other on the shoulders and say something in Mandinka that would probably translate as 'Innit!'.

'Do you know Les Amazones de Guinée?'

'Yes, I bought one of their records called *Au Cœur de Paris* in a little shop in Keighley.'

'Man o' man.'

'What about Super Rail Band of the Buffet Hôtel de la Gare de Bamako?'

'Yep! I've got one of theirs as well. Mory Kanté and Kanté Manfila played with them! Would you two like a pint of Guinness?'

'Yeah man!'

I leave the girls giggling while I crack open three cans.

Sue starts to tell a story about an old lady in the village where she was born who had the biggest mortar and pestle in West Africa. It's a story passed down over a thousand years. I swap stories about my grandad's family walking to Featherstone to find work in the coal mines. On the boat over to Holland we drink some more Guinness to wash down the Jamaican bread.

Then in the carriage as the train passes through the Dutch countryside we all fall asleep, having told each other too many tales. The Dutch ticket inspector wakes us. Sue and Ami are laying on each other's shoulders, a large bare black foot is parked on my knee. The girls speak in Dutch to the ticket inspector and later in German to the passport controller. They speak in English to me and in Mandinka to one another. Then it hits me. What have two sophisticated West African women got in common with a rough-arsed little fellow from the pit communities of West Yorkshire? Stories. It has to be our abilities to tell stories to each other that cuts across all the stuff that goes on in between.

At Cologne station we have to say our goodbyes. I'm taking my train to Mönchengladbach, they're going on a different one down to Saarbrücken. I buy a Danish pastry apiece for breakfast. They kiss me on the cheeks and I blush all the way to my carriage.

About a fortnight later when I'm back in Featherstone a postcard drops through the letter box. On the front is a very poor view of Saarbrücken. On the back it says, 'We loves ya stories. Sue and Ami.' Now I'm writing this I wish I could find that card. I'd like to write to them to tell of the pleasure that I've had listening to the Congolese singer M'bilia Bel's album *Boya Ye*, a record they recommended.

The music of North Africa I only knew from listening to a badly recorded cassette of the Brian Jones album with the musicians of the Rif Mountains in Morocco. It all changed when I discovered Cheb Khaled. I found him in a cellar restaurant on the Hafen Strasse in Hamburg that did

Lebanese food, not too far from where The Beatles used to hang out. It was a record called *Hada Raykoum*. Then Earthworks released a record called *Rai Rebels* and it had a track on it called 'Ya Loulid'. It's one of the wildest things in my collection. I can't explain how I can draw a map from the Mississippi Delta through the ale houses of West Yorkshire to the bazaars of Algeria, but it's got all those things and more in it. 'Rai' is the music of the seaport of Oran. It's dangerous stuff that you just know is sung by sailors and prostitutes. The modern Rai stuff is incredible. I've graduated from Cheb Khaled to Rachid Taha and Faudel. The three of them did a glorious live CD together in Paris a few years ago. The opening track 'Khalliouni Khalliouni' mixing an Egyptian orchestra with electric guitars and a kicking brass section gets my Sunday morning started any day of the week. It's more rock 'n' roll than anything the Stones have done since *Exile on Main Street*.

What was rock 'n' roll before The Rolling Stones? The books will tell you it was Jackie Brenston and 'Rocket 88' and before that Louis Jordan's 'Jumpin Jive'. And before that my grandad and everybody else's grandad got their thrills in the music hall where true pop music began. When Marie Lloyd sang 'Then you wink the other eye' they all knew exactly what she meant. Not quite Robert Johnson squeezing a lemon 'til the juice runs down his leg, but Blackpool Pier wasn't quite the Mississippi Delta.

In Skegness I meet two identical twin sisters who are in their eighties. One is married to an ancient clown who sits in his armchair smoking Players and puffing on an oxygen mask that is attached to a cylinder that stands on a sack cart next to his armchair. In the days of music hall the twin sisters were a mirror act. An empty gilded frame was placed in the middle of the stage between two drawn black curtains. The sisters would dance either side of the frame, 'mirroring' each other's actions until the music stopped. Then the sister at the back would step through the frame and they'd hold hands and take a bow. The sisters still have the gilded frame in their bungalow, it's in the utility room between a washing machine and an old wardrobe. In the 1930s the sisters appeared on stage with the great Harry Champion.

I know all about Harry Champion. He wore a top hat to sing 'Boiled Beef and Carrots' and 'A Little Bit of Cucumber'. The sort of songs my Auntie Alice sings. How have these ancient songs survived? Why do we still know how to sing along to them? I'm building quite a collection under my bottom shelf. There's 'Lily of Laguna' by Eugene Stratton, 'Down at the Old Bull and Bush' by Florrie Forde and '21 Today' by Jack Pleasants the shy comedian.

Who should I thank for my obsession for collecting records? Lillian McMurry perhaps for recording Elmore James, my Aunt Alice who sang 'I'm Shy Mary Ellen I'm Shy', Margaret Johnson in our corner shop who told of how cool T. Rex were?

Forty Records You Might
Want to Make a Journey to

I went to see Robert Wyatt and Alfreda Benge at their chalet at the seaside. Robert sat with his binoculars watching birds and listening to a cassette tape of his then forthcoming album *Shleep*. There are some lovely pieces on it about birds. A track called 'September 9th' became an inspiration for the soundtrack to the film *Winged Migration*. Before I came home Robert gave me the cassette. I treasure it. Sometimes I think it is the best thing I have ever heard.

Sometimes I think a recording I've got of Max Miller at the Finsbury Park Empire in 1939 is the best thing I have ever heard. Other times it's Keith Richards' guitar intro and the immortal opening lines, 'I met a gin-soaked barroom queen in Memphis.'

Yet again the voice of a Bulgarian woman called Yanka Rupkina on a track called 'The Gathering' from the first *Mysteres des Voix Bulgares* album is a wonder everyone should behold.

I'm coming to the ultimate futility of lists. I think a lot of people like to say 'I'm not a list person' and I'm one of them. It's a bit like saying, 'I don't watch *Coronation Street*', but then we all take a peek now and again. I do though get fed up of the lists that tell me that the best records ever made are by The Beatles, The Beach Boys and Van Morrison. Yes! I own *Rubber Soul*, *Pet Sounds* and *Astral Weeks*, but there are other journeys I need to make, more maps I want to read. For what it's worth here's my list.

Margaret Barry and Michael Gorman
Her Mantle So Green (Topic)

I worked on the building sites alongside gangs of Irish labourers. There was one, known to all and to himself as 'The Delaney'. He ate three fried eggs for his breakfast every morning and sang songs that he had once sung in the pubs of Dublin and London. Irish building site labourers of a certain age will tell you, 'The craic was good in Cricklewood.' The songs he sang were 'The Wild Colonial Boy' and 'The Galway Shawl'. Margaret Barry sings these on this extraordinary record from the 1950s. Her voice is otherworldly. She turns single letters into syllables and her vowels sound like something you would only hear up on the moors.

Ben Webster
Plays Ballads (Membran)

Nobody plays ballads like Ben. 'Willow Weep for Me' and 'Danny Boy' are heartbreaking. I have read that Webster was one of the few players who actually knew the words to songs. Listen to this and you can tell. I first came across him while listening to Billie Holiday records and wondering who that was whispering in the background.

Karen Dalton
So Hard to Tell Who's Gonna Love You the Best (Koch)

One of Dylan's favourite singers, or so he says in his *Chronicles* book. Everything from Jelly Roll Morton's 'Sweet Substitute' to 'It Hurts Me Too'. I read a retrospective in *Mojo* magazine and went out searching on the internet for this record.

T-Bone Walker
Complete Black and White Recordings (Capitol)

Roy Herrington gave me my first T-Bone Walker records in the late 1970s, one was *Very Rare*, the last one he made in 1973 and another recorded live at Montreux a few years earlier. This stuff is from the 1940s and is the business. Smoky jazz runs, vocals about dirty mistreaters. They're all here, 'Stormy Monday', 'T-Bone Shuffle' and 'Long Skirt Baby Blues'.

John Prine
Souvenirs (Oh Boy)

As teenagers we looked up to a man called Ralph who was a few years older than us. He was like a sage, was a film buff, his favourite was *On the Waterfront*, and an all-round expert on counterculture. He got into John Prine after the first couple of albums in 1973 and we followed him. Prine is still working, his latest album contains the line 'When you're feeling your freedom and the world's off your back, there's a cowboy in Texas, starts his own war in Iraq'. But this one features live re-recordings of many of his classic songs, including a wonderful reading of 'Angel From Montgomery'.

Buffy Sainte-Marie
Illuminations (Vanguard)

I bought a Buffy Sainte-Marie record because it was called *She Used To Wanna Be a Ballerina*, probably my favourite album title. Buffy wrote 'Love Lift Us Up Where We Belong' but on *Illuminations* she lifted gentle acoustic folk song into electronic space, amplifying what Dylan had done by plugging in his electric guitar at Newport fourfold.

Jimmy Reed
Essential Boss Man **(Charly)**

Everyone should own a Jimmy Reed record. I bought my first one *Jimmy Live at Carnegie Hall* out of a cardboard box under a trestle table at a jumble sale. Basically everything he did for the Veejay label – and this is a compilation of a lot of that stuff – is worth having. And when you've exhausted that, check the albums he made for the Bluesway label in the late 1960s.

Dwight Yoakham
Guitars, Cadillacs etc. **(Warners)**

I travelled to see the Country Music Festival in Peterborough. Billie Jo Spears sang about 'Blankets on the Ground'. But this fella was the star. I bought this album at that festival. On the cover there is a dedication to Luther Tibbs, a Kentucky coal miner for forty years and the singer's grandpa. Good enough for me.

Really! The Country Blues **(Origin Jazz Library)**

I read about this record in the early 1980s and finally tracked it down twenty years after. It's a bootleg compilation of rare as hen's teeth 78s, in fact it's probably as rare as the original 78s now. I finally found it in the second-hand list at Red Lick records. It contains Skip James' song 'Devil Got My Woman'.

'The woman I love, stole her from my best friend
But he got lucky, stoled her back again.'

Orlando Cachaito Lopez
Cachaito (World Circuit)

Some record labels are so good, you can collect anything they put out. World Circuit is one of these, they never release a duff record. Of course Buena Vista Social Club came out on World Circuit and then came a whole slew of spin-offs from that. Cachaito's is by far the best. He played bass on the Social Club sessions and pushes the experimental buttons on this.

Richard Hawley
Coles Corner (Mute)

I first heard songs from this in the snug of a Sheffield pub called Fagan's. I sat wide-eyed like Oliver Twist while the Artful Dodger himself Richard Hawley sang in that deep brown baritone voice. There are songs here about meeting loved ones outside of a department store and being born under bad signs. What more could you want?

Dusty Springfield
It Begins Again (Mercury)

Listening to old Dusty Springfield singles on a Dansette player still gives me a lot of pleasure. These days everybody rushes to quote *Dusty in Memphis* but the music she made in the middle of the 1970s is just as good.

Loretta Lynn
Golden Greats (MCA)

The original coal miner's daughter. White working-class American songs to sing along to. This includes a song 'Don't Come Home a Drinkin' with Lovin' on Your Mind'. A song that wasn't written about the street I grew up in, but might well have been.

Cheb Khaled
Khaled (Barclay)

My friend Völker bought the cassette version of this from a North African street vendor in Paris. We listened to it all the way from Wuppertal to West Yorkshire while driving in his big Dodge Ram van. The tape was called *Khaled au USA*. When the tape wore out we tracked down the CD. Rai music should have been the next reggae.

Elmore James
The Late Fantastically Great (Ember)

On one of the last Beatles sessions, George Harrison plays a slide guitar blues piece called 'For You Blue'. He says, 'Elmo James has got nothing on this, fellas.' I wondered who Elmo James was, then in a market town in Cornwall I found him. Bottleneck guitar doesn't get any better than this and if you're lucky it's the sort of LP you might still find in a cardboard box in your local Heart Foundation shop.

Norma Waterson
The Very Thought of You (Hannibal)

In the 1960s the Waterson family found incredible traditional English folk songs and breathed new life into them. By the 1990s Norma was the godmother of English song and nominated for the Mercury prize. This CD has incredible versions of popular song by writers as varied as Freddie Mercury, Harold Arlen and Nick Drake.

Ike Quebec
Blue and Sentimental (Blue Note)

When the Blue Note re-issue programme started in the 1980s I decided I would collect as many of the LPs as I could afford. Ike Quebec's *Blue and Sentimental* was one of the first I bought. The title says it all, it's the most beautiful noise that ever came out of the thick end of a tenor sax. Buy this and you'll end up like me, buying everything he ever did.

Manu Chao
Proxima Estacion Esperanza (Virgin)

Punk, politics. Rhumba, beeps, static and whistles from a street urchin who once named an earlier album after the pox you catch from a Dominican prostitute. I once laid on a hotel bed in Marseilles and listened to the track 'Me Gustas Tu' over and over again for about an hour. They call it World Music.

Billie Holiday
Songs for Distingué Lovers (Verve)

There's a debate that is ongoing amongst Lady Dayophiles. Does her best stuff come from the 1930s when she was not long out of her teens, or from the autumn years of the 1950s when her voice sounded like a scorched newspaper? I can take Billie whichever way she comes. This contains a great version of 'One for My Baby (and One More for the Road)'.

Iris DeMent
Infamous Angel (Warners)

I first saw Iris during a session for the BBC's *Late Show*. She sung like my granny about life and living it. It would be easy to think that these songs were recorded at the Grand Ole Opry in the depression years, but it's from 1992.

John Martyn
Church With One Bell (Independiente)
I bought *One World* when it came out in 1976. I have bought most of what he's done since. He has done more celebrated self-penned albums, but this collection of covers takes some beating. He takes Elmore James's 'Sky is Crying' and Portishead's 'Glory Box' somewhere else entirely.

A Century of Song (English Folk Dance & Song Society)
Chumbawamba did an album called *Readymades* and sampled folk song. One of the most successful pieces was sampled from Harry Cox's 'Pretty Ploughboy' with the refrain 'They sent him to the war to be slain'. The original is collected here alongside other examples of traditional song from 1898 to 1998.

Sainkho Namtchylak
Letters (Leo)
Leo Feigin releases far out music from his base in Devon. His mission statement is 'Music for the enquiring mind and passionate heart'. This is the album of songs that deals with letters that Sainkho sent home to her father in Tuva. About as far out as it gets!

Original Soundtrack
Kes (Compsoer John Cameron) (Trunk)

Jarvis Cocker calls this 'Music with its jesses well and truly off'. In many ways it is a soundtrack to growing up in a pit village and trying to fly. Harold McNair's flute soars as Billy takes his papers round and comes to earth when he looks for his bird, realises it's dead and finally buries his dreams.

Anne Briggs
Sing a Song for You (Fledg'ling)

Her version of 'The Recruited Collier' is the one all women folk singers aspire to. She usually sang unaccompanied. On this she is backed by a band.

Chris Farlowe / Roy Herrington
Live in Berlin (Back Yard)

This kicks off with Roy's nine-minute guitar virtuoso piece 'Born in West Yorkshire' and includes Farlowe's gutsy take on 'Stormy Monday'. The best blues album made by a Yorkshireman ever!

Chumbawamba
English Rebel Songs 1381 – 1984 (Mutt)

The history of England is not about kings, queens and politicians. The Chumbas harmonise their way through riots, strikes and acts of subversion. Proper history for the common people.

Archie Shepp / Horace Parlan
Trouble in Mind (Steeplechase)
It's an album of blues standards to play when you're sipping sloe gin or any other alcohol-based nightcap. Shepp's sax fits Parlan's piano like a jigsaw piece. The free jazz bassist Peter Kowald put this on cassette tape for my friend Jürgen, who then taped it on a twin cassette for me. Third generation copy, it still sounds right.

Following Grandfather's Footsteps
A Night in London's Music Halls (Bear Family)
These have to be great songs. How else would we still know them after more than a century? From 'The Spaniard Who Blighted My Life' to 'I Do Like to Be Beside the Seaside'. The very beginnings of pop music.

Bibi Dens Tshibayi
The Best Ambience (Rounder)
Whenever I went to London, Stern's record shop was on my list of places to visit, along with the National Gallery and a pub called The Angel near Shaftesbury Avenue. This was playing in the shop one day. It demands that you get off your arse, buy it and dance.

Kate Rusby
Sleepless (Pure)
Nobody sings like Kate Rusby, the fact that she's from near Barnsley is an added bonus. No wonder they call her, 'The most beautiful voice in the whole of England'.

Hari-Prasad Chaurasia
Hari-Krishna (Navras)
In India I listened over and over to a record by Ravi Shankar and Ali Akhbar Khan recorded live in 1972 for the Apple label. I thought it must be the best album of Indian music until I heard this. 'Janmashtami', the day of the birth of Lord Krishna, is celebrated every year by the classical flautist Chaurasia at a small private concert at his flat in Mumbai. One year they recorded it. Incredible!

Blue Murder
No One Stands Alone (Topic)
I stood at the Cambridge Festival one year lost in my thoughts and listening to this group which comprises The Watersons and Coope, Boyes and Simpson, England's best a cappella singers. When I looked round I realised I wasn't alone. The title track by itself is worth the price of the CD.

The Native Hipsters
Songs to Protest About (MRM)
MRM stands for Mechanically Reclaimed Music. Twenty years ago I was one of a number of people who lent William Wilding, a native hipster, twenty quid in order to finance an album. The album took fifteen years to come out, this second CD of theirs was paid for from the proceeds of the first. Cut-and-paste subversion of the highest order!

Harry Smith's Anthology Of American Folk Music
Volume 4 (Revenant)

The touchstone of American Depression years history. The history that not a lot of people know about.

Culture
Two Sevens Clash (Lightning)

Two albums stood in the way of punk's dominance in the 1970s. Fleetwood Mac's *Rumours* was the best known one, this was the reggae one. It got played regularly between sets by the likes of Slaughter and the Dogs and Sham 69 at Doncaster's Outlook Club. It still gets played nearly thirty years on at our house. The two sevens refer to 1977.

South Wales Striking Miners Choir / Test Dept
Shoulder to Shoulder (Some Bizarre)

A long time before Blair claimed he would stand shoulder to shoulder with Bush, industrial percussionists Test Dept did it for real with miners in South Wales during the strike of 1984/85. Half this album is noise, the other half beautiful choir singing. 'Comrades In Arms' indeed!

Fairport Convention
Unhalfbricking (Island)

When people tell me they want a New Orleans band to play at their funeral I tell them there are two songs I want playing at mine. The first is 'Rocking All Over the World' by Status Quo and the second is Sandy Denny singing 'Who Knows Where the Time Goes'. It's on this record, as is Dylan's 'If You Gotta Go (Go Now)' sung in French. How cool is that?

Jah Wobble and the Invaders of the Heart
Rising Above Bedlam (Oval)

I saw Jah Wobble alongside Martyn Bennett live at the Coin Street Festival on London's South Bank. Martyn Bennett was fusing Harry Lauder songs onto hardcore dance music. Years before this Wobble was working on his own fusions, this combines Arabic percussion, a horn section organised by Annie Whitehead and Sinead O'Connor's vocals.

Paul Pena
Genghis Blues (Six Degrees)

An extraordinary soundtrack to an even more extraordinary documentary film. I first heard the blind bluesman Paul Pena playing behind T-Bone Walker on the Montreux live album. This is a record of the journey he made to sing at the Tuvan throat-singing competition. It includes 'Gonna Move', a song from a previous and neglected album called *New Train*, and the otherworldly 'Kargyraa Moan' where Charley Patton and Blind Willie Johnson meet Outer Mongolia.

Dust to Download

I suppose I could blame Thomas Edison for my obsession with record collecting. I did a television programme about collecting things. It comprised six five-minute episodes for early evening viewing. The first episode was old comics, there were others on smoking paraphernalia and dolls' houses and the last was old gramophones.

I got a phone call from an elderly man who lived nearby in Wakefield. His name was John Turner and he wanted to invite me to an evening of talks about the hymn 'Onward Christian Soldiers'. He told me that he was giving a presentation about the various recordings of that hymn and that there would be a practical demonstration of the different machines on which these recordings would have been played. At the time I thought that this would be the wackiest meeting of eccentrics you could possibly dream up, so I booked my ticket.

It turned out that Sabine Baring Gould, the man who wrote 'Onward Christian Soldiers' was a vicar in Horbury, a town just ten miles away from where I live. Gould was a folklorist of renown, a writer of over a hundred books and had composed 'Onward Christian Soldiers' as a marching hymn to help tired mill girls to climb a hill between the factories and the town. Gould, a well-educated academic from a prosperous family later married a young mill girl and there were rumours that Bernard Shaw took this as inspiration for *Pygmalion*.

John Turner's presentation was wonderful. It turned out that he was one of this country's foremost collectors of mechanical music players. He showed carillons, gloggomobils, barrel organs and tingalaris. He had organettes, polyphons, symphonions and cylinder players. He played 'Onward Christian Soldiers' on a Victor Monarch gramophone and another recording of it on an Edison Gem player. John was fascinated by anything that made music, he even collected singing mechanical birds in cages.

After that meeting John used to come over to my house and share his knowledge. We listened to homemade cassette tapes of ancient recordings on my state-of-the-art Nakamichi cassette recorder. He was enthralled by the quality of the reproduction.

It was John who told me that in the time when records were cut acoustically with the aid of a diaphragm, Enrico Caruso became the world's earliest recording star. His voice was so powerful that it could clearly be heard above the hisses, crackles and pops. He was also the first singer in the world to realise the commercial as well as the cultural potential of the gramophone player. He probably invented the hobby of record collecting too. His very prestigious Victor Red Seal recordings were collectable even before the term 'collecting' was in common parlance. In those days listeners 'saved' the Red Seals in the same way that schoolboys 'saved' stamps, or vicars with big fishing nets 'saved' butterflies and moths. When Thomas Edison invented his phonograph in 1877 in his laboratory in New Jersey, he envisaged it first as a toy to entertain big families of children; he fastened a little dancing paper man to a diaphragm connected to a tube and spoke the immortal words, 'Mary had a little lamb, its fleece was white as snow'.

After Edison, Emile Berliner comes along and thinks a flat record is better than a cylinder, so invents the gramophone and makes records in his own factory in Frankfurt. He records Caruso and record players are no longer toys. The next stage is to find composers who will write music specifically for the gramophone rather than composers who write for orchestras and then record. The Italian composer, Ruggier Leoncavallo, is the man for the job. He composes 'Mattinata', the first ever piece composed for records. In 1904 in the Hotel Continental in Milan, Caruso sings 'Mattinata' down a horn and a disc is cut on The Gramophone and Typewriter Company label, a forerunner to HMV. This was even before HMV were using the Nipper logo.

To listen to Edison cylinders you need a cylinder player. I can't imagine listening to 'The Jolly Blacksmith', a cylinder I own that was probably cut in the 1890s, on any other type of technology. Just like I must listen to a 78 I own of 'The March of the Gladiators' on my wind-up gramophone, and a reel-to-reel recording of Ike and Tina Turner Live at Olympia recorded from the radio in 1971 on my Akai open reel. I tried transferring Ike and Tina to MiniDisc by hooking up my Sony disc player to the Akai, but it doesn't sound the same.

I think the thing that fascinates me most of all about this old technology is the fact that it allows voices to pass down and talk to us over the years. Alfred Lord Tennyson was born in

1809. He lived in the Lincolnshire Wolds. I once went to a dinner party in these Wolds at a big house called Skendleby Hall. The owner of the house proudly told the gathering that Tennyson had regularly dined at the house before us. I told the lady hostess that I had a recording of Tennyson reading 'The Charge of the Light Brigade'. That poem had originally been written in December 1854 just a few weeks after the battle at Balaclava. In May of 1890, Tennyson who was by then eighty years old and in poor health wheezed into Edison's tinfoil cylinder machine:

'Half a league, half a league,
Half a league onward,
All in the Valley of Death
Rode the six hundred...'

To complement this I also have an amazing recording of Trumpeter Landfrey playing the retreat on his bugle. The very bugle he had played at the Charge of the Light Brigade. I also have a fragment of Florence Nightingale talking. Both of these are on an album by the American psychedelic folk group Pearls Before Swine. In the sixties they did an album called *Balaklava* which I suppose is a response to the Vietnam War, America's Crimea.

The voice recordings I'm most proud of are ones I've been involved in making. In the early 1990s I worked alongside the electronics composer Trevor Wishart on a London Sinfonietta project set up by Gillian Moore in Scunthorpe Baths Hall. We led a workshop for retired people who had no experience with composition or improvisation. I encouraged the participants to tell stories about dreams they had recently had. One lady in her eighties told about a dream she had about finding a vase full of blue tulips in a friend's house. Trevor made a tape recording of the lady telling the story and then took the tape away before spending a day manipulating the voice tape into a piece. The recording found favour on Radio Three and was later released in America on the avant-garde 'Electronic Music Foundation' label.

In the mid 1980s I recorded my gran and grandad telling stories for a Radio Leeds documentary. My gran speaks in a high-pitched squeal of a voice as she tells the story of how she met my grandad on a bus travelling to Tadcaster in 1936. My grandad wheezes with silicosis like a broken harmonium as he recalls hitting pit ponies as a fourteen-year-old frightened boy in his first weeks down the coal mine. 'We had to do it,' he says in a low rumbling tone, 'else we wouldn't be paid. If the ponies didn't work we didn't get paid.'

I have an old Akai 4000 DS open reel player that I treasure. Just now and again I lace up the tapes that I made of my grandad so that Billie and Edward can hear him. 'Oooh! He's got a deep voice,' Edward says every time and deepens his own voice.

I have a cassette recording of a lady called Nellie Alexander, who was over a hundred years old when she made it. On the tape Nellie talks about the day in 1893 which came to be known as the Featherstone Massacre. In the early 1980s when Nellie made the tape she was the last surviving eye-witness. It is like listening to a ghost, the very words she uses could only be spoken by a woman who has lived so long. 'I remember the red coats on the soldiers,' she says at one point.

From the beginning of the 1984 miners strike until four weeks before Edward and Billie are born, Heather and me live in a flat above a shop that sells everything from Domestos to birthday cards. The shop owner only ever stocks cards that are covered in plastic because the card shelves are right under our bath. In the twelve years we are there we overflow the bath three times. Once I do it because I'm on the doorstep arguing with a bailiff who is trying to restrain our goods and chattels because we won't pay the poll tax. Once Heather does it because she's too busy listening to a Mary Chapin Carpenter CD. And once our lodger Elizabeth does it because she's got a boyfriend in Winchester and another one in Castleford and she's too busy thinking about which one to choose to turn bath taps off. Overflowing baths are the least of the shopkeeper's worries. At least once a month Heather and me throw an impromptu party, usually on a Saturday night after the pubs close until four or five in the morning. Whoever is still in the taproom at The Railway pub at chucking out time gets invited and this is usually the full pack of forwards of Featherstone Miners Welfare Amateur Rugby League Club, all one hundred and ten stone of 'em, and some of the backs. Arnold Millard, the only septuagenarian teenager in town sometimes comes, as do Wayne Cooper, who once climbed to the top of St Giles Church with me for a bet, and Florence Bonallie, a black-belt judo woman who likes Chumbawamba. How the one hundred-year-old floorboards stood the strain is something

I'll never know. Especially when the prop forwards, Big Windy and his brother Chris, start dancing to The Style Council and The Special AKA.

Paul Windmill, a.k.a. 'Big Windy', is my best mate at the rugby club. He is the proverbial bull at the gate, he once went head first into the fireplace and destroyed an arrangement of dried flowers just as Paul Weller got to the end of 'Have You Ever Had it Blue'. But Paul is also a big, open-minded man with a keen interest in finding things out beyond the constraints of Colwyn Terrace where he lives.

I'll never forget the day we went to the Proms at the Albert Hall. I had been invited to take part in a few workshops at the Royal Festival Hall with Trevor Wishart, who I had previously collaborated with on 'Blue Tulips'. I was invited down to the Festival Hall to meet with the rest of the team and Big Windy would drive me to London and back in the day. After the meeting, Gill mentioned that she had two spare tickets for the Proms and that if we wanted we could have them and sleep on some futons in her front room afterwards. Windy was up for it so we took the tickets. The highlights of the night were a Tanzanian timbale player and the Ensemble Modern, who were recently back from recording with Frank Zappa on the *Yellow Shark* album. Windy loved the timbale player, a big sweaty chap in an Hawaiian shirt who put his heart and soul into his playing. Then on came the Ensemble Modern. I can't remember the piece they were playing, but it was something like 'Two aliens passing each other on an escalator, each believing the other can't see them'. It was a very modern piece of contemporary composition, the sort of stuff *The Wire* magazine raves about. After the timbale playing it was difficult to penetrate, to digest. Like having ice cream pavlova after potted meat sandwiches. I felt I had to be careful what I said because Gillian's husband Bruce plays trumpet in the Ensemble Modern and I didn't want to upset anybody. In the passageways beneath the Albert Hall we were introduced to the Ensemble and assorted hangers-on. There was a lot of air-kissing going on, Mwaah! Mwaah,! and a lot of 'simply wonderful' and 'how amazing'. Everybody seemed to be giving an opinion on how 'marvellous' it all was. I was asked to say something and I think I said that the Ensemble's piece was 'interesting and thought-provoking'. When Windy was asked he said, 'I'm sorry to say this love, but I thought it was fucking shite.' After the briefest of pauses everybody carried on kissing and missing. Later back at Gill's we rolled out the futons and laid down. Gill popped her head round the door to say 'Goodnight' and when she'd gone Windy and me let out very loud harmonising farts. 'By fucking hell, I've been saving that up all night,' said Windy.

'What for?'

'Well, you've got to show your manners when you're in polite company!'

As we drifted off to sleep I told Windy about the time Harrison Birtwhistle composed a piece for the Grimethorpe Brass Band, when it was being conducted by Elgar Howarth. This too was a very spiky modern piece, which the musicians brilliantly sight-read straight from a freshly presented manuscript. When asked what they thought to it, the cornet player stood up and said, 'Well, it's alright that, cock, but it'll be better when t'tunes on t'top.'

At parties in the flat above the shop we always have a section of the evening devoted to the Grimethorpe Brass Band, usually to their versions of the 'William Tell Overture' and 'MacArthur Park'. As one big rugby player once said to me whilst rocking back and forward in my Auntie Alice's rocking chair, 'It's our fucking culture i'nt it?'

I'm not sure you can make an argument for 'MacArthur Park' being 'our' culture, or Dionne Warwick singing 'Walk on By', or Johnny Allen doing a Cajun version of 'Promised Land', or Robert Wyatt's 'I'm a Believer', or The Foundations singing 'Build Me Up Buttercup', or any of the other stuff that we played at them parties. But we had a house-wrecking old time. I'm put in mind of the house rent parties they had in the Delta towns, when they boogied 'til dawn and the walls of the houses collapsed like in the Buster Keaton movie. We broke a few pots, but the floor never did go through.

The flat was full of second-hand furniture, mostly donated by relatives, and expensive hi-fi and record playing equipment that was my pride and joy. I don't know what it is about record shops and hi-fi shops that makes me lash out money like there's no tomorrow. In a record shop in Prague once I wanted to buy a CD of The Plastic People of the Universe, they were the great underground band of the dark days before the velvet revolution. I'd only previously read about them and knew nothing about what their music really sounded like. The shop owner held up a Plastic People of the Universe box set and said, 'Complet!' It was over a hundred quid or something. I was tempted. Why would I want to spend a hundred quid on a box set of a band I didn't really know? I had to go outside and walk round St Wenceslas Square twice before telling myself 'No'. I ended up buying a compilation, which I have played twice.

My first record player was a Decca. Decca's version of the Dansette, with a blue and cream vinyl covering. It even smelt like a record player should. When it finally broke down and got replaced with a Bush one it was thrown out. I mourned its passing so much I went out in later years to buy a Dansette in the same colours, just so that I could stand it on the record cabinet that we'd had at home that I still keep Peter Sarstedt and Mungo Jerry in. Dansettes are the finest machines in the world yet invented for the playing of Dusty Springfield records.

I always wanted a gramophone player with a horn. Why? I suppose for the same reason I nearly bought a Plastic People of the Universe box set. There's no great logic behind it, but for some unknown reason, I think I ought to own one. I found a beautiful HMV machine with a tin morning glory horn in a shop in north London. A previous owner had painted it matt black, but Mick Griffiths' dad French polished it for me. Every now and then my precious relics get an airing on it, Lillian McMurry's Trumpet Records, Louis Jordan singing 'Caledonia' and a T-Bone Walker record on the Comet label called *West Side Baby*.

Once in Halifax I saw in a shop an original Edison Gem cylinder player from 1902. The man wanted four hundred quid for it and said he'd throw in a dozen cylinders. These included the Clarion Cycling Club theme tune 'Voilets', a piano solo by Albert Benzler, and 'I've Struck a Chorus' by Arthur Osmond. The cylinder boxes themselves are works of art. Most have red lids and feature a photograph of Thomas Edison with his signature underneath and the words 'National Phonograph Co. Ltd', then in beautiful gold-lined writing, 'Edison Gold Moulded records echo all over the world'. Four hundred quid somehow flew out of my wallet and the Gem player took its place on top of my china cabinet. There it stayed until one fateful party when Andy Morgan, a chunky second-row forward, fell into a woozy slumber and on coming round heaved himself from the settee by use of the precious brass horn of the player. This action had various consequences. The Edison player smashed to the floor. Andy's brother, another chunky second-row forward called Nigel, smacked him in the nose for behaviour unbecoming and I just about cried. Nose and Edison Gem were later healed.

My great dread, even in moments of drunken stupor and party mode was that the record playing equipment would be harmed. I was as house-proud about the equipment as my gran was about her polished dining chairs and three-piece suite. Party-goers could fall into the fire grate and break the furniture, but I never let anybody so much as change a record and woe betide anybody who put so much as a finger near the bass cones of my Linn Isobarik speakers.

Nowadays I hope I'm not as fussy as that, but I do wince a bit when I see people approach my state-of-the-art, valve-driven Shangling CD player, a piece of modern sculpture with a mauve light around the disc holder. The Isobariks have long since been replaced, but I couldn't bear to part with them so I have them hooked up to the telly as rear speakers. I must be the only person in the world with a pair of Isobariks behind my settee. Sometimes I wish I had a big fishing net chasing after butterflies.

When John Turner dies, his wife Joyce who has put up with his mechanical music obsession for fifty years or more, decides to have a bit of a clear-out. She comes to my kitchen and places on the table two records. One is by Florrie Forde the old music hall singer, the other a medley of George Formby songs both on pristine 78rpm. Then she takes out a record protected by a homemade perspex case. 'This one was John's favourite,' she says. 'It's the very recording that Enrico Caruso made in 1904 of Leoncavallo's "Mattinata".' The label features a 'recording angel' with wings and a quill pen inscribing onto a disc. I take into my hands a hundred-year-old relic. Just a piece of plastic really, but one that denoted the very moment when music became a thing to collect. The very first recording of a piece especially composed for the gramophone. It is like touching a revenant. Joan suggests that I play it. We fetch the HMV horn player and I put it on. Now I hear the ghosts.

'Now you will look after it, won't you?' says Joan.

'What!'

'John would have wanted you to have it,' she smiles.

I'm trying to work out how to put it onto Billie's iPod.

Breakfast with Seamus Heaney, Lunch with Tony Harrison

In 1995, the year Seamus Heaney won the Nobel Prize for Literature, I was invited to Harvard University to visit my friend Gill Moore who was on a three-month sabbatical there. At the time I was teaching a creative writing class at a Further Education centre in Castleford every Thursday afternoon. The day after the invitation to Harvard came, I went into the class, which comprised mainly of old women writing their memoirs, and said, 'I'll have to take a week off in a couple of weeks' time, I've been invited to spend some time at Harvard University.' The whole group were excited for me and one lovely lady at the back of the room, who hardly ever spoke or wrote anything piped up.

'You'll have to visit our Seamus while you're there.'

'Seamus who?'

'He's a poet. Our Seamus. They call him Seamus Heaney. He's my cousin. Have you heard of him?'

Gobsmacked! 'Seamus Heaney. Is he your cousin, Marie?'

'Aye. I write to him regular. He's been to see me. I'll bring his phone number.'

The following week Marie handed me the address and phone number of Seamus Heaney, scrawled in black felt-tip pen on the back of a brown gas bill envelope. 'I've phoned him up. He says it's alright.'

I flew into Boston Airport in the middle of a snowstorm. There was ice everywhere. Gill met me and we went to eat oysters washed down with Boston dark beer. 'Do you want to go and meet Seamus Heaney tomorrow?'

'You what?'

'Here, I've got his number.' I show Gill the gas bill envelope. 'I'll ring him now.' We rush out into the snow and from a public phone on the frozen sidewalk I ring the number. 'Hello, is that Seamus Heaney?'

'Yes. Would that be Ian Clayton?'

'It is. How did you know?'

'Marie told me you'd be ringing and I recognise the Yorkshire accent.'

'Can we meet?'

'Sure. Meet me tomorrow morning at the German restaurant on Cambridge Square. Do you like the old fried potatoes? I like the smoked salmon and fried potatoes for breakfast.'

We meet. We eat smoked salmon and fried potatoes. Later on Seamus Heaney takes me and Gill on a tour of Harvard Yard. We look at the fine statues and then Seamus Heaney finds a small relief of a construction worker who had been foreman on the building of the local underground railway station. He tells us that of all the fine artworks in this area, that is his favourite.

A few days later, not to be outdone, Gill, who is head of music education at the Royal Festival Hall, takes me for lunch with Luciano Berio, the most gifted of all contemporary classical composers. Berio has written pieces inspired by the words of Martin Luther King, by the riffs of modern jazz and by traditional folk songs. He has just completed a pencil-written manuscript and Gill is charged with taking it in a cardboard tube to the DHL office where it is to be posted to the Peak District in England. On the way to DHL we call for a pint and leave the tube under a pub table. Three hundred yards down the road I realise the tube is not under my arm and skate back to the pub. A barman is examining the package when I grab for it and tell him it's mine.

The following day Gill and me take a train out to Lexington to see where the first shots were fired in the American War of Independence. We wander about on the snow-covered fields and iced-up rivers. I feel inspired to write something. With the heel of my boot I scrawl on one of the frozen rivers, 'Baby please stop crying'. Gill has been going through a separation from her partner. I wonder about what happens when all the ice melts and the words go rushing down to the sea. Do fishermen's nets haul them in for poets to make sense of?

Arthur Scargill used to say that his father read the dictionary every day, because life depends on your power to master words. In 1987 some of my friends from the Yorkshire Art Circus were invited to be part of the audience when Channel 4 decided to record and transmit Tony Harrison reading his poem 'V'.

'V' is about an imaginary conversation the poet has with a skinhead who has sprayed the words 'fuck' and 'cunt' with an aerosol can onto the gravestone of the poet's parents. A friend of mine called Olive Fowler was at the TV studios. She recalls coughing with the smoke that was pumped into the studio for effect more than the outrage the poem caused.

But the tabloids had a field day with the obscene language. Not since the Sex Pistols had called Bill Grundy 'a rotten dirty fucker' and prompted the *Daily Mirror*'s 'Filth and Fury' headline had there been such a to-do about language.

Tony Harrison wouldn't know it, but after that he became a bit of a hero of mine. Here was a man who confronted behaviour and words with words and behaviour.

Imagine my shock, then, when about ten years after 'V' I get a phone call from a woman who is an assistant producer on a film they are making called *Prometheus*. Tony Harrison has seen me on a TV programme and thinks I have the voice he's looking for. He wants me to be one of a gang of twelve coal miners.

Prometheus is about the myth of fire set against a backdrop of the pit closure programme in Yorkshire and the pollution of Europe by industry. Much of the film's dialogue is in ancient Greek and rhyming couplets. Four of the miners though will have speaking parts in the Yorkshire dialect, also in rhyming couplets, and they'll need eight more likely lads to play miners, non-speaking.

I meet Tony Harrison and he asks me if I think I can round up some candidates to play the other miners. I tell him that there are some mates of mine at Featherstone Miners Welfare Amateur Rugby League Club who might be interested for sixty quid a day. Big Windy put his hand up and Jack Hobson, the most naturally gifted loose forward I've had the pleasure of calling a teammate, also gets a part. As does Roger Green, a devoted follower of the cult band Half Man Half Biscuit. As do 'Tetley' Dave Parker, a real-ale enthusiast who can play the ukulele, and Pete Minney, an Elvis impersonator who used to leave his BSA leaking oil in our backs in the 1960s. Best of all we took Arnold 'Sooner' Millard along for the free beer and sandwiches. We had a right laugh. Sooner was actually screen-tested for the part of the grandad in the film, a part that later went to Walter Sparrow who had appeared in *Robin Hood Prince of Thieves*. A young production assistant visited the Top House with a minicam. The conversation went something like this, 'Do you ever recite poetry Mr Millard?'

'Yes love, I know a lot of limericks.'

'Would you like to look into this camera, and when I say action, please recite one.'

'Are you sure, love?'

'Yes please.'

Sooner took a swig of his beer, a deep breath and announced:

'There was a young man from Bombay
Who modelled a fanny from clay
The heat of his prick
Turned the clay into brick
And it rubbed all his foreskin away.'

Sooner then winked and said, 'Will that do, love?' The young PA said, 'Can we get back to you on that one, Mr Millard?' Arnold's letter never arrived.

Roger Green tells me that he still smiles to this day when he recalls the first speaking he ever had to do in a film was to say the word 'cunt' to a southern actor pretending to be a northern coal mine deputy.

For about six days we filmed in the perishing cold of a disused power station near Doncaster. We marched behind a local brass band, dragged a golden statue of Zeus about and shouted swear words down a mine shaft, encouraged by Tony Harrison who was directing the film in a flat cap.

At meal times we sat on a converted single decker bus and listened while Tony Harrison swapped stories with the main actor Michael Feast about Elizabeth Taylor. Apparently they worked on a film in St Petersburg where Elizabeth Taylor had refused to come out of her dressing room until she'd opened her daily hamper from Harrods. Then Tony and Michael would listen to Arnold Millard reciting his dirty limericks and affect mock surprise when they heard about how much ale the rugby lads had supped after the match on Saturday. Talk about a clash of cultures. On the one side of a bus aisle was serious head-scratching and musing on classical Greek verse and on the other Arnold introducing us to 'the young man from Calcutta, who went for a squint through a shutter'. The buzz reached its apotheosis when Tony Harrison attempted to explain iambic pentameter to a bleary-eyed and boozy 'Tetley' Dave Parker. Dave went off and pulled out his little ukulele. He came back and struck up with:

'Up the west end, that's the best end
Where the night clubs thrive,
There's a jazz queen, she's a has-been,
Has been Lord knows what.'

Dave said, 'I think I'd sooner have Fanlight Fanny any day!' Even Tony Harrison joined in with the chorus of approval.

My favourite poem ever is 'The Wild Party', a bawdy jazz-age poem in couplets written by Joseph Moncure March in 1928. From its opening stanza:

'Queenie was a blonde and her age stood still
And she danced twice a day on Vaudeville,
Grey eyes,
Lips like coals aglow
Her face was a tinted mask of snow.'

I have been trying to learn it all off by heart. More than that I have been trying to buy every edition published. Why on earth I do that I don't know. I have talked to the poshest bookshops in Madison Avenue, New York and on Charing Cross Road in London as part of my search. I spent a hundred-odd quid on the ultra rare first limited edition of seven hundred and fifty copies and the same amount again on a signed deluxe edition from the 1960s. There is little sense and even less reason to this obsession. Why am I so interested in collecting the utterances of others in book and record form? Does it go right back to a childhood bereft of words and much music?

In Prague I lay on a narrow bed and read *The Good Soldier Svejk* the brilliant First World War satire by the Czech writer Jaroslav Hašek. In Delhi I sit scratching my bedbug bites in an infested hotel room and read Gita Mehta's take on the first hippy invasion of India, a book called *Karma Cola*. In Dublin sharing a communal bunk room in the independent hostel it's Flann O'Brien's *The Third Policeman*. Back home I constantly return to Barry Hines' book *A Kestrel for a Knave*. Since I first read it in Mr Burke's class at George Street School it has spoken to me about my life. There's a song by Chuck Prophet that goes, 'I've got a Balinese dancer tattooed across my chest, it's been my closest companion ever since my arrest'. Kes is my Balinese dancer. There's a scene right at the start of the book where Billy Casper is running to do his morning paper round, he jumps over a wire fence and tumbles into some long grass. When he gets to his feet he finds his pumps and trousers are wet through and there's dog shit on his hand. He wipes the dog shit off on some wet grass and then smells his fingers. I am that boy smelling my fingers.

I went to the pictures once with Barry Hines. We went to see *Shakespeare in Love* at the behest of Yorkshire TV who wanted Barry to review it in the form of an interview with me.

Barry told me that his favourite stories start with ordinary people getting up on a morning, going through their day and going to bed on a night. He also told me what his mother's neighbour had said to her when she announced, 'Our Barry is going to be a writer.' The neighbour said, 'Oooh! I am sorry Mrs Hines. All that education gone to waste!'

Wouldn't Swap it for a Gold Pig

Ladysmith Black Mambazo are to perform live in the Yorkshire Television studios. I ask the floor manager's permission to take Edward and Billie to watch the rehearsals. We sit in the Green Room sipping tea. Edward is beside himself. At the age of four he knows three songs off by heart, 'Fanlight Fanny the Frowsy Nightclub Queen', 'Unchain My Heart' and 'Diamonds on the Soles of Her Shoes'. He can't believe he's about to meet Joseph Shabalala the man who sang with Paul Simon.

'Will he like me, Daddy?'

'Edward, I'm sure he will.'

'When is he coming in?'

Edward must have been in and out of the Green Room twenty times, looking down the corridor for Joseph and the boys. Finally they arrive. Edward without hesitation runs headlong down the corridor and shouts, 'Joseph Shabalala' before hugging his leg. Joseph Shabalala is amazed by this little red-headed boy. 'Do you know any songs, little one?'

Edward tells him he knows 'Diamonds on the Soles of Her Shoes'. And they all begin to sing it. 'She's a rich girl she knows how to hide it. He's a poor boy empty as a pocket.' It is a touching moment, one of the moments I hoard on the shelves in my mind. This is why my house is also my head. It's why I spend my life journeying to music.

A few weeks after in the very same Green Room I was

helping myself to a cup of coffee out of a Kenco machine. The Tory MP Ken Clarke bustled in with his entourage. I ought to have told him how much I'd enjoyed listening to his *Desert Island Discs*, he'd chosen Colman Hawkins and Bessie Smith. Instead I said, 'Does tha want a cup of tea?'

When I get fed up of blowing dust off my LP collection and rearranging the CDs into some semblance of order that helps me find them, I wonder whether I ought to flog most of them and just keep my absolute favourites. I have done it on a smaller scale in the past. Before we went to India I sold a load of records to a shop for silly prices. In this way I lost George Harrison's box *All Things Must Pass* and every T. Rex single from 'Deborah' to 'I Love to Boogie'.

There are moments of musical memory that I wouldn't, as my old gran used to say, 'swap for a gold pig'.

Jürgen, me, Peter the Hamburg taxi driver and another German friend, Rainer, meet up in Dublin for a ten-day pub crawl around Ireland. Jürgen is just back from a trip selling steel to the French, Peter is back from a bicycle ride around Peru, Rainer and me haven't seen each other since the boozy night in Budapest. On the boozy first night in O'Donoghue's bar we listen to some wild fiddle players and wonder if we can sup one hundred pints of Guinness in ten days. Peter reckons that we've already had ten today and if we can pace ourselves we ought to be able to crack it. The following morning we set out by train for County Mayo and sup our first of the day in a bar beside the Clew Bay. We continue to drink our way around Sligo and Galway. Back in Dublin we're stumbling toward the home straight. On a street near St

Stephen's Green we hear a voice soaring over the tops of the houses. The voice is one of the most powerful female voices we have heard. It belongs, we find out later, to a busker called Daffy McDiarmid and she is singing the old Bill Withers number 'Lovely Day'. Whether it was the beer or the craic or just the moment, we all declare that it is the most beautiful singing we have ever heard. Ten o'clock at night on this Dublin street remains in our collective memory forever and whenever we meet up we always tell the story of the time when we stumbled across Daffy McDiarmid. I wonder if she recalls the night when she made forty quid in two minutes from four drunken, weary travellers who were about to sup their one hundredth pint of Guinness in Hartigan's bar.

The finest brass band in the world comes from a village just ten miles from where I was born. It is the Grimethorpe Brass Band, the band that featured in the film *Brassed Off*. I travelled by bicycle to Grimethorpe every Tuesday for six months to run a 'women against pit closures' creative writing group. One evening the junior section of the Grimethorpe Band were giving a concert on their home turf, the Miners' Institute, known locally as 'T'stute'.

I was given a ticket for the concert and stood at the back of the room with a pint of keg bitter. I don't know if I was prepared for what was to come, but the first number nearly blew my cap off. Grimethorpe Band can play anything and everything and they play it well. They did 'Ticket to Ride', 'Bohemian Rhapsody' and 'MacArthur Park' and by the time they got to 'Concierto d'Aranjuez' I was shaking, my hair was standing up and I started to weep. I had never, don't think I will ever, hear anything like it. Outside the club were rows of terraced houses named after seaside towns, Brighton, Margate and so on. The names belied the reality. These streets were dropping to bits. There were rats in some of the kitchens and you couldn't see the water in the beck at the bottom of the road for carpets. The pit was on its last legs and there was more glass and dog shit on the pavement outside the church and shops than anywhere I've ever been. Yet inside the club were smiling faces, shared cigarettes, trays full of beer, cries of 'Alreight old cock' and astonishing music being played.

There is a scene in *Brassed Off* where the band play 'Concierto d'Aranjuez'; I can't get past that scene without shuddering at the memory of that night in T'stute. Three or four films make me cry, even on repeated viewing. One is Ingrid Bergman's performance in *Anastasia*, another is the bit in *Railway Children* when Jenny Agutter says, 'Daddy, my Daddy!' and then there's Grimethorpe's playing in *Brassed Off*.

It all comes back to folk. Some friends were putting on a series of gigs at a club called The Wardrobe in Leeds. They brought the jazz poet Dana Bryant over from New York, even tried to get Gil Scott Heron and would have done if he hadn't got busted the week before. They also brought up the motorway from Barnsley Kate Rusby. The Wardrobe is an intimate setting, well suited to late night jazz and folk. Terry Callier gave a wonderful concert there and the audience joined in with 'People Get Ready' and turned it into a gospel tabernacle. On the night Kate Rusby played I made a bit of a closet of myself by heckling her to play the Iris DeMent song 'My Town' halfway through her set when she had planned to do it as an encore.

I wanted to meet Kate Rusby after that and hoped that she wouldn't remember it was me spoiling the ambience at The Wardrobe. I got my chance when I was commissioned to present a series called 'My Yorkshire' which explored contemporary Yorkshire through its musicians, artists and sundry other characters. Most of the filming was done at Kate's mam's house. We sat on the settee and by way of interview just talked about Kate's love of folk music and where she was from. I asked her if she'd got a guitar and would she play me something. She said, 'Do you still want me to play that Iris DeMent song?' and then giggled. Two years after I had rudely shouted out from the audience at Leeds I sat on Kate Rusby's mam's settee and got my own private concert. 'My Town' is a lovely song about where you grow up and the things you recall about what shapes you. Kate sang it through four times for different camera angles, each time I stared wide-eyed at her like a kid who'd just rubbed the sleep out of his eyes on a Christmas morning.

The Watersons have carried the banner for traditional singing in England for forty-odd years. Even when folk went completely below the radar in the late seventies and eighties the family carried on. Then in the 1990s folk came up to breathe some new air and Norma Waterson found herself nominated for the Mercury prize.

The 'My Yorkshire' programme took me to Norma Waterson's kitchen table. I sat with Georgina Boyes and her husband Jim of the No Masters record label while Norma presided like a mother. She chastised our cameraman and told him to be careful with his lights after he nearly clipped a glass ball that hung from the ceiling. 'You be very careful with that, it belonged to my great-great-grandmother, that's the ball that kept witches from her window.'

She told us about the songs she had been brought up with in Hull. I expected whaling songs and the stuff that fishermen sang about herrings. That's what a diet of Ewan MacColl and the books tell you. Norma told me different. 'It was the music hall songs that my granny had sung. The pop music of the day, the stuff that people sang in the back rooms of pubs. And George Formby. Plenty of Marie Lloyd and George Formby.'

Norma had flown back the day before from a tour of New Zealand. She was tired and her kitchen was full of camera crew. I could see that she had other thoughts on how to spend her Sunday afternoon. I wondered if I dare ask her to sing for me. In the back of my mind was the thought that I might never get this opportunity again. I steeled myself.

'Would you mind singing a little song?'

Norma raised her eyes. Then turned to Georgina. 'You didn't tell me about this when you asked about coming!'

I thought, Oh no! I've gone too far this time.

Then Norma started to sing 'Green Grows the Laurel', a heartbreaking story about a girl left carrying a baby. She sang four verses accompanied by Jim Boyes. The song apparently has more than thirty verses. We all sat hypnotised, hardly breathing.

'Will that do?' Norma smiled now.

I couldn't speak. I had a lump in my throat as big as a

piece of coal. One of the world's greatest voices had just sung a song while sitting at her own kitchen table. For me! That'll do in my book thank you very much.

Bringing It All Back Home

Knowing and Sharing

Old Mother Riley Meets Mick Ronson

I don't know what this story says about me. I have an appointment with the cemetery keeper at the Eastern Cemetery in Hull. I want to visit the graves of Arthur Lucan, better known as 'Old Mother Riley', the music hall and creaky old film star, and Mick Ronson, glam-rock guitarist with David Bowie's Spiders from Mars and Bob Dylan's guitar man on the Rolling Thunder Revue.

The keeper shakes my hand and says, 'They're buried not too far from one another. Whose stone would you like to see first?'

I pause for thought. My head is filled with a sudden strange pantomime. Mick Ronson is on his knees in glitter jumpsuit, pretending to fellate Bowie's guitar, when Old Mother Riley skips into view singing, 'I lift up my finger and I say tweet tweet, hush hush, now now, come come'. He lifts up his skirts and dances. Audrey Bryan and Hattie Jacques appear and join in with the dance followed by Bela Lugosi in his Dracula cloak. The collections in my head are like a two-hour-old jumble sale. Nothing is filed properly; everything has been picked up, looked at and chucked back onto the table. My head has become my house and even weirder than that, my house is becoming my head.

I look at the cemetery man.

He looks at me.

We smile at one another.

'Penny for them.'

'What?'

'Your thoughts.'

'I think I'll just wander about for a bit.'

'Alright lad. If you want any help I'll be in that building over there.'

Who will I find first? The bluff and gritty northern lad from Hull who dreamed of being a rock 'n' roll star? A man who found fame as the shoulder for Bowie's androgynous bisexual creation to lean on, who once worked as a Corporation gardener. Or will it be the grotesque comedian who dressed as a back street granny in clogs and shawl; a bottle-swigging washerwoman whose unsophisticated homespun humour made my grandparents laugh?

I traipse the paths of Hull's Eastern Cemetery trying to plot a route without the aid of a map, compass, signpost nor nothing. I stumble on Arthur Lucan's gravestone. It seems small and insignificant amongst a lot of other stones. Stones that were for people who were fishermen and lived on Hessle Road. Two-day millionaires who spent their money in The Alexandra pub before weaving their way back to their trawlers bound for Iceland and Baffin Bay. Flare-trousered dock workers who collapsed after nights out and flare-skirted women who once pushed babies in Tansads past the ruins of the bombed-out Cecil Cinema. Skinyard workers like my dad who stalked Stepney Lane in vile smelling overalls and washed off the grease and filth in the slipper baths on Beverley Road. There's stones here for shopkeepers, for boat builders, for men whose hands bled and women who scrubbed kitchens with Izal disinfectant. And there's this little stone for Old Mother Riley who took ill while performing at the Theatre Royal in Barnsley in May of 1954. Like a trouper he carried on to Hull and collapsed behind the curtain at the Tivoli Theatre just as the announcements were being made to the audience. Lucan had entertained at Royal Variety Performances in the thirties and starred in more than twenty films that played to packed houses across the north of England, but bewildered audiences south of Nottingham. It's impossible to imagine what American audiences thought of his appearance alongside the then past his sell-by Bela Lugosi in *Mother Riley Meets the Vampire*.

On the way back down the path the cemetery keeper appears and asks me to follow him. After fifty yards or so he stops and nods his head towards a modern stone. This is Mick Ronson's. Mick was the age I am now when he died of liver cancer. I look at the wording. The keeper stands beside me. 'Nice stone isn't it?' What do you say? I say something softly and make for the gates.

Come on in My Kitchen

In many ways the walls of my kitchen tell this story. Here a photo of the twins at the Cambridge Folk Festival, Edward under a mop of red hair with his Dennis the Menace t-shirt on, Billie sun bleached and wearing friendship bracelets she's bought from a hippy who's just got back from Nepal. Next to this is a photo of the three of us down at my allotment. Billie shows off a clutch of onions in a riddle, I hold up a leek and Edward a runner bean. Below is a poster of the early sixties film *Beat Girl* starring Adam Faith and The John Barry Seven. This was the first film to be shown on Channel 4's Moviedrome season, it's B movie incarnate, exploitative, badly acted and great fun. To the left of *Beat Girl* I run out in the colours of Featherstone Miners Welfare to play my last game of amateur Rugby League. I was nearly forty, a photographer happened to be there. To the right of *Beat Girl* a political demo, captured in acrylics by Brian Lewis, an artist friend, the slogan says 'Educate, Agitate, Organise'. Billie Holiday smoking a cigarette at Paris Airport in 1958 is at the bottom of the stairs, beneath a shot of Ackton Hall Colliery taken in 1985 just before they knocked it down. Then there's me in the Mississippi Delta in 1992, standing in a wayside bar in a pair of Converse pumps. A sign on the wall behind me reads, 'No Profanity, No Soliciting'. Heather, my partner of twenty-eight years, sits in the street in San Francisco wearing Doc Martens, a Belstaff motorcyclist's jacket and a little red

Afghani skull cap. Her nose is pierced and her head shaven. She is a prettier version of Tank Girl. This picture was taken in the late eighties when we visited Haight-Ashbury. A framed Ray Lowry cartoon from the *NME* is above a Terry Cryer photograph of Dinah Washington. The cartoon is my favourite ever. It depicts a blues singer and his wife sitting on their porch. They are both playing guitars. The woman is singing, 'He thinks he's got the blues, but I have to do all the cooking and cleaning and look after the kids, while he's out singing the blues.'

Next to Ray Lowry's cartoon is a glamorous photograph of Geraldine Farrar. Geraldine sang with Harry Roy's band in the 1940s, she was our neighbour until she died a couple of years ago. Geraldine was wonderful. I treasure the picture of Geraldine.

Near the hatstand there's a tiny postcard. On it is a message, 'Art is a means for survival'. It's signed by Yoko Ono. And finally near the sink is an abstract by a Czechoslovakian postman. He said he wanted to sell his paintings so that he could go on his holidays. I thought that it was the best reason I have yet heard to buy a painter's work. Artists need to make journeys.

Living Room

After tea we all sit on two settees facing the telly. Every house I've lived in has a telly in the front room with the chairs arranged to face it. Above our telly in this house is a painting of a line of redcoat soldiers firing their rifles at a crowd of people. The soldiers face directly out of the picture as though they might be shooting at us. In 1893, in Featherstone, that's exactly what they did. This painting by David Prudhoe recreates the events of a night in September of that year when the South Staffordshire infantry came to my home town to disperse a picket of miners and their families at the pit. When the people refused to move the Riot Act was read and the order was given to open fire. Using Lee Mitford cartridges which could kill a man at a mile distance, the soldiers fired at point blank range and killed a miner called James Duggan and a Sunday school teacher called James Gibbs. They badly wounded twenty others. The following day the *Yorkshire Post* reported that, 'Under trying circumstances, the shootings at Featherstone were a good scientific test for the new Lee Mitford cartridges.' And some time after that the Eton Public School Debating Society concluded that, 'The people of Featherstone were a very rough set and deserved to be shot at. The only pity was that not more of them were taught a lesson.' In this painting the soldiers line up between two rows of terraced houses with a pithead gear behind them like a hangman's scaffold. The soldiers look like clones, all ten of them painted exactly the same. The people stare impassively out of the picture. An old woman bends over her fallen son in a recreation of a Russian Revolution photograph. Another old woman in a pinny holds a plate in her hand, a bizarre take on the music hall novelty of catching a magician's bullet on a plate. An old man in muffler, waistcoat and flat cap stands with his hands thrust firmly into coat pockets. The sky in the painting is as grey as a slate, the streets coaldust colour. The houses are red, lit by an unseen fire. It's a scary piece of art to hang on a living room wall, especially at the back of your telly. It's the only piece in this house placed deliberately, all the other pictures and posters and photos are accidents, fastened to walls as space becomes available.

To the left of this painting on the adjacent wall are shelves for LPs and CDs. Jazz and blues LPs here; the Blue Note label, the T-Bone Walker collection, the Taj Mahal collection, Miles Davis, Ben Webster. Underneath these the folk music CDs and stuff from labels that I like; Soul Jazz, World Circuit, Talkin' Loud and Real World. I buy almost everything from these labels because I know I can trust them. Arranged around the other walls are paintings from my favourite artists. I only usually buy from artists I know personally; women prisoners in a camp in Iran by Karen Babayan from Leeds, miners returning home from work by Harry Malkin who once worked at Fryston Pit, women sewing a man by Kathryn Ensall from Huddersfield, a silk screen print of Billy Casper as he appeared in *Kes* giving two fingers by Martin Young who was born in the Mill Cottages in Featherstone. In the corner is a china cabinet, in the china cabinet a blue willow pattern Ringtons teapot which contains sacred relics of my family's life passing. This teapot used to be in my gran's china cabinet. As a little boy and even as a teenager I breathed a mist onto the glass of my gran's china cabinet while I admired this teapot.

My gran's family were farmers' labourers who stood in the squares of little Yorkshire market towns while potential employers felt at their muscles before hiring them. The family at some point in Victorian times gravitated to the coal towns to find work digging under the ground they had once ploughed. My gran had four uncles who were all killed in the First World War before they were twenty-five. She had two brothers who left the mines for the second war and never came home. During the miners' strike, Margaret Thatcher called miners and their families 'the enemy within'. My grandad swung his boot at the television and refused to ever watch the news again. He stuck to his word. In the last five years of his life, the five years that fell outside of his forty down the pit and six in the army at El Alamein and Monte Casino, he only watched the snooker.

My grandad put his knowledge down to eating sheep's brains for his breakfast at half past four on a morning before going to the pit. My gran got up with him to fry them with an egg on top and when he went off to work she'd stay up to do the washing. By half past two in the afternoon my grandad would be dozing on the rug in front of the fire surrounded by a clothes horse full of steaming and spotlessly clean shirts and towels.

My grandad has a coming home ritual. He goes straight to the kitchen sink and gargles with cold water. Hacking up great black gobstoppers of black dust off his chest. I watch him. The black phlegm hits the white pot of the sink and swirls away. He then drinks a gill of milk and lays down to sleep for an hour. Sometimes on the settee, but most of the time on the rug in front of the fire. My grandad has a set meal for each day. On Mondays he will eat the meat left over from the Sunday joint, Tuesdays and Wednesdays he will have stewed shin beef, Thursday's a chop and Friday's Finnon Haddock. For his tea he will perm any from the following: egg baked in cheese in the oven, mussels when in season, potted meat or brawn and boiled egg and tomato chopped together on a breadcake. Now, whenever Edward and Billie have egg and tomato they call it Old Grandad tea. They never knew 'Old' Grandad. When they ask me about him I tell them that he would have tickled their ribs with his poker fingers, rubbed their chops with his iron-filing whiskers and said 'I could bloody eat you.' Edward then always says, 'Would he eat us?' just so that I can say, 'No, it was just his way.' This is a signal to start telling stories about our family history. This happens at mealtimes. I have my chair at the kitchen table, Edward has his, Billie has hers and Heather hers.

It's Billie who always starts. 'What did Old Grandad look like?'

'He was a big man.'

'Was he bigger than Uncle Andrew?'

'He was six foot one.'

'How much is that in centimetres?'

'One hundred and eighty-five.'

'Oooh! that's big. What was his face like? Was it a kind face?'

'Yes. But it was a strong face. He had a right hard chin. When he gave you some chin pie, he left a tattoo of a rose on your cheek.'

'Did it hurt?'

'Oooh aye!'

'Why did he hurt you? Would he hurt us?'

'He wasn't trying to hurt you. It's just what they did in them days. He was very rough. His hand was as big as my two put together.'

'Did he kill any soldiers?'

'I don't know. He was in the war for a long time, but he mostly rode a motorbike taking messages. One day some Italian soldiers tried to surrender to him, but he told them he was too busy taking messages. He gave them some water to drink and told them to sit and wait.'

'Will you show us his medals?'

'You can have them when you're older.'

'Why didn't he want them?'

'He said he just didn't.'

'Why?'

'I don't know why really. He said he would rather have had a medal for working in the pit.'

'You don't get medals for working in the pit though do you, Daddy?'

'No. They don't give medals out to miners.'

'Were all our family miners?'

'Mostly.'

'Tell us about when they came to Featherstone.'

I've told this story a hundred times. It's partly made up and mainly true. It starts on a little stool outside of my gran's back door. 'Well, my grandad told me that his grandad lived in the countryside in a place called Staffordshire. In the Victorian times the government wanted a lot of people to work in the coal mines. These people left their pigs and potatoes and walked up to Yorkshire to work in the pits because they thought they would get more money and have a better life for their children.'

'Did Old Grandad's grandad do that?'

'He did. He made his decision by tossing his cap up into the wind. He said to himself that if his cap landed the right way up, he would set off with his family to find coal. If it landed the wrong way up he'd stop where he was with his pigs and potatoes.'

'And his cap landed the right way up!'

'It did and he set off walking to Featherstone. And he stopped when his feet were bleeding, because he walked it in his bare feet. And where he stopped was at the bottom of Station Lane. Next day he went to see Lord Masham's agent and got a job in the pit. He worked there all his life. And his son Edward, your great-great-grandad did the same and so did his brother Oliver, until a roof fell on him down the pit and he lost his leg. And his son Edward, Old Grandad, went to the pit as well.'

'Except in the war when he rode his motorbike and found them Italians.'

'That's right.'

'And that's why I'm called Edward!'

'That's right.'

'Will I work in a pit?'

'No. Because you won't have to. And besides there aren't any pits left.'

'Tell me why I'm called Billie Holiday, Daddy.'
'Finish your tea and I'll tell you after the news.'
'Dad…'
'What?'
'Have you still got Old Grandad's cap?'
'No son.'
'Oohhh!'

When my gran died I was looking at the boats in Monte Carlo harbour. My mobile phone rang in my shirt pocket. My brother Tony was standing outside Pontefract Infirmary. His voice sounded clear enough for him to be standing on the quayside next to me. 'She's gone,' he said. This woman who inspired us all with homespun philosophy, who made our clothes, who insisted we wore hand-knitted balaclavas in the winter, whose dinners tasted better than any I've tasted, even if it was just stews, meat and potatoes. This woman who left school at fourteen with a limited vocabulary, but combined the words she knew so well that she talked like a poet, was gone. When Hilda Mary Fletcher was born, in the same year as John Lee Hooker, zeppelins were flying over Yorkshire. Today her passing was marked with a brief mobile phone call between her two eldest grandsons. The day after my gran died the aeroplanes crashed into the Twin Towers. The day after that I was flying back to Leeds to help with the funeral arrangements. At Gran's house we went through her possessions. I was given an old handbag full of photographs, holidays at Blackpool, us as kids laiking in the street, a whole series taken by the back door and the two photos of my grandad departing for war. There was a wooden tray full of knives and forks, cutlery I'd used when I shared my grandad's tea of mussels or potted meat, I couldn't bear to chuck them out. Edward and Billie use them now to eat their pizza with. We told stories about Gran. The day she dropped the big stone on her toe. The day she stood up in front of the whole school after telling the headmistress she could recite poetry:

'The elephant is a funny bird,
it leaps from bough to bough.
It lays its eggs in a rhubarb tree
and sings just like a cow.'

Our Tony reminded us of the competition she'd won for the girl who looked most like Amy Johnson. Every time I see a photo of Amy Johnson I see my gran's eyes. We came to the blue Ringtons teapot. I will never know where my gran got a yellow office 'Post-it' note from, but stuck to the side of the teapot was one and on it, it said 'This is are Ian's'. The blue Ringtons teapot I had breathed on and admired all my life was to come to me.

It must have been two months after the funeral before I lifted the lid to look inside the teapot. There I found the relics. A tattered brown cutting that noted a memorial to my gran's first-war uncles. Another one that was an obituary for Uncles Fred and Edwin. Edwin blown up while trying to defuse a bomb, Fred strangely killed when a bomb landed on a cinema in Belgium. A certificate of agreement between the DER Television Rentals company and my grandad. Then a carefully folded letter on a slightly waxy paper. It says:

Dear Hilda,

I am pleased to hear about you. I hope you will do well at school. I wish you every luck in the future.

Yours truly,

Amy Johnson.

Edward and Billie breathe mist onto the glass of our china cabinet now. We still buy our tea from Ringtons, who send a man to the door with a wicker basket.

In the same corner as our china cabinet is a shrine to Lady Day. When we went to register the births of the twins we did so at the glass sliding window of an office inside Pontefract Town Hall. The lady behind the sliding glass asked, 'The little boy's name is…?' I said, 'Edward' and my grandad's hands flashed through my mind. The lady wrote Edward Clayton in beautiful scrolled handwriting into a big ledger. 'And the little girl's name is…?' I paused, even at this last minute I wasn't sure. Heather said we might as well go the whole hog if we're going to name her after a jazz singer. We debated whether 'Holiday' could be a second given name. The lady with the ledger looked up at me, 'Well?' I said 'Billie Holiday.' Billie likes to be called 'Billie Holiday', she tells people her full name 'Billie Holiday Clayton' whenever she's asked. According to John Ramsden, a joiner mate of mine who fixes stuff at our house, our daughter is the only Billie Holiday Clayton in the world. He knows about things like this because he's always on the internet.

The first song I can recall hearing was taught to me by my Auntie Alice as a sort of lullaby. It's also the first song I can remember the words to, it's called 'Poor Little Joe'.

'Poor little Joe, out in the snow,
Nowhere to shelter, nowhere to go,
No mother to guide him, no friend by his side,
Cast out in the wide world was poor little Joe.'

I don't know where Auntie Alice learned it. I suspect it is some kind of Victorian melodramatic ditty, the sort that turns sung in music halls and later in working men's clubs.

Auntie Alice was born on 24 April 1915. It was the day that chlorine gas was first used as a weapon at the Battle of Ypres. She was born on the sofa in her parents' front room. Her father was a horsekeeper at Glasshoughton Colliery. Her mother suffered regular bouts of pleurisy and was confined to the house. All four of her mother's brothers had died in the mud of the first-war trenches. Their father never recovered from the shock and took to the bottle, his liver shrivelled and he died young. I am fond of my Auntie Alice, my gran's older sister. I have visited her all my life. I have been inspired by her all my life.

On the morning of 24 April 1915, the day Aunt Alice was born, an illegitimate baby by the name of Elinore Harris was registered at the registry of births in Philadelphia, USA. A couple of weeks earlier, her mother Sadie Harris, sometimes known as Fagin, who gave her occupation as 'Houseworker' had given birth to the child in the general hospital at Philadelphia. Philadelphia is thousands of miles from

Glasshoughton; geographically, culturally, racially, politically. There are few parallels you can draw.

Elinore's father's name was given as Clarence Holiday, a musician who was posted to France in 1918 as an infantry bugler. He was honourably discharged after falling victim to poison gas in the last days before the armistice. His daughter found fame as the greatest jazz singer the world has ever heard when she combined the first name of Billie Dove, her favourite actress, with the surname of the father she barely knew.

In the middle of the 1970s I bought a book for thirty pence from the Kiosk record shop in Pontefract. It was a paperback edition of an autobiography that came out about twenty years before. It was called *Lady Sings the Blues* and I learned huge chunks of it off by heart, because I became obsessed with the singer whose life the book portrayed. Over the years I have found that most of the stories in that book were not written by Billie Holiday, not read by Billie Holiday and mainly not true.

'Mom and Pop were just a couple of kids when they got married. He was eighteen, she was sixteen, I was three.' Even the opening, entertaining and famous as it is, was made up. Since reading the book I have collected hundreds of Billie Holiday recordings. I even paid two hundred dollars in the San Francisco branch of Virgin for an ultra rare, limited edition bootleg box set from Japan. I have collected more than one hundred books and magazines about her, photos, sheet music, anything with her name on. In Birmingham, Alabama I bought a statue music box that stands about eight inches tall. When it's wound up it plays 'God Bless the Child'.

Billie Holiday, like my Auntie Alice, is a woman who has had great bearing and influence on my life.

It was the old record on Verve that did it. The one I bought in the second-hand shop at York. One night I drank until two o'clock in the morning in The Railway pub in Station Lane, playing dominoes, telling the tale. I came home, Heather was in bed asleep. I closed all the doors, dropped the needle onto the record ever so quietly and sat down at the table by the window.

'It's quarter to three, there's no one in the place
Except you and me.
So set 'em up Joe
I got a little story
You ought to know...'

Outside on Station Lane, Amigos Fresh Pizza had just closed. The man who owns the place slammed the door hard and rattled the lock. This man once gave me a well-worn tape of singing from Santiago de Compestela after I told him I had a CD of the great flamenco singer, Carmen Linares. Further up the lane I could see and hear a couple arguing. The man was shouting, 'You showed him your fucking belly button, I saw you when I was coming back from the bog.' A police car siren wailed past on Wakefield Road.

'I'm drinking my friend, to the end
of a brief episode. Make it one for
my baby and another one for the road.'

It's a long way from the sleazy bars of New York and at the same time I'm sitting right in it. I'm listening to Billie Holiday pouring out a story to a tired barman, yet I'm nowhere near. What is it that? Why in some moments do I feel more akin to a black jazz singer from America than I do to my own Auntie Alice? Why do I laugh when Auntie Alice embarks on an epic journey to Austria by herself at the age of seventy-seven because she wants to see the *Sound of Music* country? Why do I cry when Billie sings 'Gloomy Sunday'? Why do I feel silly when Auntie Alice brings me teacakes from Marks and Spencer and tells me every time I visit that there's 'two rashers of bacon in the pantry that want eating'? Why do I feel cool and a bit sophisticated when I set to discussing the recordings that Billie Holiday did for the Commodore label? I could say that Auntie Alice informs me about who I am and where I'm from. Billie Holiday takes me to places that I'd like to be from. Too simple minded that, though.

An old pianist in a pub once told me that when Billie Holiday toured England for the first time in 1954 her first gig was in Manchester and her second was in Nottingham. In between she did a late-night spot in Wakefield. For a long time I believed it. I wanted to believe it because Wakefield is six miles away and that's the nearest I could ever have been to Billie Holiday, even though I wasn't born until five years after. When I read Max Jones' book *Talking Jazz* and the chapter about Billie's tour, I realised that although Billie was at the Free Trade Hall in Manchester and the Astoria Ballrooms in Nottingham, the Wakefield gig never took place. I still like the old pianist's story.

During July of 1959, my father spent hours trying to repair an electrical fault on a vacuum cleaner. My parents had married in March of that year after falling for each other on a waltzer ride in Bridlington. My father was still making the girls scream in those days spinning the cars; 'The louder you scream girls, the faster we go.' They rented the house in which I was born in Mafeking Street, opposite my gran's. I was due to be born in the September. My father proudly pushed the mended hoover over to my mother. My mother switched the hoover on and electrocuted herself, almost inducing my birth. In New York in the early hours of the morning of 17 July in the Metropolitan Hospital, Billie Holiday's heart failed her.

For a number of years before he died I corresponded with the most knowledgeable man in the world on Billie's recordings. His name was Jack Millar. Jack had written the definitive discography of Billie Holiday after almost fifty years of research. He was founder of the Billie Holiday Circle, a club he had formed as far back as 1946. Jack owned a little radio repair shop somewhere in Kent. He had seen Billie at the Albert Hall in 1954. He was asked if he'd ever actually met her. He replied in his modest way, 'Why would she want to meet me?' On 2 January of the year he passed away while quietly reading a jazz book, I phoned him. I just wanted to wish him a Happy New Year. My daughter was standing by my leg. She said, 'Can I say Happy New Year?' I passed her the telephone. She cheekily shouted down the phone, 'Happy New Year, whoever you are,' passed the phone back to me and scurried off to play with her dollies. Jack was thrilled to bits. He said, 'I am the only man in the world today who can say that Billie Holiday has wished him a Happy New Year.'

Allotment

When we move from the flat above the shop to the new house, our near neighbour is Geraldine Farrar, a lady in her eighties who once sang in front of the big bands in the 1930s and 40s. Geraldine is the original gin-soaked ballroom queen. Not from Memphis, but from Featherstone. Her father was the concert secretary at the Rat Trap Working Men's Club when Ernie Wise was a clog dancer in his father's act. He named his daughter after the great American opera diva of the same name.

To say Geraldine had a smoky, dark brown voice by the time I knew her would be like saying that Capstan Full Strength are toy cigarettes. We met in a taproom. Geraldine leaned on the bar from a high stool, cigarette poised like a black and white film star, her glass of gin leaving wet rings on the bar like Ray Milland's did in *The Lost Weekend*.

Geraldine has lovely stories about Geraldo, Harry Roy, Lew Stone and Sid Philips, ancient British band leaders who survive on the scratchy 78s she keeps in a box in the back bedroom of her bungalow. She had made hundreds of live BBC broadcasts from Oxford Road studios in Manchester. She tells me about nightclub cocktails with Elizabeth Taylor, Richard Burton and Shirley Bassey. She has tattered, nicotine-stained photos in scrapbooks.

Geraldine loves Edward and Billie and plies them with sweets and expensive Belgian chocolate. She tells me that I need an agent and offers to arrange one for me through contacts in the West End. She shows me a letter from a showbiz agent in Tin Pan Alley that was written to her in 1952.

One day when me and the twins are out walking we see Geraldine feeding feral cats on Marks and Spencer's chicken. She calls us over.

'Dahlings, do come and talk with your Aunt Gerry for a little while.'

She speaks in the clipped accent of a 1940s BBC radio personality. She learned breathing at the Wigmore Hall alongside Deanna Durbin.

'I'd like to arrange elocution lessons for the little angels.'

'Why do you want to do that, Geraldine?'

'Because, my dahling, I wouldn't want them to grow up talking like you!'

My dad told me, in his cack-handed way with words, that you find your lot in life when you grow stuff. My dad grew enough cabbages and cauliflowers to feed the whole street and to prove it sent me round with a homemade wooden barrow selling them to our neighbours. It was embarrassing, nearly as embarrassing as him sending me out with a shovel and bucket every time Clarrie Copley's milk round horse shit in our street.

When I was about ten I discovered that my dad couldn't read or write. I had my suspicions. He never helped me with my homework and I'd never see him with a paper in his hand. He had copies of *Mayfair* and *Penthouse* in his allotment shed, but you don't really swap them with your mates at work for the reading matter. My mam filled his sick notes in when he was off work or 'laiking' as they say round here.

I was watching *Grandstand*. In the late sixties and early seventies the BBC had Eddie Waring, a son of Dewsbury commentating on the second half of rugby league matches. The BBC in a patronising attempt to introduce northern sport to the Saturday afternoon masses sent a couple of outside broadcast cameras to far-flung places like Wilderspool at Warrington, Fartown, Huddersfield, and occasionally Post Office Road at Featherstone. Eddie Waring was like an old-fashioned music hall turn, with half a dozen catchphrases and a battered trilby hat. Once at Wakefield's Belle Vue ground, the fans in the stand that backed onto Wakefield Theatre Club chanted, 'Eddie Waring for Vietnam'. Half of the people in Yorkshire and Lancashire despised this grotesque caricature of northerners, the other half put up with it because he put our towns on the TV map and he really did know his rugby. The BBC and viewers in the south thought that northern rugby folk looked and talked like Eddie Waring. In our house they probably did.

Batley and Hull Kingston Rovers are slugging out a dour Yorkshire Cup second-round match in the mud at Mount Pleasant when my dad kicks off his rolled over wellies and says, 'Hey up young 'un, how's tha spell rabbit?'

I say, 'Don't you even know how to spell rabbit?' He says that of course he does, but he's checking to see if I do. I tell him it's 'R. A. B. B. I. T'.

'Correct, lad. Full marks.'

Later I see him looking through an Uncle Remus colouring book that belongs to our Andrew.

On the Sunday morning when I visit our allotment there is a homemade sign taped to the fence. My dad has made the sign by cutting out the back of a big cornflakes packet and attaching it to a cane. The grey side of the packet faces into the street and on it my dad has written, 'Brer Rabbits FOR SALE. BY APPOINTMENT'. The first two words in scrolled handwriting, the following four in block capitals copied from an estate agent's sign. Clever man in his way, my dad.

He was the first man in the street to get BBC2. At the time you had to have a specially adapted aerial. The aerials looked different to the older type. After he erected the aerial on our chimney he spent ages across the street admiring his handiwork. He told anybody who was passing, 'See that aerial. It can pick up BBC2 that.' We watched a lot of serious documentaries on a snowy screen for the first three weeks after that. And of course, *The High Chaparral*.

We were also the first in our street to have doors flushed with corrugated hardboard and painted in pastel shades, as opposed to the dark panelled ones that everybody else had. And when sliding doors became fashionable, we had a glass panelled one fitted between the kitchen and front room. It became known as 'the middle door'. The door that separated the area where you sat to watch the telly from the area where you sat to eat your dinner. One Sunday morning my dad wanted to take a sledgehammer to the separating wall to make a serving hatch. My mother pointed out that a serving hatch would be absolutely no use to us, because we ate at the table next to the gas oven. So he ripped out the cupboards in the alcove next to the chimney breast instead and made a stand for a record player and a shelf for his Ink Spots and Platters records.

One day at work in 1968 a huge roll of packaging fell onto my dad and fractured his pelvis. He waited ages in agony for his compensation and slept on the old middle door for months in front of the fire in the front room. He accepted the company's solicitor's first offer, before my grandad got home from the pit to tell him not to. He bought us a caravan so that we could have holidays at Withernsea, a crumby terraced house in Hull and, before that, a new shed for his allotment.

I vowed and declared that I would never ever follow in the family tradition of renting an allotment off the council. When the kids were four and I wanted them to eat organic produce I signed up for an allotment. My partner in digging things is Max Morley who I lost at the Bob Dylan Blackbushe gig over a quarter of a century ago. I found Max again when we moved to North Featherstone and started drinking in The Bradley Arms. We get drunk together on Saturday teatime sometimes and demand our favourite music be put onto the pub's MiniDisc system; Neil Young, Jimmy Reed, Bob Dylan, John Prine, Janis Joplin, Curved Air. Curved Air! Max's King Charles locks have long gone.

At the allotment we do more talking than digging. We sit on a pair of deckchairs that my gran and grandad once took to Blackpool to save on the hire charge. We watch kestrels hanging in mid-air and then diving for mice and the police helicopter hovering over the town looking for Asbo kids.

'Do you know, Ian, I'm sometimes working in my back yard and I can hear my dad whistling. He's been dead more than twenty years. When I look I see a blackbird. That bird's ancestors must have heard my dad and mimicked him. My dad's whistling has passed through a lot of eggs to get to that bird I hear now.'

We talk about gigs and beer and our families growing up. About house prices and holidays.

'I'm looking forward to the Cambridge Festival this year. I've seen some of my musical heroes and heroines since we started going as a family. Joan Baez, Taj Mahal, John Prine, Kate Rusby, The Watersons, Afro Celt Sound System. Do you know it's the only festival that plays *The Archers* through the PA on a Sunday morning?'

'I bet that's fuckin' lovely.'

'It's nice though.'

'Do the kids like it?'

'What, *The Archers*?'

'No, the chuffing festival.'

'Oh! Aye. They love it, they're full of confidence when they're there. It's the only place where they go where they don't think about being more than fifty yards away from us. We'll be sat supping and watching Cajun music and they go off and twirl plates on sticks at the circus skills area.'

'Don't you natter?'

'No. Folkies are lovely, aren't they. Besides everybody's been going there since they were kids so everybody knows one another. Paul Simon played at the first Cambridge Folk Festival you know.'

'He did, did he?'

'Oh Aye! For twenty quid I think.'

'Did he sing?'

'Aye. Like that blackbird.'

'Is your Edward still playing his piano?'

'Yes, he goes for a lesson every week.'

'You want to make sure he carries on. You'll always have the price of a pint if you've got a piano player in the family.'

'He reminds me of my grandad.'

'Well he's spit and dab of you an' all.'

'I can't see it. I think he's more like Heather. Billie's more my side. She's got them grey eyes like me gran.'

'Shall we get them shallots planted?'

'Right then.'

We start planting shallots and a bag of garlic cloves somebody in the next allotment had given us.

'When we came back from our holidays last year we got on the train at King's Cross and sat opposite a family who'd had a weekend in London. They'd been to see *Chitty Chitty Bang Bang* and they had bags full of toys from Hamleys toy shop on Regent Street. I said to Edward that Hamleys was the finest toy shop in the world; he asked me if we could go there one day. I never thought any more about it until the other week when I had to go to London to do a job with English National Opera. I took the kids to school on the Monday morning and when I kissed them at the gate I told them I'd see them on Friday. Edward said, "When you go to London, Dad, will you be visiting the world's finest toy shop?" The little bugger had remembered after all that time.'

'They do do. I'll tell you what. You'll learn that as they grow up and before you know it, you'll be like me, running about all week planning for their wedding. Let's get these fucking plants in.'

We finish the rows and roll a cig apiece. Max hums the old Buddy Holly song, 'Raining in My Heart', to himself.

'You know the kids would be three else four, we were invited to Sunday dinner at a school teacher's house. The teacher was eager to entertain and educate the kids. She gave Billie a book to look at and asked Edward if he knew any nursery rhymes. Edward just said "Mmm". The teacher said, "Do you know 'Goosey Goosey Gander Whither Shall I Wander'?" Edward said, "Mmmm," then she said, "What about 'Little Boy Blue Come Blow on Your Horn'?" "Mmmm." "And 'Hickory Dickory Dock', do you know that?" Edward just went "Mmmm" again. When she'd used up all the nursery rhymes she could remember, Edward just gave her a look and said, "Do you know any Joe Cocker songs?" The teacher squealed, she didn't know what to say. So Edward broke into "Unchain My Heart".'

Max likes to remember the time we went to see Dylan at Blackbushe. His latest idea is to hold a fancy dress party and everybody who comes has to dress as a character from a Dylan song. He's undecided whether to turn up as 'the diplomat who carries on his shoulder a Siamese cat' or 'the vandal who stole the handle'. I muse on what happened to the top hat that Dylan wore at Blackbushe. Max stops planting again and studies. 'Do you know what kid, we'll be telling our grandkids about the day we went to see Dylan at Blackbushe.'

I remember trying to hitch a lift down the A1, a flight from Karachi to Delhi, the hire car we used to tour the Delta and the start of another journey when a bloke I knew at school saw me with a rucksack on my back in Station Lane. 'W'ere's thy going?'

'California!'

'What on t'chuffing Wakefield bus?'

After

I handed the first draft of this book to my publisher just before Easter. We then planned a family holiday in Hay-on-Wye. Heather and me had longed to go there for the bookshops. We knew that Edward and Billie would be bored traipsing around one musty store after another, but we thought they would enjoy the countryside and fresh air. On the second day the kids were already fed up with bookshops. We made a plan. Heather would spend the afternoon browsing and I would take Edward and Billie on a canoe trip down the River Wye. We went to an organic juice bar and while Heather and the kids sipped their drinks, I nipped to a record shop two doors away and bought an old Ben Webster LP that I'd spotted the previous afternoon. I called in to a little bakery and bought some Welsh cakes and then we went to the river.

Edward sat in the front seat of the canoe and told everybody he was the driver. Billie in the middle marvelled, as usual, at the lovely things to see. She was overjoyed when some swans swam right up to the side of the canoe. She said more than once, 'Oooh! Daddy I can't wait to get back to school to tell my friends about this adventure.' I took a quick snap of them. Billie looking over her shoulder with that smile and Edward winking his cheeky eye.

We had been on the river for an hour and a half travelling downstream back to Hay. The canoe hit a tree and overturned. I was thrown out into the water, Billie and

Edward were trapped underneath the canoe. I tried to pull them both up, but I only found Edward. We were half an hour in the freezing water before I could get him onto the bank. My beautiful Billie Holiday didn't make it. She never surfaced and drowned trapped by currents and tree roots. The emergency services later recovered Billie and flew her in a helicopter to Hereford Hospital. Heather, who had been waiting by an empty river for us to arrive home, Edward and me were taken in a police car there. A broad-shouldered male nurse was attempting to resuscitate Billie, but the woman doctor said she was medically dead and was seeking our permission to stop trying. I looked at the male nurse, he was wet on his face with sweat and tears. I just said, 'She's gone hasn't she?' He simply nodded. I wanted to put my hands on her and say the little fairy story ditty, 'Healing hands will you heal this girl', but I didn't. I stroked her cheek and ran my finger across her eyebrows, the bit in the middle where they joined together. I looked around the room, I think there were eight or nine doctors and nurses standing quiet with their heads down. 'Look at those beautiful eyebrows!' They looked. 'What shapes all this to take it away before she's even ten?' Nobody answered. I started to remember fragments of the Wilfred Owen poem 'Futility'. 'Are limbs, so dear-achieved...O what made fatuous sunbeams toil.' Heather started to weep on my shoulder, Edward held my leg and roared.

Billie always asked me if one day we could live in the countryside. I used to say, 'But we already live near the countryside.' Then she'd say, 'I mean far out in the countryside.' To stop her I would say, 'Yes yes yes.'

'And will there be mountains behind, Daddy? And animals and woods and a fast river?'

There was a moment in the river when everything stood still. I looked up and saw two new lambs on the grass. A big bird of prey circled above and stopped crucified in mid-air. Behind and to one side were the Brecon Beacons. I shouted Billie's name at the water. I shouted it at the trees.

We told the funeral director that we wanted a non-religious funeral. He found us a humanist woman from Hebden Bridge who had once set up a feminist bookshop in London called Sisterwrite. He leafed through the catalogue of wickerwork coffins that were, he said, ecologically sound and made specially to order in Somerset. He said he had guessed that we might like one of those. We chose one and he said he would have it made directly. He told us that Billie had been five feet tall.

In the days leading up to the funeral Heather noticed that a collared dove who had never visited us before kept landing on a fence post in our back yard. Every time we remarked about it, it flew away.

Our friend Judy phoned. Judy runs a massage company and tours the summer festivals massaging musicians before they go on stage. She reminded us that last year Billie had had a non-permanent tattoo of a leaping dolphin done on the small of her back. Terry Mullaney called. He knew, he said, what we were going through. Some years ago, his son Stephen, a promising young rugby league player who had captained Wakefield schools at Wembley, had been run over by a car outside school. He said that there would be a light at the end of the tunnel. He also told me that sometimes he would smell rugby players' liniment while he was sat reading the paper and know Stephen was still around.

Sixty-seven cards of condolence came on one day. The postman, who was from an agency and didn't know us said, 'All them birthday cards and no parcels.' One letter came from a lady who Billie had taught to play dominoes in a pub taproom. Another from a Yorkshire branch of the Laurel and Hardy fan club 'Sons of the Desert'. The writer of *Chocolat*, Joanne Harris sent a card, as did Alan Plater who had known Billie since she was a bump in Heather. Featherstone Cricket Club who Billie never saw play wrote and Featherstone Male Voice Choir who she had enjoyed did as well. Painters, sculptors, jazz photographers all sent lovely letters. As did a woman I don't know who said she had lost two children in the sea at Skegness in 1964. Ray Hearne the folk singer said that he felt uselessly sorry to hear and that his singing was heavy now.

I phoned the local hospice to ask about some counselling. While I waited to be connected, Mozart's piano concerto No. 21, the andante part was playing. When Billie was a few weeks old I had played this while I shushed her to sleep. The image of me rocking her gently while my tears fell onto her cheeks came to my mind. I had felt so connected to my daughter at that moment. I often told her that story as she grew. She always asked me, 'But why were you crying, Daddy?' I told her, 'Because I was so happy.' She would give that big easy smile of hers and say, 'I didn't know people cried when they were happy.' Most nights she wanted me to sing the old Carter Family song 'You Are My Sunshine' to her.

'You make me happy, when skies are grey,
you'll never know dear, how much I love you.'

A lot of people wanted to come to the funeral, so many that we ended up issuing tickets. Big Paul Windmill flew over from Guernsey. Two Muslim mothers whose children went to Billie's school asked if they could come. Apparently Billie had once been kind to their children. My mate Miki Salkic and his wife Alma who are seeking asylum because they daren't go back to Bosnia came. Richard Hawley told me he wanted to play a lullaby but daren't ask.

Billie laid in her open wickerwork coffin in our music room for half an hour before we set off. Miki Salkic kissed his fingers and touched Billie on the forehead near her joined-up eyebrows. Big Windy pecked her on the cheek. We transferred some of her favourite songs from her iPod onto a CD and played it quietly as people queued to say goodbye. Donovan's 'Jennifer Juniper', which Billie called 'Jennifer Juniffer', followed by Loreena McKennitt doing 'The Coventry Carol'. James Blunt's 'You're Beautiful', Lindisfarne's 'Meet Me on the Corner', Nelly Furtado's song 'I'm like a bird, I'm gonna fly away' and Linda Thompson's 'Oh Mary you may have to run'. Billie had already developed taste.

Gillian Moore caught the seven o'clock train up from London and made it to the house just in time. She said at first that she wasn't sure about coming in to look at Billie. The last time she'd seen her, she was eating an ice cream outside the Globe Theatre on the South Bank. She did come in to the music room and she phoned later in the night to say she was home safely and she told me that she was glad that Heather had held her hand and encouraged her to look. Hawarun Hussein our friend from Bangladesh put her best white sari on and held my hand when I started to cry.

We all walked down the lane to All Saints Church. Nearly two hundred of us. Bosnian asylum seekers, Sikh corner shop keepers, friends from school, Yorkshire Television presenters, neighbours, mates from every year of our lives, family who we never see from one year to the next. Billie would have loved all of it.

The service was relayed to the churchyard. Mozart's piano concerto drifted over the fields. Dean Smith had placed some freshly cut blackthorn blossom next to the lectern. I stood up and listed things that Billie loved; porridge with Lyle's Golden Syrup, grapefruit cut into the shape of sunshine, playing the violin, looking through windows she hadn't looked through before. Edward played piano. He played a piece called 'When You Grow Up What Would You Like To Be'. He played it from memory because he had forgotten to bring his book. Heather stood up and read 'The Lady of Shalott':

'And at the closing of the day
She loosed the chain and down she lay;
The broad stream bore her far away,
The Lady of Shalott.'

She read it beautifully.

We chose three pieces of music. First was Van Morrison singing 'Sometimes We Cry', second was Sandy Denny doing 'Who Knows Where the Time Goes'.

'Come the storms of winter
And the birds in spring again
I have no fear of time.'

All that joking about playing that song at my funeral came into my mind. Third was Neil Young's 'Unknown Legend':

'Somewhere on a desert highway
She rides a Harley-Davidson
With her long blonde hair blowing in the wind.'

I looked across the pews at Max. He was gritting his teeth and forcing back some tears. Only weeks before he had helped Billie catch a chub. At the grave the humanist officiant Lynn mentioned that as we came into the cemetery she had seen the first swallow of summer. When the wicker coffin was lowered into the hole, the swallow swooped down low over our heads. At the cemetery gates, two little girls stood watching the crowd file out. One was holding a small doll. They reminded me of the end of Billie's favourite film, *Whistle Down the Wind*. Alan Bates has been arrested, a little girl says to Haley Mills, 'Has he gone?' And then says, 'Will he come back again?' That bit made Billie cry. We went to the Old Featherstone Working Men's Club and drank some pints of Guinness and ate vegetarian quiche. When the caterer had asked me how many pork pies I wanted, I told him that Billie was a vegetarian.

Two days before we went to Hay-on-Wye, I'd watched Featherstone Rovers struggle in a dour game of rugby league with Gateshead. I stood with some Rovers committee men and ex-players in the boardroom. On the wall is a photograph of young Stephen Mullaney. I remembered looking at the photo and thinking, 'What would I do if a child of mine was to die in an accident?'

Heather and Edward have been incredibly brave. Edward is dealing with the death of his twin with extraordinary dignity. Just after we got back home from Wales he said, 'Dad, I've been thinking that Billie came so that I could.' Heather and me are holding on to that one.

Knowing what to hold on to and what to let go of have become engrained in our daily life. Sometimes I look at Billie's beautiful photo on the kitchen wall sixty times in an hour. I don't know who I am or what I believe any more. Some Christian neighbours told me that 'Heaven must have needed an angel'. I told them that Earth needs angels. Heather keeps me sane. When I said to her one day that I didn't think I could get through this, she pulled me up sharp and said, 'You've no choice, it's not a matter of trying to, you have to!' Earth needs angels like my Heather as well. When I feel sorry for myself and declare that I might go mad in the next six months, it's Heather with the humour typical of round here, who says, 'You can't go mad when you arc already!'

We decided that we can't keep Billie's room as a shrine. It's still called Billie's room and Edward goes in every morning to open her curtains to let the sunshine in, but it's a guest room now. Jürgen Bredebusch was the first to stay there when he drove from Germany one Friday night with his condolences. Billie's telly has been moved into our bedroom. A picture of Dusty Springfield with panda eye make-up and a pink dress that Billie cut out of a magazine is stuck to the side of it. There it will remain. Billie liked Buddy Holly, particularly that song 'Everyday':

'Everyday it's a gettin' closer
Going faster than a rollercoaster
Love like yours will surely come my way.'

She made me copy out the words on a piece of scented notepaper. We stopped and started the record until we'd copied them all, like teenagers did in the olden days.

My boss from ITV phoned and said that they would like to donate £1000 in memory of Billie. Heather and me talked about what we would do with the money. We decided to put £1000 of our own savings to it and buy violins for local schoolchildren. We set up an account called 'Billie's Violin'. Within weeks people in the local community wanted to put on events for us. Roy Hampson, who sells nostalgia CDs on the markets, organised for a 1930s Palm Court Orchestra to play a benefit. Paul Harper who sings like Al Bowlly came to sing 'The Very Thought of You'. A few weeks later Featherstone Male Voice Choir, all eighty of them, did a joint concert with the Trinity Girls' Brass Band from Wigan and donated £1600. Heather and me have now gone into partnership with the local authority's music education department. We hope to buy at least three instruments a year for the next ten years for junior school kids in Featherstone. Billie will never realise her ambition of playing her violin at Whitby Folk Festival, but another local kid might achieve that ambition for her. That would make us proud.

Last year we went to the folk festival at Whitby as we

nearly always do. At nine o'clock one morning we found ourselves walking on the beach and splashing in the sea's edge. Billie found a stick that she called a wooden snake. It is a well washed stick that has been in the water a long time. It has a knot like an eye and a split in it like a mouth. She carried the stick about with her all day; in and out of shops, in the Magpie Fish Restaurant and through a lot of impromptu sing-rounds. She even took it on a pleasure cruise on the sea on a boat made up like a replica of Captain Cook's *Endeavour.* At ten o'clock that night the kids fell to sleep outside the Middle Earth Tavern during the umpteenth badly sung and played version of 'Cheer up sleepy Jean'. We piled into a taxi and went back to the tent and forgot about the stick. Next morning at six o'clock Billie woke me up and wanted to know if I'd brought her stick back last night. She was upset when she found out that I hadn't and said that we should go back to the pub straight away to find it. After breakfast we did. Some cleaners were in the pub and I asked them if they had found a stick outside. They looked at me gone out as I described the wooden snake with its knot-hole eye. One man said that the road sweeper had gone by half an hour before and that he had probably thrown it into his mobile bin. Billie said that we should set off and search the streets of Whitby 'til we found him. The sun shone on bleary-eyed mandolin players and blokes with beards carrying bodhrain drums as we scoured the harbour side. Finally we dropped on an old bloke with a roll-up dangling out of his mouth who was pushing a bin on wheels. I offered him the price of a pint if he would tip his bin onto the pavement. Billie delved and found her stick. She smiled like a breakfast grapefruit piece. After the funeral I found the stick propped up under the desk in her bedroom. One day I will do something with that stick. One day I will write stories not about my own life and what music has meant to me but about my children and what they mean. I will write about my Edward who plays boogie-woogie like Meade Lux-Lewis and my Billie Holiday who should've played her violin at Whitby and Cambridge Festivals. My Billie who should have flown. But I can't do it yet.

Everything reminds me of something.

Ian Clayton

Ian Clayton is a jobbing writer, story teller and broadcaster. He loves books, films and music. He is a traveller, a collector, a gatherer and is passionate about finding the voice of the common people. He still lives in the town where he was born and lists his hobbies as tap-room conversation and gentle subversion. Amongst other things he is a recognised authority on the life and works of Billie Holiday, has a fondness for the comedy songs of George Formby and aspires to play blues harmonica like Jimmy Reed. His partner of twenty-eight years Heather is a social worker and their son Edward is a budding pianist.